Men of Peace

Books by Bradford Smith

BIOGRAPHY

Bradford of Plymouth
Captain John Smith
Men of Peace

SOCIAL HISTORY

Americans from Japan
A Dangerous Freedom
Yankees in Paradise
Why We Behave Like Americans
Portrait of India

RELIGION

Meditation: The Inward Art

NOVELS

To the Mountain
This Solid Flesh
American Quest
The Arms Are Fair

FOR YOUNG READERS

William Bradford—Pilgrim Boy
Daniel Webster—Union Boy
Stephen Decatur—Gallant Boy
Rogers' Rangers & the French
 & Indian War
With Sword & Pen
 (Adventures of Capt. John Smith)
The Islands of Hawaii

EDITOR:

A Handbook of English & American Literature
The Story of Jesus

Men of Peace

by Bradford Smith

J. B. Lippincott Company
Philadelphia & New York

Member of the Authors League of America

First Edition

Printed in the United States of America

Library of Congress Catalog Card Number: 64–23478

Contents

Men of Peace

1. Escape to the Future

 A radical operation for cancer forced me to face the fact that I too must die. It also forced me to look at the world with new eyes—detached, sympathetic, disinterested, and in a perspective not limited to the alarms and urgencies of the moment. It was as if the present, along with the recent past, had already become history. The fizz and the fuss dissolved; the essence remained.

We tend to see events as the headlines see them. All is conflict, disaster, and threatened collapse. Hourly newscasts by radio and television compound these urgencies, until we feel that we are living always on the brink of disaster. Perhaps we are. But if we are, the disaster is different from the multiple of all these headlines—different from the conflict between communism and capitalism, or even between have and have-not. Our preoccupation with present fact blinds us to long-range significance.

We worry about Castro, and suddenly a little island a few miles off our shores assumes a size and a menace out of all proportion to its place in history. We find ourselves shoring up or undermining a government in Vietnam half a world away. From the headlines one would guess that it must be as close as Cuba and that our existence as a nation depended on what happens there.

We look at all the divided countries—Korea, Germany, the Congo, Cyprus, and somehow we are involved in all, we scarcely know how. Why have we become involved in everybody's life, when all we want is to enjoy our own?

This basic frustration lies at the root of all our thinking about world affairs.

It is hard for us to see that even if communism had not become a world force, the end of World War II would have brought on the same world-wide demand for an end to colonialism, the same thrust toward self-government throughout the world, and the same battle to replace poverty and ignorance with at least minimal standards of living and of education.

All this ought to please us. We have always stood on the side of freedom. We were the first to throw off colonialism, and our example inspired people all over the world.

Then how has it come about that in this struggle we have somehow become identified with imperialism and have lost the spiritual leadership we once held? How is it that, although we have spent a vast treasure to help other countries get on their feet while maintaining our own huge military establishment, we are regarded with dislike and mistrust in many parts of the world?

The answer is an easy one, though we don't like to face it. We are comfortable, therefore we don't want anyone to rock the boat. We have done well with a system which holds private property sacred, therefore we don't want to upset it. We are in the position every great and powerful state comes to: the status quo suits us, therefore we do not invite change. This is the surest sign of imminent decline.

The United States has always welcomed change. In occupying a continent we had to learn the art of meeting sudden emergencies, changing our ways to keep alive in a changing environment. We are a people who immigrated from everywhere to fill up this land. So we had to learn, not only how to live under new circumstances, but how to live with each other. And we have shaped our social and political institutions in the direction of increasing opportunity and equality for all.

How then can we be otherwise than delighted to see the rest of the world following the same course?

Our worry arises from the fact that, having won the battle for an open and mobile society and become comfortable doing it, we see in communism a threat to what we have built for ourselves. The other people of the world are in a hurry to catch up with us. They are not going to take the century or so we, as pioneers, took in blazing the trail. They want to get there in a hurry, and they will choose what looks like the straightest road.

Whenever they choose a road that looks different from ours, we cry communism, and assume they are involved in a plot against us. What looks like communism to us may indeed be that, or it may be the adoption of socialist or even totalitarian instruments to hasten economic growth—nationalization of basic industries, control of the means of communication, even a one-party system.

In our fear of communism we have come to brand all socialism as communist, thus lumping our friends with our adversaries and driving them away from us. The irony is that we are more social-ized than many of the nations whose socialism we deplore. India, for instance. Nehru frequently said that India is a socialist country. He meant that India, in its effort to cope with poverty, ignorance and disease, has found it necessary to finance and control some basic industries and to tackle the problem of agricul-tural underproduction by a program not very different from our agricultural extension service.

But India cannot afford the social security, the unemployment insurance, the care of dependents and all the other social services we have. These things are the envy of poorer countries. Yet here at home we use the word socialism as if it meant leprosy. This mental set against change which benefits the less privileged is a sign of that national hardening of arteries which if not corrected will lead us straight downhill in the same direction other fully developed societies have taken.

It is our "socialism" as well as our private enterprise which has kept us from going stale. If only we could realize that we need not choose between these two, but continue to work both their benefits together, we would overcome one of the mental blocks that stands in the way of our being liked and trusted as world leaders. An economy which can turn out goods at the rate ours does *needs* socialism as a way of distributing those goods to keep the economy running. If we did not have the graduated income tax, old-age and unemployment insurance, farm price supports and all the other forms of government "interference" with the economy, those who complain about socialism would soon find their dividends drying up, and surely they must know it.

We worry about such things as socialism and communism, Castro and Khrushchev, subversion and "un-Americanism" when the fact is that these are but manifestations of something bigger and more hopeful. The peoples of the world want what we want —recognition of the freedom and dignity of the individual, employment and a fair return for their labor, education for their children, medical care and the assurance of help in the case of emergencies their own resources cannot handle.

Once upon a time this was the sort of program each nation had to work out for itself. Now, as a result of interlocking trade and markets, it requires cooperation among nations. A fall in the price of tin or coffee or rubber can plunge a nation into insolvency through no fault of its own. Increased automation can put thousands out of work in Detroit unless we can find overseas markets for our increased productivity.

A new world is coming to birth: this is the big fact about the times we live in. Nothing can stop it. Nothing can fundamentally alter its shape, except inexcusable stupidity on our part, in which case communism despite all its built-in disadvantages will fall heir to our birthright.

We are like a woman in labor who complains of pains in her

[14]

legs and back and neck as if they had nothing to do with what she is about. Castro may be a pain in the neck to us, but he is only a symptom of something else. And we cannot get rid of that pain until we have accomplished the birth that must come.

As Americans, we have reacted in various ways to these signs of birth. The reactionary would like to stop the labor and go back to the bridal night. The conservative advises his wife to hold onto the baby as long as she can, for by doing nothing the dangers of birth can be avoided for a while, and maybe in a month or two an even bigger and better baby will result. The middle-of-the-roader is reluctantly willing to call in a midwife, whose long experience in dealing with such crises persuades him that she probably knows better than an obstetrician what should be done about it. The liberal is all for summoning the best medical care and getting the thing over with as soon as possible. The leftist puts the whole matter in the hands of the state or party and lets it decide what to do, while the anarchist is willing to leave the whole thing up to the woman and let her get out of it the best way she can.

In spite of them all, the birth will occur, and it will be the child of the same parents. But we can take some responsibility for it if we will, in order to make sure that the child has a fair chance for survival and suffers no injuries at birth.

This new world is one in which all mankind will be united by cultural, economic and political ties at least as strong as those which now bind the people of one nation together.

Indeed that world is half born already, and part of our trouble comes from the fact that we are halfway through a difficult delivery.

Personal history illustrates this. I intended to teach English in some New England college. But I graduated into the midst of the depression. The only firm offer I received was a mission appointment to teach in a Christian university in Japan. I knew nothing of Japan, but the offer was generous and I wanted to get married, so we accepted. It never occurred to me that I was part of a world movement Jesus had begun two thousand years ago, and that even then he had foreseen the birth of this new world in which all men would live together as brothers.

After five years in Japan, we returned to our own country and I took up the career I had intended from the first. Only by now I had published books and articles on Japan. So I was asked to talk about that country. I was invited to join societies interested in Japanese culture. I could not keep Japan out of my life.

When war came, I inevitably went into the Office of War Information, ultimately with the task of setting up printing and radio operations in the Pacific aimed primarily at hastening the end of our war against Japan. When the war ended, I found myself back in Japan, then writing a book about Americans of Japanese ancestry, hoping to modify in some small degree the injustices we had done them in wartime.

All this led to an invitation to work up an introductory program for Japanese coming to study in our universities, and that in turn led to a similar program for Fulbright students from all over the world. I ran that program for eleven summers. Meanwhile the interest in international education led to another trip to Japan to conduct shipboard orientation programs, and a long study tour of Europe to confer with Fulbright students who had returned to their homes. And then to two years at an international center in India, where in a small way we tried to help with the birth of a world in which men and women of all nations could meet in an atmosphere of receptiveness to each other.

Without intention, almost against the current of my own plans and hopes, I was drawn into this international world. The same thing has happened to others, and with increasing frequency. Today it is so common that we take it for granted.

The young men and women who come home from Peace Corps assignments, or from study overseas, or from duty with the armed forces, or who go out as air pilots and stewardesses, or as bankers, traders, teachers, missionaries, business executives or

[16]

even as travelers will find that their lives have been changed. If they are sensitive and open to new experience, they will know that the international world which is coming to birth will be a richer and more exciting one than we have ever known.

The signs of this world are everywhere—in foreign aid programs, the founding of the United Nations, the European Common Market, the Alliance for Progress, the international work of foundations like Carnegie, Nobel, Ford and Rockefeller, the rise in world travel and study abroad. The World Bank, the International Labor Organization, the General Agreement on Tariffs and Trade and all the other international agencies are proof of the fact that we cannot live in a narrowly national world.

Since the world is going to be one, whether we like it or not, it is quite clearly going to be neither communist nor capitalist, but something both camps and those outside either camp will accept as a satisfactory way of life.

With our mental bias toward polar thinking, we imagine that the world must be either communist or capitalist. Yet we have lived for nearly fifty years now in a world which is both. If we were not blinded by our disposition to see everything as either black (perhaps I should say red) or white, we would know that in politics as in optics we have a spectrum—a rainbow—which merges so imperceptibly from one color to another that you cannot put your finger upon a spot and say, "Here red ends and orange begins." One grows into the other.

We pretend we are a nation of private entrepreneurs, when in fact we have from early times used socialistic practices when it suited us. The Pilgrims tried communal living. For several decades the Oneida Community did so successfully. Government has always come to the aid of business when needed. It gave away an empire to the cross-country railroads. It gives away a fortune today to keep farmers in business, to keep oil men happy, to support those who cannot support themselves. We are a socialized democracy, and the sooner we accept this fact instead of denying it, the more effectively we shall react to world challenges and opportunities.

Russia, on the other hand, has discovered that communism doesn't work very well. For a long time now it has paid premium salaries to those whose work is valued—scientists, writers, performers, engineers, industrial managers. Khrushchev tells his farm managers that they had better start thinking like capitalists in order to boost production. Russia, in short, has found it necessary to provide incentives in order to get output.

The differences between communism and capitalism are narrowing. If we manage to avoid annihilating each other, the differences will continue to grow smaller until we can no longer tell them apart, any more than we can put our finger on the precise point where red turns to orange.

But this is assuming that we are perceptive enough to understand that communism changes just as capitalism does. Today we would regard the predatory capitalism of the nineteenth century as a danger equal to that of present-day communism. Yes, times change, and so do all social systems. Our strategy therefore should be to encourage everything that makes for change in the communist world. Those who think communism can be destroyed are like those who wanted to destroy witches. They killed thousands of people before discovering that there was no such thing as a witch. The witchery was all the time in their own heads. The communism we are resisting is largely in our heads. There is Russian imperialism, just as there is American or Chinese imperialism; all great powers in our present world are imperialist whether they want to be or not; their strength makes them so. There is Russian deprivation of liberties, just as there is American deprivation of liberties. We are entitled to think theirs worse than ours, but a Negro living in Mississippi may not.

Russia permits only one political party. We talk a lot, but is our situation really so very different? We, in effect, have outlawed communism. Public opinion is so manipulated that we would not get far either with a socialist party or anything other than the middle-of-the-road sort of coalition which elects our presidents. The system has great advantages, including the right to disagree, but it does not permit a broad spectrum of choices.

The new world coming to birth, then, will not be capitalist or communist, but an amalgam of the two, as it is already. And it will have to wipe out the deprivation of liberties that can happen both in Siberia and in Mississippi, or anywhere else. Whoever fails to be for that kind of world will fail to be a leader in it. That is precisely our problem today. The world is looking for the physician who can guarantee a safe delivery, and much of the hesitation and hostility we feel results from the fact that men are not sure we can do it. Can we? If not, mankind will go off in another direction. Nothing—not our vast nuclear power, nor our wealth, nor our willingness to give material or technical aid—will do us any good. We shall be bypassed, and the world will march on.

If, on the other hand, we recognize what sort of world is coming to birth and will prepare ourselves for it, all that we have dreamed of shall come to pass.

How do we go about it?

First, we must have the courage to imagine a free, world-wide society. There can be no compromise on this. By "free" I mean that men must be able at all times to say what they think and vote as they please. Neither of these conditions exists at present in the United States. The mentality of the Birch Society and the House Un-American Activities Committee has made people afraid to speak their minds. The men and women of other nations discount everything we say about freedom when they see this, or when they observe our failure to send colored children to the same schools with white children, or to give every Negro in the South his Constitutional right to vote.

Suppose for the moment that we have the strength to impose our ideals upon actuality and to give all Americans the freedoms we say they are entitled to.

Let us then imagine what a world society might be like.

Thousands of years ago, when men were groping towards being human, they formed themselves into tribes. For thousands of years these small tribes fought each other until the ceaseless wars and miseries led a strong man, here and there, to impose his will upon several tribes. So kingdoms came into being, and after kingdoms, empires. The common people may have felt some sort of allegiance to their king, but the idea of a nation did not yet exist—that is, of a polity within which all were bound together like an extended family.

During the Middle Ages the Catholic Church provided that sort of cohesion in Europe. Then, as feudal barons fought and then joined under a king, as languages came to have a uniting effect, and as the feud between pope and emperor flared up, the modern nation-state was born. Men began to feel a familylike allegiance to this larger unit. The petty wars between states died down as men learned that they could live together as Germans even though they might be Prussian, Bavarian or Hessian. In the United States men learned this lesson with amazing speed. Immigrants became Americans within a few years, and their children were never anything else. In spite of a lingering sentiment for the old country, most of the foreign-born and their children felt themselves to be American.

The growth of nationalism also ushered in an era of devastating wars. If every country regarded itself as superior, the struggle to prove this superiority was bound to lead to dispute and conflict. The period of world wars began.

Men learned to identify their interests with tribe, kingdom, empire, nation. They can learn to identify with mankind. The notion that this will somehow wipe out national loyalty is another evidence of that either-or fallacy which invades all our thinking. A man can love his family, his community, his church, his state, and still be a loyal American. He can be a loyal American and still go on to the inevitable final step, that of a world society.

There is nothing new in this idea. Jesus preached it. Buddha understood it. Other men have glimpsed the vision. But until our own time the difficulties of distance and communication have made it as impossible as our present facilities now make it imperative.

We have already begun to build the instruments, organizations and agencies of such a world, not only in the United Nations and its agencies, but in the world-wide exchange programs for students, the arts, professions and sciences, in the International Geophysical Year, in some small space exploration projects which have joined Russian and American resources and manpower.

We have begun to build, but we lack the confidence and the vision to go on with it. We are afraid; we stop halfway, like one who must give birth but is afraid to bear down for fear of the pain.

Imagine for a moment a free world society in which problems like overpopulation, unemployment, surpluses of food and raw materials, hunger, education, transportation and other things could be handled on a world-wide basis.

Unemployment, for instance. Millions of Indian farmers are unemployed a good part of the year for lack of irrigating water to make a second crop. Suppose we supplied enough wheat so that some of these farmers could dig ditches and build dams for an irrigation system. Hand labor is still the rule in India, so thousands of picks and shovels would be needed. Factory hands now idle, say, in Illinois might be reemployed to make them. Somewhere trees would need to be felled for handles. Forest owners and lumberjacks would be paid. Ships would have to be loaded and sent off.

The world is full of such opportunities. Men and resources are lying idle for lack of something that could be supplied if the world were an economic unit.

Imagine a world development authority which would coordinate these needs. Imagine national planning commissions which would figure out capacity, production, overproduction, underproduction, unemployment, needed skills, necessary educational facilities to produce them, and all the other details of the economic life which each nation could and should analyze. Imagine then that all the surpluses and lacks are brought together in one balance sheet, and the program undertaken which would set them right.

But where would the money come from?

Where does the money now come from which the nations of the world squander upon military establishments because they cannot trust each other? One hundred and twenty billion dollars a year or more, poured out into channels that are totally unproductive, like pouring milk into a sewer.

Imagine for a moment that the nations of the world agree to take one tenth of their military funds and divert them into this world authority, and that if the first year goes well, they will divert a fifth the second year, and so on until perhaps half the military expenditures are diverted to peaceful uses. The other half, or much of it, could soon be phased out because we would have met the problem which is causing most of the world's unrest: poverty. Not communism, not subversion, not creeping socialism, not inbred national hatreds or tribal vendettas. Poverty, with its inevitable companions, ignorance, hunger, ill health.

What could we not do with that first twelve billion! We could build schools and send teachers to train other teachers, badly needed in all the developing countries. We could immensely expand the training of teachers, doctors, agricultural experts, industrial engineers—all vitally needed in the first phase of raising production. And we could use our now embarrassing surpluses to balance present shortages in other parts of the world. Much of the money we as a nation paid into this fund would come back to us in the purchase of foodstuffs, industrial products and salaries.

Much of the unemployment we now suffer from could be alleviated by world planning and development. It cannot be solved in any other way. Private enterprise has not been able to solve it. Government has not been able. Automation will continue to wipe out some jobs while creating others. Only a world market can generate the need for goods which will, along with education for upgrading of jobs, put our people to work.

The fact that we turn out huge food surpluses we do not know what to do with, and at the same time throw men out of work whom we cannot deal with either, makes plain the need for world-wide planning. The fact that many nations cannot at present grow enough food to feed their people, or generate enough capital to get productive industries going, shows the same need.

But what about Russia? It always comes back to that.

If we seriously and sincerely proposed the launching of such a program, could any great nation stay out without insupportable damage to its prestige and place? We cannot go into any such program looking for national advantage over others, yet to enter such a program, to be in at the birth of such a world, is bound to be advantageous to those who take part and disadvantageous to those who do not.

To take part in specific programs of world cooperation would build confidence in a world community; each step would make the next easier.

There is a politic beyond politics which is concerned with the freedom of man's mind and spirit. It looks beyond communism or capitalism to the welfare of the human family. Whoever builds upon this politic will serve humanity and, in serving, gain its allegiance.

There is an economic beyond economics, which concerns itself not with loans, interest, discount rates and production figures but with the needs of man and the best ways to fill them. Whoever puts idle resources and manpower to use instead of hoarding them will vitalize the economy for all.

There is a civilization beyond civilizations which seeks the fulfillment of life to the farthest reach of each individual's capacity. Since everyone is crippled by society's failure to develop every individual to his fullest capability, a true civilization rises by what it receives from those members who have been educated to give all that they have.

There is a religion beyond religions which recognizes the brotherhood of man in the great miracle of a creation which demonstrates that it lives according to law, and that its laws are universal. Such a religion sees all faiths as paths leading to the same summit and welcomes every insight of science or art which clarifies the essentially spiritual nature of man's pilgrimage.

Man, the only creature in all this creation who can meditate about his condition and seek to understand it, has earned the duty of this privilege: as his gifts are godlike, he must use them in the service of the society, the family, the creation from which they come. For no man owns himself: he is the product of cosmic history. The sun was truly his father, and the salt of the sea still flows in his veins.

The following chapters deal with men of courage who believed that "there is no way to peace; peace is the way." We have been deluged with good books dealing with all the technicalities of world government, arms control disarmament, and world economics. They provide the information with which to build such a world, and a forum in which to hammer out differences. But it seemed to me that another sort of book might also have a place— a book telling the stories of those men who throughout the ages have known that mankind is one and that war—any war—is civil war, is fratricidal.

What did they say, what did they do to help bring this world of mankind nearer to reality? How can they guide us today?

[24]

That is what I have tried to discover in the life stories which follow.

As the lives of these men will show, peace is basically a religious concept, announced and delineated by religious men. It is the ultimate concern of those who believe that man is fundamentally spiritual, not limited to flesh, bones, desires and greeds but capable of rising above them.

It is the fashion of our time to seek the secret of human consciousness in nucleus and proton, in nerve ganglion and cell chemistry. Valuable as all these discoveries are, each one of them as it is made merely deepens the mystery. Why all this at all?

To find an answer we have to look at the totality, not the fraction. Love and selflessness are facts, as demonstrable as protons and ribonucleic acid. The demonstration occurs in the lives of great men.

History could be written as a symbolic working out of individual aggressions, drives and frustrations through identification with the tribe or nation. We would then see how personal hatreds get converted into such socially acceptable ways of behavior as patriotism and hatred of the enemy. Men may love their families and communities, but they often hate the restraints imposed upon them by family duty and social custom. Through the symbol of the god-king or the nation that can do no wrong they merge themselves with a larger self, thus overcoming their individual limitations. In return, they may be rewarded for killing, pillaging, taking women—all in the name of the inviolable symbol. Men who love power manipulate all this so as to use the little men for their own ends.

Peacemakers have always known this, have always sought to challenge the better nature in man and thus lead him into the ways of peace. Some of these leaders have been enunciators primarily, like Buddha, disclosing the truth that frees. Others have been organizers, like Asoka. Some have been both, like Penn, Wilson or Gandhi. Each of the men whose story follows has opened the way to peace, and each has failed because we do not yet have peace. Are we nearer to it than we were in the day when we hacked off the loser's head and bore it home as a trophy? Even the Pilgrims did that. Or has nuclear warfare made permanent the threat of war by giving us weapons we can neither use nor lay down?

Through these life histories we seek an answer.

2. Ikhnaton:
(c. 1385-c. 1354 B.C.)

The Pharaoh Who Gave an Empire for Peace

 The royal palace at Thebes stood at the edge of the desert near the western hills, which turned from pink to yellow and back to pink again as the hot Egyptian sun crossed the sky. It was a large palace, but lightly built, its walls gaily decorated, its big artificial lake reflecting the sacred sun disc, the clouds of evening.

Amenhotep III had built it for his wife Tiy—a small-featured, pretty woman with a stern and willful mouth and a queenly look about her narrow face. The pharaoh himself, with his long, slightly curved nose and sharp chin, had the look of a man who was in the habit of pursuing his pleasures and having his whims attended to. Of the two, Tiy seemed the stronger person. As she grew older, the willfulness carved unerasable lines in her forehead and from nose to chin. But Amenhotep seemed to lose energy as she gained it. He died young, like so many of the pharaohs, when his son and heir was only about twelve years old. Tiy took over the reins of government and held them tight. Perhaps she found it hard to give them up, when the time came, to her dreamy young son.

He had been named Amenhotep at his birth about 1385 B.C.

Not until the sixth year of his reign did he come to be known as Ikhnaton—"Aton is satisfied." Growing up in the spacious, sun-drenched palace by the lake, young Amenhotep responded to the gracious surroundings, both man-made and natural, in a way that was to change history. For something grew in him that had never found expression by any man before. What he was to express was universal. Once uttered, any man could recognize it and respond. But young Amenhotep was the first to give it form.

While still a boy of sixteen and shortly after his coronation he was married to Nefertiti, whose young, smooth-featured beauty still lives in her widely known portrait bust. The cleanly molded young face with its lovely planes and faint hollows has a look both regal and warm, both young and dignified. No one knows for sure who her parents were. She may have been the daughter of the powerful grand counselor, Aye.

The young pharaoh's delicate features bear a strong resemblance to Nefertiti's. He has a rather dreamy look, his eyelids are heavy, his lips full, his nose imperially long and straight. Only the forward thrust of the chin suggests the pharaoh and the man of iron will who was to wipe out every mention of gods other than Aton on every temple, mausoleum and carving in Egypt.

His head was too large—he may even have been an epileptic, his health in any case none too good. It is possible that fits or hallucinations may have had a part in forming his religious vision. No one has satisfactorily explained the thighs heavy almost to deformity or the outthrust stomach which appear in his portraits.

Shown together, the two young rulers have an appeal that stretches fresh and clear across three thousand intervening years. Nefertiti comes to him offering flowers, her flowing robes half exposing a lithe body, smiling as she comes and welcomed by a dreaming affection. Or they sit, each with a child in arms, he kissing his little princess. A father before eighteen, he made

[28]

domestic felicity the center of his world. Nefertiti is often shown with an arm around her husband, or even kissing him or sitting on his lap. Compare this with the stiff formal poses of the pharaohs before and after, and you see how remarkable a revolution Ikhnaton was the center of, though it died with him.

Children, flowers, gardens, animals, even the chick in the shell were his delight. He had a truly Wordsworthian love of nature, and a sense of being at one with it.

About the time the first of his four daughters was born (he never had a son), Ikhnaton seems to have taken up the reins of government from a mother who was reluctant to let go. By then this remarkable young man had already conceived the main lines of his religious faith. At twenty it was fully matured.

Thebes was then under the firm control of a vast hierarchy of priests—priests of the god Amon-Ra. Amon had originally been a mere local god at Thebes. By combining him with the sun-god Ra, the priests had been able to elevate him and themselves, for in one way or another Ra was worshiped everywhere. Even before Ikhnaton was born, a tendency had begun to give equal prestige to the god Aton, whose symbol was also the sun. Men had begun to think of Aton as a universal god, acceptable to people throughout the enlarged empire, and as one who could unite them all.

When young Amenhotep renamed himself Ikhnaton—he was about sixteen then—it was clear that he had decided to make this god his own and the empire's. He was to carry the concept of one god far beyond what any man had dared think before him.

But Thebes, crowded with the priests and temples of Amon-Ra, was too hostile an atmosphere for the young pharaoh's new vision. He wanted a whole new city which would harmonize with his concept.

In search of a fitting site, he sailed down the Nile. Three hundred miles he sailed, until at last he came—a hundred and sixty miles above modern Cairo—to a place where an island rose from the river. Along the river bank ran a thin strip of cultivated land where he could plant his palace gardens. Where the desert began he would build his palace and temples. Beyond that the sandy wilderness sloped upward to a stone cliff where he would carve his tomb and those of his family and officers.

"I will make the city of the Horizon of Aton, for the Aton, my father, in this place," he said. Boundary stones went up with his promise graven upon them. Happy in his dream, the young pharaoh returned to Thebes.

Architects, sculptors, craftsmen, laborers went to work to transform the dream into walls and murals, roads and courts and lake.

Eager to see his vision take shape, Ikhnaton embarked with his family and attendants for the new city in 1369 while the city was yet abuilding. He was still only about sixteen—young enough to be impatient.

A hundred barges set out down the river, the great golden prow of the king's own barge pointing the way. With him rode his lovely young wife Nefertiti, already the mother of a daughter, whose delight in the voyage can be imagined from the other intimate family scenes we have of them.

"Sweet love fills my heart for the Queen," said Ikhnaton in one of his poetic outbursts. "Grant a great age to Nefertiti, and may she keep the hand of Pharaoh for many years."

Somewhere in the leading barges rode the chief counselor Aye; also a man named Nakht, who was to take the place of Ramose as chief vizier when the court was established in the new city, and Thutmose, the chief sculptor.

The night before they reached the new city—"The Horizon of Aton," as Ikhnaton called it (it is now Tell-el-Amarna)—the pharaoh ordered the barges to tie up along the shore so that they might reach the city just at sunrise.

That was the way he showed it to Nefertiti, its tall columns and smooth new walls shining in the early light. So eager had he been to leave Thebes that the palace was only half done. But colored pennants fluttered above its walls and from the temple to Aton.

[30]

As the royal barge eased in to the wharf, priests and workmen and soldiers stood deep to greet them:

"Life, health and strength!"

Riding perhaps in a single chariot as we see them on one of the bas-reliefs, Ikhnaton and his queen drove up the wide royal road to the palace. A bridge arched across the great road, connecting the palace with the royal chapel, and in the middle of the bridge was the window of appearances where the king could appear to his people and look down the long, straight avenue across the whole city. It looked clean and spacious, its big courtyards and garden surrounded with walls, but open to the sun, to nature, as Ikhnaton wished.

"When one sees her," a nobleman said of the city, "it is like a glimpse of heaven."

Ikhnaton wanted it to be a happy city, for the common people as for himself. Already he had ordered that a city of Aton should also be built in the other main divisions of his empire, in Syria and Nubia.

It may have been another two or three years before he made Akhetaton his permanent residence, leaving behind him a Thebes which seethed with hatred for the young pharaoh who had despoiled the temples of Amon, overthrown his worship, and cut off the rich revenues upon which thousands of priests and their hangers-on had fattened. For when Ikhnaton moved to Akhetaton, the royal revenues pouring in from all over the empire followed him, leaving proud Thebes shorn of the riches which had once been unloaded at its docks.

As for Akhetaton, it had become everything the young monarch had dreamed. Grand as Thebes was with its rich complex of temples, it had nothing like these enormous halls, these tall pillars. The Aton shrine alone stretched out for two hundred feet, while the temple enclosure was half a mile long. Here Ikhnaton himself officiated as high priest, aided by Nefertiti of the sweet voice and beautiful hands.

[31]

Ikhnaton now turned his attention almost entirely to the religion which, in his vision, would unite all men in its warm and unifying light.

Ikhnaton's concept was of a god whose energy comes to man on the sun's life-giving rays. But Ikhnaton conceived god as a formless essence, as the loving force which permeates time and space. To symbolize it, he used the sun's spreading rays, each ending in a hand. So the hand of God was in every affair of life. God was an active presence in all things—in the growth of plants, in the flooding of the Nile, even in the fledgling who chirps before breaking out of his shell.

Ikhnaton wanted his people to look for the divine not in battle or in blood sacrifice, but in flowers that opened, in birds arcing through the sky, and in human relations.

Aton was intangible yet manifest as an ever-present father and sustainer of life—a far cry from the animal gods Egyptians had been taught to worship. He was visible in the joy that caused young animals to frisk and play, or birds to flutter among the reeds. He was god of the simple delights of living.

He was also the loving father and mother of his whole creation.

"Your love is great and large," says one of Ikhnaton's poems of praise. "You fill the two lands of Egypt with your love. . . . Your rays encompass the lands. . . . You bind them together with love."

Ikhnaton's god was compassionate, tender, without anger—a gentle personality as on the whole Ikhnaton seems himself to have been. Of all men Ikhnaton was the first to grasp the truth about religion—that the divine is goodness incarnate, dwelling in men. Aton is a beneficent creator, a spirit informing and vitalizing all life, a creator who loves what he has created.

"Sole god, beside whom there is no other," wrote Ikhnaton, poet of the divine.

And again, on one of the great boundary stelae at Amarna:

"My reminder of eternity, my witness of the things of eternity, who fashioned himself with his own hands, whom no artificer knew."

Perhaps, if all his poems had survived, Ikhnaton would strike us as the greatest of all psalmists. As it is, we have two remarkable poems, the longer one so reminiscent of Psalm 104 that the Jews must have heard it in Egypt. Indeed, the distinguished historian, James Breasted, asserts that the idea of a god who cares for man came to the Jews from Egypt, and perhaps their ideas of monotheism, righteousness, and a personal relationship between god and man as well.

Here, from the longer hymn of praise, is a sample of Ikhnaton's thought:

You dawn in beauty at the far horizon,
O living Aton, source of life!
Rising in the east,
You fill all the land with your beauty.

Creator of the germ in woman
And of the seed that becomes man,
Giving life to the son in his mother's body,
Then soothing him that he may not weep,
His nurse even in the womb,
You give the breath of life to every one you create.

When the fledgling in the egg chirps within the shell
You give him breath even there to preserve him alive.
You gave him his term in the egg, and when to break it.
Forth he comes from the egg to chirp with all his might,
Going about on his two feet
When he has come forth.

How manifold are your works!
Yet are they hidden before men,
O single God, beside whom there are none.
For you have created the earth according to your heart.
The world lives in your hand. . .

Yourself are length of life,
And through you do all men live.

To grasp the virtuosity of this very young man's vision, we have to compare it with the primitive concepts that surrounded him—the gods in animal shapes, the stiff and complicated rituals of the temples, the preoccupation with death and the afterlife. Ikhnaton's was a religion of living. It overleaped the centuries to grasp a cosmic theism like Spinoza's, Emerson's, Whitman's.

God, author of the universe, showed himself to man in light, in life itself, in beauty, in love. The sense of an immanent divinity was strong:

"Though you are far away, your rays are upon the earth; though on high, your footprints are the day."

So, communing with himself, strong enough to turn aside all the influences that should have bound him to the old gods, and through his own happy marriage brought to understand that love is the basis of religion, Ikhnaton established a new faith. He expected that it would be the sole faith of his land and people, for he believed it to be as universal as it was self-evident.

There was no superstition in it, no ancient myths or rites, no appeal to fear. What it asserted, experience and reason could prove.

To bring it home to the people, Ikhnaton planned ceremonies in keeping with its sunlit, positive spirit. The temple he built at Akhetaton, though half a mile long, was not dark and secret like those of Thebes. It was full of airy courts open to the divine rays of the sun. There was no image of god, for Ikhnaton knew that god had no form—that instead he informed, he dwelt in, all of life. Never before had man conceived a formless deity.

Worship took place in the open where all could see. Near the high altar gathered the permanent choir and orchestra which, attached to the temple, performed several hours each day. Music —intended to induce a spirit of joy in the worshipers—was the

[34]

most prominent part of the ceremonies, which were simple and joyous.

When Ikhnaton installed Meryra as high priest, girls threw flowers in his path as he was borne upon the shoulders of his friends. Music, poetry, flowers, youth: it was the gay and informal and beautiful rather than the secret or ascetic that set the tone for Ikhnaton's religion as for his domestic and even his official and artistic life. No pharaoh before him would have dared to ride intimately through the streets, be seen at close hand by his people, even give a kiss to his queen as she rode beside him in his chariot! Youth was in the saddle, riding across an open, flowering countryside of eternal summer, and love united everything, from the chick in the egg to the beautiful young queen, to the universal spirit which created all.

The spirit carried over into the arts, which under Ikhnaton's bounteous and friendly hand were transformed from a stiff formality to a charming intimacy and an amazing naturalness.

On the walls and floors and ceilings of his palace calves gallop, fish swim, ducks fly, kingfishers plunge toward the water, and grasses bend in the wind. Nature, caught in all its moods, looks as if it had paused a moment for the artist and would then resume again. In everything it is as if life had suddenly been infused into the scene by Ikhnaton's universal life-force. The revolution he created in art was quite as remarkable as that in religion. For Ikhnaton, the two could not be separated. He would have agreed with Sir Thomas Browne that "Nature is the art of God."

To share this youthful joy of life with others, Ikhnaton made rich gifts to his favorites, showering down golden collars and other jewelry from the window of appearances.

At night he might lead Nefertiti up the stairway to an open balcony where they might sit in the cool of night, looking up at the bright stars in a clear sky, or out across the city to the river and to the watch fires of the guard.

So life went on in the gleaming, flower-decked city of Aton.

Never had there been a city like this, nor a ruler so fired with a vision combining artistic impulse with prophetic insight and rationality.

To celebrate the twelfth year of his reign, Ikhnaton held a great holiday. He was now twenty-nine, his queen twenty-eight. Down the great fifty-foot highway he came borne in his golden chair upon the shoulders of eighteen soldiers, the high crown on his head, the golden crook and flail in his delicate hands. Behind him rode Nefertiti and their daughters, led on with flags and the blare of music to the great temple.

Although Ikhnaton regarded himself as the special son and vehicle of Aton, he seems to have gone out of his way to have himself shown as a natural man—not as a stiff, depersonalized pharaoh. This too was part of the purposive consistency of his thought. If all nature is one, and if vital creativity is its core, then a dynamic naturalism is the only proper art, whether for king or commoner.

The art of Ikhnaton's reign revels in the joyous creativity of life itself, from the chick in the egg to the great pharaoh. The whole chain of being stems from one source. As he smells the flowers Nefertiti holds out to him, or gathers her into his lap, or kisses the little princess, he merges into that greater life which all the living share. That is how he wanted it to be. But what courage it took to be the first man to want this!

Ikhnaton saw religion as a total attitude toward life rather than as a set of prescribed rituals to be enacted. His view was total: all life should be religious, as all life had one source. "Living in truth" was his motto and philosophy.

This was not a new idea. Ikhnaton supported the ancient morality which traced back to the age of the pyramids. Foremost was Maat—truth or justice, a broad concept somewhat like the Hindu Dharma. Aton was the sustainer of truth. The moral order was an inseparable part of the universal order.

Unfortunately we know little more about "The Teaching," as

[36]

Ikhnaton's religion was called. If he left an ethic—and it seems that one so deeply concerned about religion must have done so—it has been lost. Perhaps it was destroyed by vengeful priests.

Because when he died, the priests whose power he had curbed made every effort to destroy his memory and his religion.

It is hard to think of Ikhnaton as a fanatic. Yet the fact is that he was so determined to establish monotheism that he ordered every mention of the name of the rival god Amon to be chiseled out of every temple, tomb and carving, wherever it occurred. Even his father's mausoleum did not escape, for his father's name included that of the god. The wealth of the temples was carted off to Amarna, golden statues melted down, priests driven out.

A few years later Ikhnaton ordered the names of every other god but Aton to be similarly erased.

Was this his response to a growing resistance on the part of the priests of Amon, with whom he had struggled ever since the vision had come to him? Or was it an attempt to deal with an even wider resistance?

Ikhnaton's religion amounted to more even than a complete change of faith for all his people. It involved a revolution which overturned old customs, old employments, which struck at the customary economy and even the continued existence of Egypt.

When Ikhnaton forbade the worship of Amon-Ra, he destroyed the livelihood of thousands who had made or sold amulets and charms, statues of the gods, mortuary figures, temple offerings and all the rest. His decree wiped out their employments at a stroke.

He wanted his people to be happy. Yet he could not avoid turning many against him. Atonism never became popular—it was too much for most minds to comprehend. Its simplicity and reasonableness were beyond the grasp of a people steeped in Amonism.

The logic of Ikhnaton's religion made him a pacifist. Aton, god of love, was inevitably the lord of peace. He was the first deity ever conceived by man who was not limited to a tribe or nation. He was for all. And such a god would not permit men to kill each other.

So, although the faithful General Horemheb kept warning the young pharaoh that he must act against treacherous men like Aziru the Amorite who were breaking up his empire, Ikhnaton refused to act. When the Hittites moved down into Syria, Horemheb begged permission to strike them down. But Ikhnaton, man of peace, would not go to war. Letter after letter came from lesser kings who were loyal to him, begging him to send support in order to hold the empire. He ignored them. He would not get embroiled in a war over Syria. Tribute stopped coming in. The pharaoh no longer knew where to find money. Egypt was fast being reduced from its position as the world's strongest power to that of a petty state.

Other disasters came. His mother died, then one of his little daughters. For two years the Nile did not overflow. It seemed as though god—or could it be the gods?—was working against him.

Ikhnaton's father had sired two sons by lesser wives before his death. Each was to marry one of Ikhnaton's daughters to keep the royal line firmly within the family, for Nefertiti never had a son. One of these boys, Sakere, became co-regent with Ikhnaton about 1356 when he married thirteen-year-old Meritaton. The other boy was Tutankhamen, who followed Sakere to the throne while still a young boy.

Ikhnaton was only a little over thirty when he died his religion rejected, his empire shattered, his faith in peace as a way of life a failure. Yet he was the first man in human history to understand the nature of the divine and to turn his back upon barbarism as a way of life. As husband, father, poet, teacher, patron and inspirer of the arts, and as philosopher, he was a great man. But he was too early. So were Gandhi and Thoreau in their time. Must it always be too early for such men?

Under Aye's direction, Tutankhamen returned the capital to Thebes, revitalized the army, and put Egypt back upon the road to empire. Under the influence of the priests of Amon he allowed the name of Ikhnaton to be chiseled off wherever it could be found. His burial place was also desecrated. Thus ended the great experiment.

It was not until General Horemheb took charge that Egypt grew strong again.

Ikhnaton's vision was complete. It was universal. He saw that the cosmos was one, that life had a single source, that it arose out of love and that God was love. Conquest and oppression had no place in this scheme. Ikhnaton was willing even to surrender the conquered part of his empire to this conviction. What looks to us like his worst act—expunging the names of the other gods from tomb and temple—was in his view an act to release men from bowing to false gods and an oppressive priesthood so that they might be free.

So pacifism had its first champion and its first failure. Yet the militarists of his time are forgotten; Ikhnaton lives.

3. Buddha
(563?-483? B.C.)

The Religious Teacher Who Gave Up God for Peace of Mind

 Two men might have changed our world beyond recognition, if those who profess to be their followers had really followed.

The two, of course, are Jesus of Nazareth and Siddhartha Gautama, known as the Buddha—"the one who has been awakened."

Something like 904 million call themselves Christians; Moslems come next, with 434 million; then Hindus with 336 million and Buddhists with 153 million. Buddhism has lost ground since its heyday, when much of India and China accepted its teachings. As with Christianity, its present forms differ greatly—sometimes it seems diametrically—from the teachings of its founder. Yet the kernel of a unique and noble teaching remains.

To distinguish between the teachings of the founder and the practices of the religion which bears his name is perhaps dangerous, surely difficult, and yet necessary as a means of understanding both the founder and his followers. Like Christianity, Buddhism developed in several directions over the course of the centuries. This in itself indicates either that there were ambiguities in the original teaching, or that different aspects of the

[40]

teaching were accentuated by different groups, or that the original teaching was ignored. All these things happened to Buddhism.

Siddhartha Gautama has often been called the prince, the son of a king. It is natural for followers to exaggerate the origins of the leader they venerate, especially in an age when kings amounted to something. The fact is that Siddhartha was the son of a large landholder, a sort of feudal baron of the Kshatriya or warrior caste.

The fact? To separate fact from invention is even more difficult in the case of Buddha than Jesus. Great men attract myth and story to themselves as flowers attract bees. Even in our own day we can see this. How many Lincoln stories are true, and how many invented? As with Washington, every hero has his Parson Weems, happy to imagine the things that ought to have happened because they aptly illustrate the man.

So with Buddha, the impact of his teaching was such that men tried to fill in the story of his life in a manner that would do justice to his stature. The few facts came to be so encrusted with the jewel of legend that some historians in despair have doubted the very existence of the man.

We need not go that far. Yet we may as well admit that the facts can probably never be known. To reject what strikes us as fanciful or miraculous may make Buddha more acceptable to our rationalist bias but does not guarantee accuracy either. Perhaps the best guarantee of Buddha's authenticity is that the great emperor Asoka within a century or so of his death, which occurred somewhere between 483 and 383 B.C., erected a memorial pillar at the place of his birth. The stupa (cairn) erected by the Sakyas near the boundary of Nepal, over their share of Buddha's ashes, has also been found.

His birthplace was in northern India not far from Nepal, in what is now known as the state of Bihar. North of the Ganges, in the sixth century before Christ, lay the kingdom of Kosala. Its northeastern tip—now known as Oudh—belonged to the Sakya princes. This was the family of Buddha. Northward the great Himalayas rose into cloud and snow. Winter nights were cold, but even in winter the hot sun and clear sky made this a clear, bright and happy land.

Legend has made the Buddha a wealthy prince and given him a palace for each season as well as forty thousand dancing girls to please and entertain him. The fact is that his family probably managed a modest country estate even though he was able to "wear silks and use toiletries brought from Benares"—the equivalent of Bond Street tailoring and Parisian perfumes.

Naturally enough, legends have gathered about his birth and childhood. His mother Maya had not known her husband when she became pregnant. Strains of heavenly music were heard as the infant came undefiled from his mother's right flank. Soon Kaladevala, a recluse, appeared from the Himalayas, prophesying Buddha's greatness as a religious teacher and shedding tears because he himself would not live to see the matured Buddha and hear his teachings.

Or there is the story of the young child being placed under a rose-apple tree one day while his father was doing the ritual plowing required of a prince at the start of the season. When the nurses returned to him, they found that while the shadows of all the other trees nearby had turned with the sun, the rose-apple's had remained still in order to shade the child.

Such stories have their value, not because they supply facts about Buddha but because they reveal how deeply those who followed him loved him and therefore sought to give him immortality among men.

It need not surprise us that he married at sixteen, or even that his wife, Gopa Yasodhara, was a cousin. The only child we hear of is a son named Rahula, who did not arrive until Siddhartha had reached his late twenties.

One of the many legends of Buddha's early life is worth telling, though it is clearly the sort of thing that gets invented after the fact to explain how the great one arrived at his teaching.

Suddhodana, Buddha's father, was determined that his son should be protected from the knowledge of sickness, disease and death. His reason for doing this was that a holy man had predicted the son would either become a great king or—if he chose to be a recluse—a supreme Buddha. So Siddhartha was surrounded by all things youthful and delightful, and so he spent the first twenty-eight years of his life. But in his twenty-ninth year, he begged that he might go out of the palace.

Driving with his faithful charioteer, Channa, he saw an old man with bent back painfully creeping along while leaning upon a staff.

"How did he arrive at this deplorable condition?" Siddhartha asked.

"It is the course of nature that all men must grow old and feeble, if they do not die young."

"I also, Channa?"

"Thou also, Master."

On their next ride, Siddhartha saw a leper, and next a decomposed corpse.

"What is the use of kingly splendor, all pomp and all enjoyment," he asked, "if they cannot guard me from old age, sickness and death?"

Struggling with this question, he met an ascetic whose features clearly reflected a deep inner peace. Siddhartha felt that if he could discover the causes of human misery, he might find a way of life which would bring him this inner peace.

This fourfold story illustrates far better than any verifiable biographical fact the nature of Buddha and Buddhism.

Siddhartha knew now that he must follow a course of life which would lead to a happiness more firmly based than the pretense that ill health, old age and death did not exist.

He arose at night, picking his way among the sleeping women, for a last look at his wife and his son, Rahula. A lamp of scented oil burned within the room, so that he could see Yasodhara lying on a bed strewn with jasmine and other flowers, her hand on her son's head.

"If I move aside the queen's hand and take my son," he thought, "the queen will awake and this will be an obstacle to my going. When I have become a Buddha, I will come back and see him."

Silently he left the room, the palace, taking his charioteer with him. When they had ridden some distance, he gave all his ornaments and fine clothes to Channa and sent him home. As Indians had done for centuries, he retired to the forest to seek the truth in silence and solitude.

He found there a holy man, and then another, but neither satisfied his longing for the truth. He went to the temple priests, only to be offended by the cruel animal sacrifices. Finally in the jungle of Uruvilva in Magadha he found five ascetics. Admiring their austerity and self-control, he too devoted himself to the search for truth through self-denial.

He fasted so severely that when he thought to touch his stomach, he found that he had hold of his backbone.

"The mark of my seat," he reportedly later told his disciples,

was like a camel's footprint through the little food. As the beams of an old shed stick out, so did my ribs stick out through little food. And as in a deep well the low-lying sparkling of the waters is seen, so in my eye-sockets was seen the deep low-lying sparkling of my eyes through the little food. . . . When I thought I would touch the skin of my stomach, I actually took hold of my spine, and when I thought I would touch my spine, I took hold of the skin of my stomach, so much did the skin of my stomach cling to my spine through the little food.

Finally he grew so weak that when he tried to rise one day from his bath in the river Nairanjana (today's Phalgu) he sank back into the stream. By grasping a branch that dipped toward the water, he managed to crawl out. But then he fainted by the way and might have died if Sujata, a herdsman's daughter, had not happened by. She revived him with rice gruel.

At last it was clear to him that this sort of self-torture led nowhere, and in disgust he gave it up, convinced that such abuse of the body was as bad as indulgence. His five friends then left him in disdain.

One night while he was in deep meditation under a fig tree, he perceived that the source of all suffering was desire, and that man could free himself by leading a pure life. At this moment he became a Buddha—an awakened or enlightened one.

When he considered how men condemned themselves to sorrow and suffering because they were the victims of desire, compassion overcame him. In the morning he set out for Benares, which even then was a holy city.

On the way he met an ascetic who stopped him, saying:

"Your faculties, friend, are clear, the color of your skin is pure and clean. Whom do you follow, friend, in leaving the world? Who is your teacher, and whose doctrine do you approve?"

Buddha answered that he had taught himself. "To Kasi City now I go, and in the blinded world the drum of the immortal will I beat."

In the Deer Park of Isipatana outside Benares he found the five men with whom he had lived an ascetic life, but who had left him in disgust when he had abandoned it. So when they saw him coming, they agreed that they would not greet him, nor would they rise in respect, nor would they take his bowl and robe.

"But as I approached," Buddha later told his followers, "the five monks were not able to abide by their decision. One approached and took my bowl and robe, one prepared a seat, and one set water for my feet."

Here the Buddha delivered his first sermon. Like himself, the five monks attained Nirvana—the state beyond desire. Soon he had sixty disciples, whom he sent in all directions to teach the truth to all men. Twelve of them became famous preachers.

Now for forty-five years the Buddha carried on his work of teaching men how to become free by overcoming desire.

His habits were simple. He would rise early in the morning— as who does not, in India? After washing and dressing, he would meditate in silence until it was time to go begging for his food. Sometimes alone, sometimes attended by disciples, he would walk to a nearby town or village and go from house to house until he had in his bowl food sufficient for his one daily meal. Sometimes he would eat the meal in a home, then talk to the family about the Dharma, the Buddhist law of life.

Returning to his residence, he would recommend subjects for meditation to his followers, then retire for the short rest the Indian climate encourages during the noontime heat. In the afternoon, when followers and neighbors had gathered, he would speak to them in the lecture hall. At the close of the day he would bathe again, explain difficult points of his philosophy to his disciples, and then spend the night either meditating, while he walked up and down in the cool of the evening, or sleeping in his chamber.

During nine months of the year he customarily traveled from place to place, walking fifteen to twenty miles a day. But during the three rainy months, he stayed at one of the monasteries which had grown up to serve his disciples.

Although intellectually tough, his teaching was not esoteric. He did not restrict it to the elect, but rather welcomed the opportunity to explain it to all, even to the simplest villagers. So it was natural that he should often, like Jesus, teach through parables and stories. Indeed the voluminous Buddhist scriptures contain thousands of such stories. Our difficulty in undertanding the teachings of Jesus is that we have so little text to work with. Our difficulty in understanding Buddha is that we have so much.

Once when Buddha held out his alms bowl to a Brahman farmer, the man said:

"I plough and sow, and having ploughed and sown, I eat. It

[46]

would be better if you were in like manner to plough and sow, and then you would also have food to eat."

"O Brahman," Buddha answered him, "I too plough and sow. Faith is the seed I sow; devotion is the rain that fertilizes it; modesty is the plough-shaft; the mind is the tie of the yoke; mindfulness is my ploughshare and goad. Truthfulness is the means to bind; tenderness, to untie. Energy is my team and bullock. Thus this ploughing is effected, destroying the weeds of delusion. The harvest that it yields is the ambrosia fruit of Nirvana, and by this ploughing all sorrow is brought to an end."

Then the Brahman poured rice gruel into a golden bowl and handed it to the Buddha.

"Eat, O Gautama, the milk-rice," he said. "Indeed, you are a husbandman; for you accomplish a ploughing which yields the fruit of immortality."

Were these truly the words that Buddha spoke?

Probably not. We need to remind ourselves again that absolute historical accuracy is impossible. But undoubtedly the story is accurate on the high level of truth to the significance and value of the Buddha's teaching.

So many are these stories—there are thousands of Buddhist "scriptures"—that one hardly knows how to select a few that will best illustrate the Buddha's teaching.

Should it be the story of the thirty wealthy young men who had been sporting with their wives in a grove? One of them, unmarried, had brought a courtesan along. While they were all busy at some game or other, the courtesan robbed them of their things and ran off.

As the young men ran seeking her through the forest they met Buddha. When they asked whether he had seen her, he said:

"What do you think, young men? Which is better, for you to go in search of a woman, or to go in search of yourselves?"

That search of self, so deeply implanted in Indian culture, is the beginning point of the Buddha's teaching. For what he discovered as he sat in meditation under the Bo tree was that knowledge comes only by experience. He swept away all speculation about things that could not possibly be known, even including all guesswork about the nature of God or his existence. To know the true nature of cause and effect was the bedrock of his system—an eminently practical thing. For it was in the nature of cause and effect that he found the key he had been looking for, the key that would open the door of release from suffering.

The cause of growing old and dying (those sorry creatures glimpsed from his chariot!), he now saw, was birth itself, and the desire of birth. Only by killing desire can new births and new misery be prevented. And the only way to accomplish this is to lead a pure life.

The conditions that go to make an individual are the very conditions that give rise to sorrow. As soon as individuality occurs, disease and decay begin.

This was the lesson Buddha had to teach the sorrowing young mother who, when her baby died, could not accept the fact but in her grief wandered from place to place with the little body in her arms, seeking a medicine to restore life. Finally she came to Siddhartha.

"Lord and master," she said, "do you know any medicine that will be good for my child?"

The Buddha knew that grief had taken her reason away, but he also knew how to bring it back.

"Yes, I know of some," he said.

She immediately asked him what herbs she should gather, since it was then the custom for the patient to bring the necessary simples to the doctor.

"I want some mustard-seed," he said. This was one of the commonest ingredients. But the Buddha added: "You must get it from some house where no son, or husband, or parent or slave has died."

"Very good," she said, and went off, still carrying the dead child with her.

The seed was easy to come by, but when she asked, "Has any son died here, or husband, or parent or slave?" the answer came:

"What is this that you say? The living are few, but the dead are many."

At each house where she stopped the answer was similar. "We have lost a son," or, "We have lost our parents."

At last, when she saw that every house had been visited by death, her mind began to clear and she understood that her suffering was common to all humanity. She buried the dead child in the forest and returned to Buddha.

"Have you the mustard-seed?" he asked.

"My lord, I have not. The people tell me that the living are few, but the dead are many."

Then Buddha explained to her the impermanence of all things. Accepting her lot, she became a disciple.

Buddha formulated his discovery in Four Noble Truths:

    I.   Life is suffering.
   II.   Pain comes only from desire.
  III.   Pain can be overcome only by overcoming desire.
  IV.   Desire is overcome by means of the Eightfold Path, which turns out to be self-discipline, self-therapy:
       1. Right knowledge (the Four Noble Truths)
       2. Right aspiration (wanting to overcome desire)
       3. Right speech (our speech exposes us; rightly channeled, it can lead us)
       4. Right behavior (do not kill, steal, lie, drink intoxicants, or be unchaste)
       5. Right livelihood (work that promotes life instead of destroying it)
       6. Right effort (constant striving toward the good life)
       7. Right mindfulness ("All we are is the result of what we have thought")
       8. Right absorption (mental concentration arrived at through repeated and habitual exercise and discipline)

In his first sermon, Buddha made it clear that the religious life must steer between two extremes.

There are two extremes, O monks, from which he who leads a religious life must abstain. What are those two extremes? One is a life of pleasure, devoted to desire and enjoyment, that is base, ignoble, unspiritual, unworthy, unreal. The other is a life of mortification; it is gloomy, unworthy, unreal. The Perfect One, O monks, is removed from both these extremes and has discovered the way which lies between them, the middle way which enlightens the mind, which leads to rest, to knowledge, to enlightenment, to Nirvana.

Nirvana, though usually translated as nothingness or oblivion, is actually a much more meaningful concept. Buddha would only say, "Bliss—yes, bliss, my friends, is Nirvana." It was a state which might be attained temporarily through meditation, here in this life, or ultimately after death—but only by one whose cycle of rebirths had finally reached to that perfection where he no longer had to be reborn.

Westerners have jumped to the conclusion that Buddhism is a counsel of despair, withdrawal, and inaction. The reason for this is that Westerners for at least 2500 years have suffered from the illusion of either-or, black or white, positive or negative. Two minutes' reflection would prove even to a moderate intelligence that experience rarely if ever can be described as either-or, nor that all colors are black or white, nor that all deeds are positive or negative. If experience proves anything, it is that good is mixed up with evil, joy with sorrow, rain with sunshine. Even such terms as a past and future or time and space are not mutually exclusive; for the future is always being affected by the past, and our own era has shown us how time and space have intermingled.

The East does not thus divide experience into two heaps, or insist upon divorcing this aspect from that. So Buddha, though he perceived the elements in life which made for suffering, did not therefore conclude that life was evil and nonexistence good. Salvation, he saw, depended upon modifying one's inner nature through one's own exertions.

[50]

Because he was not misled by the philosophy of black or white, Buddha began with the idea that the individual could not and must not differentiate himself from his neighbor. Since evil comes from suffering born of desire, good implies the victory over selfish desire and an equal respect for the rights and persons of others, even enemies.

Life is one. Whatever separates one aspect of life from another causes suffering. We must learn to regard each other as facets of one underlying reality. The way to escape from suffering, therefore, is to escape from narrow self-interest and to recognize ourselves for what we are—inseparable parts of one vast and universal life.

Compassion therefore became the overruling virtue in Buddhism, as love in Christianity, and Siddhartha Gautama was remembered of men as the Compassionate Buddha.

"As a mother, even at the risk of her own life, protects her son, her only son, so let him cultivate love without measure towards all human beings," the *Metta Sutta* counsels the faithful. "Let him cultivate towards the whole world—above, below, around—a heart of love unstinted, unmixed with the sense of differing or opposing interests."

This compassion manifested itself in the doctrine of ahimsa—nonviolence—which even then apparently was not new in India and which Gandhi was to take up again with consummate statesmanship. (See Chapter 14.)

When Buddhism divided and spread over Asia after Buddha's death, the Theravada (Way of the Elders) or Hinayana (Small Vehicle) which captured Ceylon, Burma, Thailand and Indochina accentuated wisdom as the key virtue and man as individual. Mahayana (Great Vehicle), which spread northward through India to Tibet, Mongolia, China, Korea and Japan, emphasized the oneness of man and the virtue of compassion. It was the Mahayana Buddhism of compassion which converted the Emperor Asoka (Chapter 4), whose enthusiasm started it on the way to being a world religion.

[51]

Hinayana was to remain a religion for monks and ascetics, demanding a strong intellectual discipline of meditation. Mahayana became a popular religion, complete with rituals and prayers to the Buddha regarded as a god. This he would have abhorred. While Theravada held together like Roman Catholicism, Mahayana continued splitting up like Protestantism into a bewildering number of sects. And why not? Man may be essentially one, but his ways of showing it are amazingly various. Different temperaments require different ways of religious expression.

Buddha's teaching is usually referred to as Dharma, which means more than any single English word. It means the teaching, the doctrine. It also means the law which rules the universe. The word is still widely used by Hindus today to mean something like religious duty or obligation. Each individual has a dharma to which he must be obedient if he would be happy. These individual dharmas provide patterns of right conduct and duty which are somehow related to Dharma, the universal law.

The Dharma which Buddha taught was not a dogmatic statement about the universe or the gods. Buddha swept away as idle all speculations about the unknowable. He made no assertions about divinities; he did provide a psychological attitude which, he claimed, would end suffering.

But our special interest is in what Buddha did about peace, and how his Dharma led men in that direction.

Buddha, like Jesus, loved to tell stories. He knew that a narrative which made people react to one another had far more effect than abstruse arguments.

Here is one of those stories.

Brahmadatta, a great king, destroyed a lesser king named Dighiti, killed his wife, and took over his kingdom. Dighiti's son Dighavu, however, managed to escape. Unknown and unrecognized, he got a humble job in the palace of Brahmadatta. One night the king heard him playing the lute and singing. The music moved him so deeply that the next morning he sent for the young man, was pleased with him, and made him his charioteer and companion.

A day came when the king, having driven into the forest with Dighavu, grew sleepy. Brahmadatta dismounted from the chariot, lay down under a tree, and slept. Now, Dighavu realized, he had the king in his power and could slay him in just revenge for the injuries done his family.

At that moment the king started from his sleep.

"I dreamed," he told his charioteer, "that Dighavu the son of Dighiti whom I killed was about to slay me."

Dighavu stroked the king's head with one hand and drew his sword with the other. Then he told Brahmadatta who he was. The king begged for his life.

"How have I the power to grant your majesty your life?" said Dighavu. "Your majesty, however, might grant me my life."

So each granted the other his life. And Brahmadatta restored to Dighavu all the lands and possessions he had taken from his father and gave him his daughter in marriage.

All this because Dighavu had remembered the dying words of his father:

"Hatreds are not quenched by hatred. Nay rather, dear Dighavu, hatreds are quenched by love."

To the Buddha, all war was unholy because it ignored the oneness of life.

"Every victory begets hate," he said, according to the Dharmapadda, "because the one you overcome is not blessed. Only the one who forgoes both victory and defeat, content and glad at heart, is truly blessed."

Or again: "Although one might conquer a thousand thousand in battle, the man who conquers himself is the greatest warrior."

And finally: "Better than a thousand idle songs is a single song which brings the hearer peace."

No one knows the details of the Buddha's forty-five-year ministry. There are stories of his return home, of his father's displeasure when even there he insisted upon begging for his daily meal, of his wife and son becoming followers and even entering the Buddhist order. But none of this is certain. And there are the touching stories of Ananda, a cousin who became towards the end Buddha's beloved disciple.

At eighty, Buddha perceived that his life was drawing towards its close. One day he stopped in the home of Chunda, a smith, where he ate some mushrooms. Some of them were of the poisonous variety, and he was tortured by violent pains. Followed by his disciples, he crossed the river and lay down in a grove of sal trees.

Even in his last hours he continued his teaching.

"Expect nothing from pitiless gods, themselves subject to the law of Karma, who are born, grow old and die only to be reborn, and have not succeeded in throwing off their own woe," he told them. "Expect all from yourself: nor forget that each can gain a power greater than that of Indra himself."

Tears were trickling down Ananda's cheeks.

"After all I have taught you," the Master gently reprimanded him, "how can you still feel grief? Is it so hard then for a man to get rid of all suffering?"

He repeated his doctrine of the Four Noble Truths. He named the four objects of pilgrimage—his birthplace, the place of his enlightenment, the Deer Park of his first sermon, this place where he would achieve Nirvana. He even gave the monks some advice about women.

"How are we to act, Lord, with regard to women?" Ananda had asked.

"Not seeing them, Ananda."

"If we see them, how are we to act?"

"Not speaking, Ananda."

"What must be done by one who speaks?"

"Mindfulness must be exercised, Ananda."

Wise man!

Then the Buddha praised his beloved disciple for his virtue, made one last convert, and said:

"Now then, O monks, I tell you that all compound things are transitory. Therefore strive diligently!"

As he lay there on his right side under the trees, though it was out of season, flowers in full bloom fell upon him and covered his body. Sandalwood powder fell from the sky, adding its perfume to the air, while divine music and singing came from above.

How the Buddha himself would have reproved his disciples for making up such stories! Yet they have their value, for they tell us how simple souls longed to see that this wonderful teacher had his due of praise.

As far back as we can see, India has been full of men seeking answers to the riddle of life—that all its joys are based upon its inescapable transience, that the basis of its unity is its diversity, that the way to gain is to give. Buddha was a product of centuries of such seeking. The answers he found, based upon universal experience which anyone could test for himself, seemed so satisfactory that they spread for thousands of miles to men and women of many countries.

Buddha's approach was honest. He did not promise divine intervention. He did not agree to do the thinking or the suffering for his followers. He told them they must do it themselves, but he did promise to lessen the suffering by telling them how to think about it. He told them how to overcome ignorance, and then desire. His teaching was not abstruse, metaphysical, or theological. It was practical. Through knowledge of self, it led to compassion for all.

Did he change men?

Yes. His most important convert, as the next chapter will show, was an emperor who made Buddhism his guideline, carrying it not only to the whole of India but to lands beyond—an emperor who actually seems to have given up the waging of war.

The following generations, especially the young and the old, flocked to Buddhist monasteries in such numbers that society became alarmed at the possible economic and social effects. Thousands of men and women took up the begging bowl and the life of contemplation. Large monasteries flourished, some of them apparently built by Asoka himself. And all these members of the Sangha (monastic community) accepted the principle of non-violence as a basic part of the discipline.

Wherever Buddhism went, compassion and nonviolence went too. In Ceylon, Devanampiya Tissa, who is supposed to have accepted Buddhism as a result of an embassy from Asoka, founded the great monastery at Anuradhapura. Pieces of it may still be seen there, along with the sole surviving offshoot of the famous tree under which Buddha attained his enlightenment. Wandering among the ruins of temples, the huge white stupas pointing at the sky while pilgrims enter for a look at the revered tree, one gets a sense not only of a living religion but of the vast backward and abysm of time through which it has survived.

Buddhism entered China in the later or Eastern Han Dynasty around the beginning of our era, first by way of central Asia and then from India. The Emperor Ming spoke favorably of it in a decree of the first century. Flourishing by the close of the Han Dynasty, it had been transformed into an institution that included gods, rituals, images, ten heavens and ten hells, and salvation for individual souls. Chinese scholars made the long trek to India between the years 200 and 600 to locate authentic texts. Under imperial patronage shrines, images, temples and monasteries multiplied. But in China Buddhism lost the emphasis on self-knowledge, self-discipline and Nirvana that Buddha had taught. Instead, it compromised with the popular demand for answers to prayer, rebirth in a happy heaven, and salvation. Omit'o (Amidha) and Kuan-yin became popular gods to whom the simple might pray and through whom, rather than through self-discipline, they might achieve heaven.

The Ch'an sect, however (the word comes from Sanskrit *dhyana*, meditation), emphasized the Buddha-nature in every man, the value—even the necessity—of meditation, and therefore of self-discipline and self-knowledge. In Japan this stem of original Buddhism came to be known as Zen. Internationally, it is the strongest survivor of original Buddhism.

About 972 the Buddhist canonical books were printed by imperial order in Szechuan. One hundred and thirty thousand wooden blocks were required for the job, which was repeated with additions in the next century in Fukien and elsewhere. This was 1500 years after Buddha's birth. Until recent times, Buddhism has been a strong and seminal force in China's intellectual and artistic life.

Buddhism was the most popular religion with all the Mongols. Kublai Khan (1214–1294) himself gladly accepted relics of the Buddha from the raja of Ceylon. But this did not prevent him from raiding, invading and pillaging like his predecessors, until the Mongol hand had been felt all the way from Russia to Japan. By now Buddhism, following the usual history of religions, had been corrupted into something the Buddha would not have recognized as his own.

In 372 Buddhism reached Koguryu, northernmost of the three kingdoms into which Korea was then divided. By 552 or thereabouts it began to play a significant role in Japan, where it remains important to this day in a variety of forms and sects. Emperor Yomei became a convert shortly before his death about 587. His clan, the Soga, continued their sponsorship. During the reign of Suiko, first officially recognized empress, the Crown Prince Shotoku (593–622) imported the Chinese form of government and firmly established Buddhism by founding several great monasteries, including Shitennoji, Hokoji and Horyuji. Horyuji, said to include the world's oldest wooden building, remains today as a stirring reminder of the long journey Buddhism made from India, and of the intellectual and artistic force it still was able to exert upon the receptive Japanese.

In the many beautiful stone, wood and bronze statues of Buddha and of the goddess of mercy Kwannon, Japan still shows the visitor in tangible form the compassion and peace of the Buddhist philosophy. Although Buddhism has had its ups and downs in Japan, it has never been submerged. The world-wide interest in Zen has stirred a revived interest in its homeland, and several other Buddhist sects also show signs of vigor. Whether the Japanese in their earnest quest for peace can draw sustenance from the essentially pacifist bloodstream of Buddhism it may be too early to judge.

An interesting offshoot of Japanese Buddhism is that of our own Hawaii and West Coast temples, founded by Japanese immigrants and sustained by their descendants. All the principal sects of Japanese Buddhism reproduced themselves in Hawaii during the first quarter of this century—Shin (both branches), Hokkekyo, Nichiren, Jodo, Shingon, Tendai, and Soto-shu, a subsect of Zen.

Carriers at first of the home culture for which the immigrant workers felt a natural nostalgia, the temples gradually began Americanizing themselves in order to hold the rising generation. They inaugurated Sunday services, a thing then unheard of in Japan. They installed pews. They brought in pianos, organs, choirs. They used Japanese and English instead of Sanskrit. They formed YMBAs and YWBAs. They held young people's meetings and old people's meetings. They opened Sunday schools where you could hear childish trebles singing:

> Buddha loves me, that I know,
> For the Sutras tell me so.

They even began to conduct marriages and to emphasize the aspects of Buddhism which the surrounding Christian community stressed—peace, love of man, equality.

Southeast from India Buddhism spread into lands where it has entered even more fully into the lives of the people than in China and Japan. You cannot walk down a street in Burma, Thailand or the Indochina peninsula without seeing the men in yellow robes, often with bowls in their hands. The temples and pagodas of Rangoon or Bangkok, with their startling color, their prodigality of ornament, their striking shapes and designs, are the dominant features of the cities. Everything else by comparison seems pale and neutral.

Yet the Buddhism of these countries is closer to the original austerities than the Buddhism of the north. Most young men spend a period of their lives as monks, following the contemplative life. Buddha in these lands is not a god to be worshiped but a paragon to be imitated. Buddhist priests are firmly integrated into community life. They visit the sick, manage the festivals, officiate at funerals and naming ceremonies, teach, supply books and even bathhouses, act as safe depositories and give counsel to those in trouble. Governments have also used them to teach hygiene and modern agriculture.

These men are often politically active. In Burma it was the monks who led the independence struggle, in Ceylon Buddhism has become the dominant element in the political struggle, while in Laos Buddhism is the state religion and the two controlling groups, religious and political, are interrelated. In these lands families often give as much as five to ten per cent of their income to the temple.

Ironically, the religion which captured the hearts of most of Asia, where over half of mankind lives, gradually disappeared from its homeland until there was hardly a Buddhist left in India. The decline began at least as early as 900 A.D., when Hinduism incorporated its best features. It lingered on in Bengal and Bihar for another three hundred years until the Muslim conquests brought in a new and militant religion.

The hard, inescapable question now has to be asked: Did Buddha and Buddhism, in their tremendous impact upon Asia, make it measurably more peaceable?

As soon as the question is phrased that way, it becomes clear that we do not know. There is no experimenting with history—no way of deciding what would have happened if this or that particular element had been omitted from the mix. We cannot even know whether the nature of human history is such that, if Siddhartha Gautama had not played his role in it, another and similar man might have done so. Yet the history of India, with its parallel development of another peaceable religion, Jainism, suggests that perhaps this would have played the role of Buddhism. It remains a small but sturdy influence today. A country so full of spiritual seekers would surely have found another Buddha. But whether his personality and his persuasiveness would have set off a reaction of equal proportions, no one can say.

Looking at the wars for sovereignty in India, or the waves of aggression from the Mongols, or the continuous struggles between rival houses or clans in China and Japan, one can hardly call Asia's history any more peaceable than that of Europe.

So what, after all, did the Compassionate One accomplish with a message which aimed at changing the nature and behavior of men? Would human history have been even more bloody if he had never lived? Were his standards so high that he really did not alter men's behavior at all, so that they either withdrew from the world, and thus left it free to go its old way, or stayed in it and ignored him? Does the great teacher of peace ask too much and end by getting nothing? Is pacifism self-defeating, because it lies beyond human capability? And is it always the fate of the spiritual leader to ask so much of men that they corrupt his teaching, chopping it down to something they think they can control? Is that the melancholy history of all religions?

One way of answering the question is to look at a human group before it has been touched by such a religion.

Before Captain Cook visited Hawaii, these small islands were in the grip of a dual tyranny, the chiefs and the priests. The common people could be struck down on the spot if even unwittingly they allowed their shadow to touch a chief. Priests went after victims in the dark of night so as to be able to make their human sacrifices. Commoners had to do whatever the chiefs required of them, living under a constant cover of fear. Meanwhile the chiefs fought each other continuously, and the commoners suffered the results. Infanticide was common. Maiming, including the gouging out of eyes for slight offenses, prevailed. Life oscillated between fleeting pleasures and an underlying fear.

And here in Hawaii we do have a sort of laboratory, since the coming of Christianity completely renovated Hawaiian society, putting an end to ritual murder and all the other inhumanities, and establishing a regime of peace and justice. It is also true that the coming of the white man with his diseases nearly put an end to the Hawaiians, but that is another story.

Similarly, Buddhism did lessen if not end animal sacrifice in India. Though it was no more able than Christianity to end war, it did tend to make the arts, meditation, compassion and a concern for ethical conduct more important to men than they would otherwise have been.

Perhaps the final test is this. Who can name the thousands of kings, emperors, chieftains and warriors who carried on their bloody work throughout the centuries while the teachings of this one meditative man swept the whole Asian world? What other man ever made half the impact upon Asia that this one made? Do we then call him a failure because few could live up to his teachings, or a success because so many wanted to be identified with him even though they could not do as he would have them?

The empires have fallen, but the teachings are still there—as fresh, as challenging, as exciting as when the five disciples first heard them 2500 years ago. They have only to be tried.

4. Asoka
(295?-c. 232 B.C.)

The King Who Tried to Merge Religion and Empire for Peace

 In the year 327 B.C. Alexander the Great, a young man with a thirst for far places, crossed the Hindu Kush Mountains with a body of light troops and cavalry. Impatient to reach the heart of India, he hurried through mountain valleys, battling the fierce mountain tribes in their walled villages, then pressed on until he had reached the Indus River.

Here, after his generals Perdiccas and Hephaestion had built him a bridge, he crossed over into the Punjab in 326. Taking advantage of a quarrel among local princes, he made an alliance with one, then moved on to the Hydaspes just as the monsoon rains flooded the river. Rajah Paurava (Porus) awaited him on the other side with two hundred elephants, India's version of the tank.

While the sheeted rain drummed through the night, Alexander took some of his men farther up the river, crossed, and bore down upon Paurava and his elephants. The tough Macedonian army, shrewd in all the ways of fighting, surprised and routed the Indian prince, wounded him, and took him prisoner.

But Alexander knew how vast a distance separated him from home, and that he must now win his victories by alliance rather than annihilation. Making friends with Porus, he headed east again, lusting like a lover to thrust himself far into India.

But at the banks of the Beas even Alexander's tough troops refused to go farther. Alexander raged. He thirsted to reach the Ganges, as if he were dying for a drink of its water. He longed to seek out and subdue the rich kings he believed to be there, see the magnificence of their courts and palaces, take a few more women, and enforce his sovereignty over all.

For three days he fought the stubborn resistance of his men. In the end, even he, the great emperor who had seized everything from the Danube to the Indus, destroying the great Persian empire, had to give way to the will of his troops and turn homeward. The lands he had conquered east of the Indus he left in Indian hands. To the west he left Macedonian governors. Three years later he died at Babylon, aged thirty-two.

At about this time Chandragupta Maurya began his rise as ruler and unifier of North India. Plutarch says it was he who urged Alexander to advance beyond the Beas. If this is true, Alexander's own troops prevented it. In any case, Chandragupta did for himself what he advised Alexander to do: he overthrew the Nanda emperor and took his capital, Pataliputra (modern Patna).

Chandragupta finally locked horns with the Greeks in the person of Seleucus Nicator, a general of Alexander's who was trying to make the eastern parts of Alexander's empire his own. About 305 B.C. the Indian defeated the Greek. Nicator had to give up part of Afghanistan in return for five hundred elephants. He also sent an ambassador, Megasthenes, to Chandragupta's court—no doubt to keep an eye on this rising emperor and report what he was up to. It is through what survives of Megasthenes' writings that we know what Chandragupta's court was like.

The emperor lived in an enormous wooden palace, surrounded with luxuries in such variety and quantity that Megasthenes, no stranger to opulence, was astounded by what he saw.

The capital city, standing on the banks of the Son above its merging with the Ganges, was defended with huge palisades of timber, a broad moat, sixty-four gates and 570 towers.

The palace itself, resembling that of Persepolis which Alexander had burned, was vast, its many pillars clasped by circling vines artfully decorated with gold, and with silver birds perched in the branches. Royal courtesans followed the king with umbrella, golden pitcher and fan, waiting upon him as he traveled in his litter or sat upon his throne. To divert himself, the king watched elephant fights or bet upon races in which oxen and horses were yoked together. When he rode out in his chariot, four horses pulled him.

Before Chandragupta, the government of India had belonged largely to princes of small territories who sometimes joined in confederations. But Chandragupta, aided by an adviser known as Kautilya, or Chanakya, or Vishnugupta, worked out a centralized form of government. Kautilya has been called both able and unscrupulous; perhaps he was both. Both as Kautilya and as Chanakya he has been perpetuated in the place names of the diplomatic enclave of New Delhi—no doubt with good reason.

Administrators and magistrates controlled the economic and political life of the state, maintaining order and collecting taxes. Traveling inspectors checked the work of local administrators. An elaborate secret service system operated everywhere, with courtesans and prostitutes among its ablest members.

Some sort of caste system was already in existence and to a certain extent was related to occupations—already specialized into activities as varied as executioner, acrobat, potter, barber, dancer and snake charmer. Plural wives were common, sexual activity comparatively free and unrelated to the idea of morality.

A change was taking place from a nomadic to an agrarian, and from an agrarian to a trading, economy. Guilds of artisans and merchants came into being; trade routes stretched beyond India into Burma eastwards and through Taxila towards Iran and Europe. Good roads bound the empire together; the road known today in Delhi as the Grand Trunk Road ran through

[64]

the Punjab to Taxila. Traders followed a sea route to Ephesus and Africa, and those crossing the deserts traveled at night, using the stars for guides.

Craftsmanship reached a high level. Many metals were mined and manufactured into objects of use and decoration. The wonderful stone carving seems to spring from nowhere, since nothing of a previous period has come to light.

A productive, centralized, taxable economy was necessary to support Chandragupta's opulent court and his army of a million men, divided into specialized groups. The cavalry carried lances into combat, while the archers used a bow so strong that they held one end of it with the foot, shooting an arrow three yards long. But the backbone of the army was its elephants. No respectable king thought he could win a victory without them. Chandragupta had them in thousands, each one attended by three fighting men and a driver.

Chandragupta accomplished his great work of unification in twenty-four years. Hardly anything is known of his son, Bindusara, who followed him, except that he asked Antiochus I, king of Syria, to send him figs, wine, and a sophist. He got the wine and figs, but Antiochus refused to send a sophist. Greek philosophers, he said, were not for export.

About 269 B.C. Bindusara's son Asoka (pronounced Ashoka) came to the throne while still in his twenties, after a four-year interregnum. He had probably spent some time at Taxila as viceroy. There the currents of Europe would have touched him, for Taxila was not only the center of trade with central Asia and the West but a great seat of Hindu learning as well. Here Panini, the great scholar who had reduced grammar to a science, had taught a century before.

As with Buddha, it is difficult to get at the real person of Asoka, to separate legend from fact, or to get hold of enough solid matter to revitalize the man. Yet, because we do know that he too was one of the great men of all time, it is worth the effort to

[65]

puzzle out what manner of man he was and what made him an apostle of peace.

Ironically, the first major event in his life that can be pinned down is his conquest of Kalinga. Kalinga was the area in the south between the eastern Ghats and the sea, and between the Godavari and Mahanadi Rivers. The conquest happened during the ninth year of his reign, that is, in 260 B.C. Happily, we have his own account of it, preserved in one of the rock edicts which even after the passage of more than two thousand years bring him close to us.

"150,000 people were taken captive," he wrote, "100,000 were killed, and many more died. Just after the taking of Kalinga, the Beloved of the Gods began to follow Righteousness, to love Righteousness, to give instruction in Righteousness. . . . Today, if a hundredth or a thousandth part of those who suffered in Kalinga were to be killed, to die, or to be taken captive, it would be very grievous to the Beloved of the Gods."

By the time Asoka began to feel remorse over his conquests, he had seized an empire greater than both India and Pakistan today, since it included present-day Afghanistan. Although the southern tip of India remained unconquered, its rulers probably acknowledged Asoka as suzerain. And though he did not take Ceylon by force, he did, as we shall see, take it by love.

So here was the greatest emperor India had known, repenting himself of the way of conquest in the ninth year of his reign and devoting the rest of his life—some thirty years—to the way of peace.

Skeptics might say that having conquered everything in sight, he found it convenient to hold what he had through conciliation. But the story of Alexander makes it plain that those who love conquest rarely recover from it. And for Asoka there was still that southern tip, and the island of Ceylon.

Something happened to make him begin to follow righteousness.

[66]

The thing that happened was contact with the ideas of Siddhartha Gautama. In the hundred years since his death, his teachings had spread, monasteries had grown up, and thousands of monks were practicing the austerities which they believed Buddhism demanded.

At this time no big temples had been raised, nor were there any images of the Buddha. In keeping with the great teacher's own spirit and teachings, he was memorialized only by such symbols as an empty chair, a pair of footprints, a wheel.

Ritualism had not encrusted the original ethical teachings. But stupas enclosing the relics of Buddha or a Buddhist saint had become centers of devotion.

The appeal of Buddhism, then, was not through the elaborate art and ritual which developed later, but as a guide to living. Its system of social ethics made each individual responsible for his own behavior. This spirit of social consciousness was well suited to the Maurya period—to the growth of commerce and cities, and to a more sophisticated system of political administration. Indeed the parallel might be drawn between a rising Buddhism and—centuries later—the rise of Protestantism and capitalism in the West.

Economic and political change, as always, offered opportunities for able men who had been kept in the lower ranks of society. In India the caste system made social mobility especially difficult. Rigid Brahmanism, resisting change of all kinds, was out of step with the times. Buddhism, which renounced caste, offered a way out. It was part of the current which was sweeping through all things. Although its central message was to put an end to useless speculation and empty ritual, concentrating upon right living, it also praised prudence in business.

"The man grown wealthy," says one text, "should divide his money in four parts: on one part he should live, with two expand his trade, and the fourth he should save against a rainy day."

Such a text was well designed to draw the allegiance of the

rising classes of traders, manufacturers, administrators—even of an emperor.

Buddhist legend would like us to believe that Asoka started life as a thoroughly wicked man. After his conversion, he became a paragon of righteousness and died in sorrow, owning nothing but half a mango. Such a story was obviously invented to teach the power of Buddhism, even over the great, and the inevitability of suffering. It tells us nothing about the historic Asoka.

Asoka, like many royal heirs, had to fight his way to the throne. Perhaps the orthodox Hindu elements opposed him. Buddhism, though not anti-Hindu, was essentially protestant—a protest against dead ritual, social standpatism and moral stagnation. It welcomed any to its ranks. It may therefore have looked to Asoka like a way of gathering wide support. He may even have guessed that it could supply that underlying symbol structure he needed in order to hold a vast empire together. This, in fact, is what Constantine and Charlemagne were to do with Christianity centuries later.

"I have been a Buddhist layman for more than two and a half years," Asoka confessed in his Minor Rock Edict, "but for a year I did not make much progress. Now for more than a year I have drawn close to the community and have become more ardent."

The conqueror of Kalinga, sickened by the close-up view of carnage on the battlefield and suffering among the innocent, was clearly looking for a better way of life and governance. Those words, so human, so close after more than two thousand years, have the sound of a living man in them.

So in the ninth year of his reign, sick of conquest, he began to look for a better way of ruling and joined the Buddhist community as a layman. Two years later he became a member of the order, and after another two years felt himself to be on the eightfold path which leads to Nirvana—the end of desire and suffering.

In the thirteenth year of his reign he began to compose the inscriptions which, carved on rocks and pillars throughout India,

[68]

tell us most of what we know about him, providing the first solid documentary evidence in Indian history.

These edicts—there are some thirty of them—center on one thing, the conduct of life. And the conduct of life is to be shaped upon one principle—Dhamma (Dharma).

What did Asoka mean by Dhamma?

As a ruler, he had come to see that good government depends upon a proper attitude among the governed. To create, encourage and foster this attitude in his people was the essential purpose of the edicts. And the key to this attitude was a sense of social responsibility.

Asoka's Dhamma seems to have been his own invention. Though the word was ancient and the idea of a moral law deeply embedded in Hinduism, Asoka created something new. He separated moral conduct from ritual. He conceived of Dhamma as a universal law, applying equally to all men and not differentiated by caste. He separated it also from theology. This insistence upon right living rather than ritual, this disregard for theological speculation which could never be proved, was of course a faithful following of the Buddha's original teaching.

"Thus speaks the Beloved of the Gods," says the Second Pillar Edict. "Dhamma is good. And what is dhamma? It is having few faults and many good deeds, mercy, charity, truthfulness, and purity."

For Asoka, Dhamma was a way of life based on the highest concept of social ethics and civic responsibility. Like any ethical teacher, Asoka speaks out against cruelty, anger, pride, envy. But what he seems to have been seeking was a practical guide to conduct—a guide so simple that all men could follow it. Specifically, he asked that men fulfill their family obligations, show courtesy toward slaves and servants, reverence toward elders, gentleness toward animals. He recommended moderation in owning goods and dispensing wealth, tolerance toward all religions.

Men should practice restraint in the way they speak about other sects. To honor another man's religion is actually to gain security for one's own. Each sect—Asoka was thinking of Hindus, Buddhists, Jains—should listen to the teaching of the others and profit from it.

His aim, clearly, was to lay down so firm and broad an ethical base that men of all faiths could embrace it as their own.

Asoka's genius was in recognizing that human relations are what matter most—not ritual, not memorizing old texts, not a slavish following of tradition.

He must also have had the genius to see that by stressing Dhamma he was shifting the sanction of moral values from the king as a person to the idea of virtue itself. Kings might come and go, but the idea of righteousness was universal and eternal.

Yet he could not entirely let go of the personal relation.

"All men are my children, and just as I desire for my children that they should obtain welfare and happiness, both in this world and in the next, so do I desire for all men," he says in one of the edicts.

Again, in the Fifth Major Rock Edict: "It is hard to do good, and he who does good, does a difficult thing." This was the conclusion Alexander's teacher, Aristotle, had reached. But Asoka, being an emperor, goes on: "I have done much good."

In the succeeding edict:

"I consider that I must promote the welfare of the whole world, and hard work and the dispatch of business are the means of doing so. Indeed there is no better work than promoting the welfare of the whole world."

Ceremonies Asoka regarded as a waste of time.

"The one ceremony which has great value is that of dhamma," he announced in the Ninth Rock Edict. Then he went on to explain what he meant. "This ceremony includes regard for slaves and servants, respect for teachers, restrained behavior toward living beings, and donations—these and similar practices are called the ceremony of dhamma. So father, son, brother, master, friend, acquaintance and neighbor, should think, 'This is virtuous, this is the ceremony I should practice, until my object is achieved.' "

In the place of animal sacrifices, ablutions, fire, the burning of incense—all empty of meaning, in his view—Asoka would substitute the deeper ritual of right conduct. His point of view is similar to that of the Quakers, who observe no rituals or sacraments, believing that the conduct of life itself is sacramental.

Perhaps it was his aversion to killing which led him to his dislike of religious ceremony. For the way of nonviolence and peace is the strongest, the most repeated item in his code.

First he asked his people to refrain from the killing or sacrificing of any living thing. As an example to them, he reduced the large number of animals killed daily for food in his palace to two peacocks and a deer, promising that even this would not continue long. He put an end to royal hunts, once the chief sport of kings and nobles. Instead, he made pilgrimages to holy places or visited distant parts of his empire to see how the people were living. And he asked that prisoners, children, and the aged and afflicted be kindly treated. In the Seventh Rock Edict he asked the various communities and sects not to stay apart but to mingle and to learn from one another. A policy of toleration and understanding was central to his thought.

Then in the Thirteenth Rock Edict he expressed a new idea. He had seen the horrors of war and killing. He had seen the force in an idea—the idea of Dhamma. Now he put them together. Dhamma itself would become the conqueror by winning the minds of men to righteousness, and war would not be necessary any more. It was a grand idea, one that Ikhnaton would have understood, one that really breathed in the teaching of Buddha and exhaled it in a new form.

"This inscription of dhamma," he said, "has been engraved so that any sons or great grandsons I may have will not think of gaining new conquests, and in whatever victories they may gain will be satisfied with light punishment. They should consider

[71]

conquest only by dhamma to be true conquest, and to delight in dhamma should be their whole delight, for this is of value in this world and the next."

It is easy to see in this the prudence of a man who has grabbed all he wants and would like to hold onto it. But Asoka's acts showed that he meant what he said.

First, he established throughout his empire a network of Dhamma mahamattas, or overseers of righteousness. Through them he hoped to offer social services to the lower castes and the unfortunate. These officers were to have access to the king at all times, whether he was eating or sleeping. How much they accomplished we really do not know. But the setting up of a nationwide social service was itself of historic importance.

We do know that Asoka ordered wells dug every mile or so along the principal roads so that travelers might refresh themselves, that he planted shade trees against the hot sun, grew medicinal herbs to treat the ailing, and took an interest in medical care for both man and beast.

Eager to spread his gospel, he sent missionaries beyond his own borders in all directions—to Kashmir, into the Himalayas, to Burma and South India and the lands bordering the Indus, and even to five Hellenic kings: Antiochus II Theos of Syria, Ptolemy II Philadelphus of Egypt, Antigonus Gonatas of Macedonia, Magas of Cyrene and Alexander of Epirus.

There is no evidence that he succeeded with these five, but King Devanampiya Tissa really did become a convert. Legend says that Asoka sent his own son Mahendra (Mahinda) to Ceylon. In any case the Ceylon Chronicle asserts that Tissa became a convert as a result of Asoka's urging and considered the great emperor his mentor. Perhaps Tissa saw that Buddhism would provide a better authority than military power for the control of his own island. His conversion had unexpected consequences, since from Ceylon Buddhism spread to Burma and Thailand.

The edicts Asoka caused to be carved on rocks and pillars throughout India are a remarkable evidence of his mind and interests. It was not to perpetuate his name and fame that he made them, but rather to let his people know about dhamma and persuade them to follow it. Yet the incidental information they give us about himself supplies most of what we really know about Asoka.

Some of the edicts are personal epistles directed to the Sangha—the Buddhist community. Asoka concerned himself in its affairs, fought schism, and was the patron of the third great Buddhist council, held at his capital, which led to the expulsion of heretics and the final canonization of Pali scripture. The edicts manage to convey a sense of the identification Asoka felt with the Buddhist community and his desire to see it grow and prosper. The Schism Edict, written about 240 B.C., threatens nuns and monks with expulsion if they cause disunity in the Sangha.

Twelve years passed between the rock edicts and the pillar edicts. The pillars, quite apart from their content, are remarkable both as works of engineering and of craftsmanship. Some of them, as high as fifty feet, weigh fifty tons. The one at Sarnath is surmounted by the four lions bearing the wheel of the law which independent India adopted as its national symbol.

A warm and human touch comes into those edicts, which speak of Asoka's disillusionment with war and his planting of banyan trees for shade and mangoes for the refreshment of travelers along well-maintained roads. But even these things are of little value, says Asoka, compared with the practice and the spread of Dhamma. For this is what gives the king, the Beloved of the Gods, his deepest satisfaction.

Asoka did more than preach Dhamma and erect sermons in stone. He was a great builder. In his time, and under his patronage, the skill of architects and artists reached high peaks of performance. Stone cutters achieved results that cannot be duplicated today. Huge slabs of hard sandstone as long as forty feet were dressed and polished with a finish so fine that no modern mason can reproduce it. Enormous surfaces of the hardest gneiss were burnished to the smoothness of a mirror. At Pataliputra, Asoka added masonry walls and stone buildings to such an extent that it all seemed to his successors beyond the power of man to have conceived and carried out.

Sculpture, always in India the companion of architecture, adorned public buildings, bringing proof down to our own times that Asoka's India with its chariots, its fabrics, its dress and its furnishings had reached a stage of culture quite the equal of Mogul India two thousand years later.

Asoka's artisans built spacious buildings of wood, brick, stone. They made irrigation works of impressive size and skill. They built the great stupas or tumuli.

The origin of the stupas, by tradition, goes back to the mounded shapes—apparently based upon a hut with a bamboo roof—which were erected over the divided ashes of Buddha. Asoka unearthed the ashes of Buddha from their several places and divided them still further, building great hemispherical masonry stupas for them all over India. These, rather than temples, were the meccas of the faithful. Worshipers walked clockwise around the stupa, prostrating themselves and strewing flowers. At Sanchi, in mid-India, the greatest of these still stands—110 feet in diameter at the base of the dome, and 77 feet high. The four large gateways, however, were added after Asoka's time.

Asoka's most extensive building program may have been the monasteries, some big enough to house a thousand monks, which he placed all over India.

He built; he also traveled. Both building and traveling, so consistent was the man, fitted his religion, expressed his love for the Dhamma.

Four places of pilgrimage associated with the life of Buddha had become popular, and Asoka as a devotee visited them all. In the tenth year of his reign (259 B.C.) he went to Bodh Gaya to see the tree under which the Buddha had sat when he achieved enlightenment. Tradition says it was Asoka who sent the cutting from that tree which still lives at Anuradhapura in Ceylon. Thereafter he kept up a series of Dhamma yatas, described in the Eighth Rock Edict—tours of the country to encourage men to live by Dhamma.

In 249 he traveled as far as Nepal, where he had four great stupas built which remain to this day. In 249 he also visited the Lumbini Grove at Kapilavastu where the Buddha was born. He made pilgrimages to the Deer Park near Benares where Buddha had preached his first sermon, and to the grove near Kushinagara where the Compassionate One had died.

The Minor Rock Edict at Brahmagiri suggests that Asoka also traveled to the southernmost edge of his empire. State visits are, apparently, as old as states. But Asoka went in the hope of conquering not men's bodies but their hearts.

Including the years when he was getting control of the country before his coronation, Asoka must have ruled about forty years—roughly from 273 to 232 B.C. He would have been in his sixties when he died.

The political system Asoka built up required a strong king. It made little or no distinction between executive and judicial functions. It was a noble idea to incorporate ethics into government in the persons of the Dhamma mahamattas—perhaps a revolutionary idea. To base government upon morality, politics upon ethics—how naïve and how superb! We cannot very well judge the results at this distance, but we have Calvin's Geneva and Winthrop's Massachusetts to make us cautious. The difference, perhaps the important difference, was that they wanted to impose a theology as an integral part of ethics, while Asoka took pains—though he professed Buddhism—to welcome all religions and to assume that there was an overarching ethic which joined them all.

After his death, the Maurya empire declined for fifty years, then collapsed and gave way to another. What a brief span for a noble idea!

Some historians have tried to prove that the collapse was a result of Asoka's commitment to nonviolence, but there is no evidence for this. Rather, the corruption of weak rulers seems to have been the true cause.

Or perhaps there was another. In India the social order of caste, community and class had its own self-contained laws. Even to this day the concept of loyalty to the state, the nation, is weaker than the bonds which tie a man to his caste and to the council which administers its laws and judgments. So in Maurya India there was no sense of national loyalty.

Asoka's great idea, of binding men to a universal loyalty of righteousness, failed to take hold.

"The greatest of all victories is the victory of righteousness."

This was the core of his great discovery, the main pillar of his faith. What perhaps he did not know was that it was a victory always to be striven for, never to be won.

So his empire fell apart in weaker hands, the Dhamma he believed in was forgotten, men even forgot how to read the language of his pillars, and the ethical teachings of Buddha were distorted and then forgotten in the land of his birth.

Two thousand years went by before the edicts were redis-covered and deciphered. By then they preserved almost all that we know of their author. Now we see him more clearly than he has been seen since the decade of his own death—an earnest, energetic, hopeful man, certain that men would be happy if they would only be good.

But how? By nonviolence, consideration, kindness, and all the rest—yes. But how do you make this sort of man?

Asoka doesn't tell us. But he had the vision—of an ethic that would merge into politics, of a just prince who would do good to his people so that they might in turn be good, of a state that would live without war or violence, of an allegiance to goodness rather than to a prince or a purse. He sought practical measures to bring this vision to birth—officers to encourage social justice, highways where travelers could move in comfort, pillars of good admonishment to keep a people in the right way, works of irrigation for prosperity, encouragement to trade, stupas to remind the faithful of their compassionate guide so that they might try to be like him, works of art and architecture to lift the mind.

How far did he succeed?

Not far, perhaps. Yet he still speaks to us. He saw that men may differ in religion but unite in a standard of conduct; that social welfare is the basis of good government; that to achieve nonviolence one must overcome desire as Buddha had taught.

"The greatest of all victories is the victory of righteousness."

Greatest—not only because most effective, but because hardest to achieve.

5. Jesus
(c. 6-39 A.D.)

The Saint Who Could Find Peace Only in the Coming of God's Kingdom

 He knew nothing of political science, this man from Nazareth, yet his words were to have a greater impact upon history than those of a thousand forgotten emperors who ruled wide dominions. He was most of all a man of peace, yet in his name thousands were to die cheerfully, or later to kill thousands who did not believe in him, or were in their turn themselves to be maimed and burned alive.

Living in a world that was in ferment, where Rome had imposed its rule upon his people—who considered themselves uniquely the sons of God—and had bloodily put down their effort to repossess their freedom, he counseled an inward victory instead of an external one.

For those raised in Christendom it is almost impossible to regard this figure dispassionately, or in the same light in which we examine other historic persons. Approaching him by way of an encyclopedia article makes the point come clear. Other entries deal with men who are born in the normal way, get educated, make their mark and die. But with Jesus, everything is miracle— the nature of his birth and the way it is made known, the way he cures and restores life, the way he triumphs over death.

If such things were asserted of some other person in the encyclopedia, your eyebrows would turn skeptics. Or you would consign the article to those dealing with myth and saga. Or, like Thomas Jefferson, you might be moved to compose your own gospel by removing all that is miraculous in order to see more clearly the person whose teachings retain their firmness and immortality even when the miracles are removed.

Yet even when the miracles are set aside—and we know that to an era which did not recognize and had not discovered many of the laws that control nature, miracles were an acceptable evidence of godhood—difficulties remain. We can if we like explain the miracles as psychological events or as stories interpolated to gain converts.

Who, then, was Jesus?

John the Baptist, although he had received and baptized Jesus as "the Lamb of God, which taketh away the sins of the world," must have had second thoughts. For after being thrown into prison by Herod, he sent messengers to Jesus inquiring, "Art thou he that should come? Or look we for another?" To which Jesus replied, "Go your way, and tell John what things ye have seen and heard."

Who was he?

In the furore over the discovery of the Dead Sea Scrolls some were eager to make an Essene of him. It is true that he showed some preference for ascetic self-denial, baptism, holding of property in common, contempt for money, and communal dining. Yet he was no monastic. And he flouted the ritual law in a way the Essenes would have rejected. He did flee for a time to the desert of Judaea with its strewn rocks in a waste of sand, but, unlike the Essenes, he did not remain there shut off from the workaday world. He preferred to walk the roads, stop at the wells, dine in the villages where the plain people lived and worked.

Who was he?

To Mark, he was the unique son of Yahweh, the writer on

whom Mark based his Gospel, the good one come to earth. To Matthew he was the Messiah of the Jews, to Luke an intensely human being. John made of him God translated into human flesh, and the Apocalypse made him the lamb slain for the sins of mankind.

As each of the Gospels was written to prove something, and with a particular audience in mind, each has its own distinctive view of Jesus. The Gospels have come to us, moreover, as reworked texts, based upon earlier texts and oral tradition which can never be recovered in their original forms. It is clear to us now that they are collections of the sayings and acts of Jesus assembled during the first Christian generation and handed down in the manner of folklore to those who then gathered and put them in written form.

Controversies with other sects stimulated early Christians to preserve sayings that demonstrated the authenticity of the faith. Ethical problems in the Christian community accounted for the gathering up of Jesus' words about marriage and social relations. Competition for popular favor led to the stories of miracles.

It is from these materials that we have to derive the life of Jesus. Since the Gospels themselves present different points of view, the biographer of Jesus has many hard choices to make. In a sense, no biography of Jesus is possible, since we cannot produce an authentic geography or chronology of his ministry, or assert with finality that he was the person Luke wrote of, or Mark, or John.

Mark, as the oldest of the Gospels, generally has the favor of historians. John is clearly an allegory of man's search for union with the divine. Yet the Jesus we know would be diminished without John.

I know a Bible student who wrote a book (unpublished) to prove that the Gospels describe four different persons. It does not seem necessary to go that far. If we were to ask four persons—a southern Democrat, an historian, a Russian and a Cuban—to write accounts of President Kennedy, we would probably find as much discrepancy as exists among the Gospels. Together, they would certainly give us a more dynamic portrait than that of a campaign biography. Out of such a dynamic we have to form our picture of Jesus. Any reader of the Gospels must do this.

The biography of Jesus is in its fullest sense the story of his impact upon two thousand years of history. What he has meant to men is, historically, quite as important as what he truly was in his earthly career.

So it need not surprise us that men saw many things in him from the beginning—the Son of Man Enos had described, the Suffering Servant of Isaiah, the beloved whom John had baptized, the compassionate physician to the maimed and the blind, the teller of stories so full of point and pith that they are part of our vocabulary and way of thought even today, the voice of conscience, the teacher of a bold new way of life, the man who was close to God, the reader in the synagogue, the carpenter, the lover of nature.

Jesus lives because he brought the very essentials of true religion and universal ethics together in a way the simplest could understand. He taught so compellingly that hearers thirsted after this life for themselves. And he embodied his teaching in his own behavior. This is a simple truth, but all great truths are simple.

Abbé Steinmann says: "He knew himself to be king, priest, prophet, judge and sage; soon he would add to these the role of victim and hostage." In the end, he knew himself to be the suffering, martyred servant of God whom Isaiah had prophesied, the innocent one slain for the sake of mankind.

But in the early part of his ministry, he was the teacher of the poor, the weak, the humble. Under the skies of Galilee his message had a simple, endearing quality which thrust, both sharp and tender, into the heart.

A good part of the ministry of Jesus was in Galilee, and the charm of the Gospels comes in part from this rural setting. Unlike the barren area around Jerusalem, Galilee with its lake and hills made a lovely landscape. Its palms and fig trees, the fields of wheat in the Gennesar Valley, the warm waters of the lake gave this country a comfortable, well-to-do air. Its people worked at the simple tasks of fishing, watching their flocks and raising grain and grapes. Their vineyards, their boats and threshing floors and jugs and nets and lamps, have a familiar, timeless quality in our minds.

They lived and worked close to nature, in a fine climate of clear skies, warm sun and brilliant starlight which made life something of an idyl. An average amount of industry supplied a family with necessities, and there was fish aplenty in the lake.

To the quiet life and the gentle climate we need to add the factor of scale. These places where Jesus taught were villages. Much of his ministry was limited to half a dozen of them near the shores of the Sea of Galilee (Lake Tiberias). His farthest journey took him no more than ninety miles from home.

He does not seem to have cared for cities. Though he went to Jerusalem, and though Sepphoris, a cosmopolitan city with men of many races, was only four miles from Nazareth, he obviously preferred the country, the fields, the lakeside to the crowded streets. He preferred simple people to the scornful priests and men of high station, and among them even he sought out the disadvantaged, the most humble, the sinners. Or the sick, the maimed, even the dead and the dying. Among all these who were weakened by birth, by sin, or by youth or age he seemed to find strength. So he walked among them, healing, "casting out devils," teaching, admonishing, urging. For he had a message to share with them.

Although he could talk learnedly in the synagogue, having studied the sacred books until he knew much of them by heart, Jesus liked best to carry his message to people where they lived and worked—to the streets and public squares, to lakeside and field and mount, and to that center of village life the world over, the well. In these places he could talk to the plain people rather than to scribes and Pharisees—to farmers and artisans and fishermen, housewives and children and servants. A carpenter's son, he was one with them, and he spoke the universal language of story which goes home to the heart when abstract theology slides off the skin and disappears into the sand like water spilled in a desert.

The popular image of Jesus as a gentle, forgiving, compassionate person ignores entirely the frequent harshness with which he attacks the evil-doer.

"Woe unto you, scribes and Pharisees, hypocrites! for ye compass sea and land to make one proselyte, and when he is made, ye make him twofold more the child of hell than yourselves" (Matthew 23:15).

"Ye serpents, ye generation of vipers, how can ye escape the damnation of hell?" (Matthew 23:33).

Nor was he content with words only.

When he found the money changers and those that sold sacrificial animals in the temple at Jerusalem, he made a scourge of small cords and with it drove them all out, beasts and men alike, and spilled the money upon the floor.

"Take these things hence; make not my Father's house an house of merchandise" (John 2:16).

Jesus had already had his brushes with the Pharisees, those strict sectarians who insisted on a rigid conformity to all the rules and taboos of their faith—at the expense, it seemed to him, of true religion. The irony of it was that Jesus himself believed in a life of religious devotion, as did the Pharisees. Yet he found them stressing the wrong things—washing before meals, strictly observing the Sabbath laws, avoiding contact with Gentiles.

Jesus found the practice of strict orthodoxy forever standing in the way of true religion—love of neighbor or stranger, help for the sick or the deprived. He wanted men to think about God—even if in the process they slipped up on a dietary law, even if they did a good work on the Sabbath.

So he was beginning to appear as a dangerous person—dangerous to the strict conformists of his own community; dangerous to

[83]

Herod, who ruled as a Roman pawn and who feared that any trouble brewing in his country might threaten his own position; dangerous to the Romans who were always on the lookout for disturbers of the peace in their vast empire, and who found it easy to snuff out the lives of men who even appeared as if they might be trouble makers. Rome knew the Jews as a proud, dissatisfied, exclusive people with a religion which told them that they had been chosen by God and that He would restore their lands and their independence.

For all these reasons, a man who preached the coming of a mysterious kingdom, and who was beginning to be regarded as the restorer of their ancient freedom to the Jews, was bound to be watched by the secret police.

The world Jesus lived in was one of political ferment. The Jews hated both the Romans and their puppet, Herod. Their powerful Sanhedrin which ran the temple was quite ready to resume the governing of the people if by some miracle the Roman power should wane or weaken. The Zealots, terrorists who wanted to drive the Romans out, had already had a try at it. Many of them had been caught and executed at Sepphoris near Nazareth, where Jesus as a boy might have seen the crosses of execution.

The Publicans and their assistants, on the other hand, cooperated with the Romans, gathering taxes from their fellow Jews and doubly hated both as collaborators and as tax collectors.

Divided politically, the Jews were also split into three religious parties. The Sadducees believed that the soul dies with the body; they were strict observers of religious law. The Pharisees lived more humbly and on a modest diet, believed in immortality and emphasized the virtue of reason as a guide. The Essenes, though mentioned nowhere in the New Testament, lived well if ascetically in their own communities, sharing what they had.

Both the political and the religious divisions were active in Galilee where Jesus taught. In Jerusalem Galilee was thought to

[84]

be boiling with revolt, so Galileans coming up to the holy city got a suspicious and doubtful welcome.

If Jesus had chosen to ally himself with the religious hierarchy as a popular leader whose genius for speaking the language of the people and gaining their allegiance was already proved, he might have saved himself. But in alienating all the centers of authority—synagogue, tetrarch, Rome—he set the stage for his own tragedy.

Over against the idyllic but politically fervid Galilean scene we have to set the popular conviction that this world was near its end.

"The Kingdom of God is at hand." This was John's message, and Jesus at times seemed to agree.

But what did he mean by the Kingdom of God? Some scholars, and they include Albert Schweitzer, have argued that Jesus expected the literal coming of the Kingdom of God and the end of the world within his own lifetime.

Older Jewish thought, they say, had made a distinction between the kingdom of the Messiah—"the anointed one"—and the end of the world which it would usher in. But Jesus held the newer apocalyptic view that they would come together. His work was to prepare men for the coming of this new order. All were to be changed, "in a moment, in the twinkling of an eye, at the last trump" (I Corinthians 15:52). Then the lowly would be raised up and the high cast down.

Jesus, Schweitzer has said, expected that the change might even take place before his disciples could get back from the missions on which he had sent them throughout Israel, to gather in the lost sheep of the house while there was yet time (Matthew 10:23). These disciples, by the way, included men who had followed John the Baptist, and two, Simon and Judas, who belonged to the terrorist Zealots. Two others may have had connections with the Publicans—those who collaborated with the Romans. There were no Pharisees, Essenes, or aristocratic

Sadducees. Zealots and followers of John were sure to be watched as potential trouble makers.

When the end of the world did not come, Schweitzer would have us believe, Jesus retired into heathen country near Tyre and spent a whole fall and winter there, wanting to remain unknown. And there he came to the conclusion that the great change would not come until by suffering and death he had atoned for the world's evil and thus become the Messiah (Mark 10:45).

In Jewish thought the Messiah is an offshoot or descendant of David, an angelic being in human form who, as described in Daniel (7:13–14), "like the Son of man came with the clouds of heaven. . . . And there was given him dominion, and glory, and a kingdom, that all people, nations, and languages, should serve him; his dominion is an everlasting dominion, which shall not pass away, and his kingdom that which shall not be destroyed."

Sharing this Jewish vision of a better world that would soon come, Jesus saw himself as the sacrifice, the atonement, the one who would usher in the end of the world, the last judgment, and the Messianic kingdom. It was a grand vision, and one not at all out of tune with the knowledge of its time. Indeed the first Christian generation continued to live in expectation of seeing the world's end and the return of Jesus as Messiah. That was why they so easily gave up property or held it in common with their brothers, generally did not marry after becoming Christians, and had little use for the things that attach men to earth.

But other scholars tell us that Jesus did not think of the Kingdom as the end of the world but rather as the reign of God on earth. This would be a kingdom of kindness, peace and good will. Jew would no longer scorn Samaritan, blood sacrifice would end, and the rich would care for orphans and the poor. In his parables, Jesus spoke of the Kingdom as a feast to be set before all men.

[86]

As for the end of the world: "Of that day and that hour knoweth no man, no, not the angels which are in heaven, neither the Son, but the Father" (Mark 13:32). Rather, the Kingdom was within man's grasp, a new way of life which a man could enter whenever he chose.

The religious message Jesus gave was singularly free of rites, ritual, observances and patterns. It was to be a religion of the heart, of inner purity. In contrast with the leaders of Judaism in Jerusalem, it was a religion in which the humble, the meek and the lowly would inherit eternity. It was not theological but ethical, not external but internal, not one of observances but of feeling and attitude, not one of wealth but of poverty.

"Be ye therefore perfect, even as your father in heaven is perfect."

There perhaps is the heart of it—the belief that men as the sons of God could dare perfection.

Was Jesus a revolutionary? A pacifist?

No doubt the Romans feared that he might stir up a revolution, as had Jews before him. Varus, Roman governor of Syria, had visited Judea after the death of Herod the Great and had ordered two thousand suspected rebels executed. The Romans burned Sepphoris and enslaved its inhabitants because the rebel Judas of Galilee (not the disciple) had obtained weapons there for his revolt. While it seems clear to us that Jesus was concerned, not with political revolt like the Zealots, but with a revolution in the minds of men which would turn them to love as a way of life, the words he used were—in that uneasy land—subject to political interpretation. What was this kingdom of his, if not a return to political independence for the Jews? So Pontius Pilate, though he found no fault in Jesus, may have been content to see another potential trouble maker put out of the way.

Those who welcomed Jesus into Jerusalem with hosannahs, spreading their garments as well as palm leaves before him on that festal day, were clearly hoping that he would prove himself a leader, an emancipator. Politics and religion were never very far separated among a people who thought of themselves as chosen by God, and if they worshiped him as Messiah, there would be those who expected the Messiah to bring the divine power that would free them from foreign rule.

The crucial exchange between Pilate and Jesus makes this clear.

"Art thou the King of the Jews?" Pilate asks.

The synoptic gospels have Jesus answer merely, "Thou sayest." But John gives us more. He tells us that Jesus answered:

"Sayest thou this of thyself, or did others tell it thee concerning me?"*

"Am I a Jew?" says Pilate. "Thine own nation and the chief priests delivered thee unto me: what hast thou done?"

"My kingdom is not of this world," Jesus answered. "If my kingdom were of this world, then would my servants fight, that I should not be delivered to the Jews: but now is my kingdom not from thence."

"Art thou a king then?"

"Thou sayest that I am a king. To this end was I born, and for this cause came I into the world, that I should bear witness unto the truth. Everyone that is of the truth heareth my voice."

"What is truth?" said the Roman skeptic. Yet he went on trying to save Jesus from his persecutors, first by sending him to Herod, then by offering to release him according to the custom of freeing a prisoner at the Passover. When they chose Barabbas, Pilate said:

"I am innocent of the blood of this just person: see ye to it."

According to John's account, when Pilate continued his efforts to release Jesus, the Jews kept raising the political issue.

"If thou let this man go, thou art not Caesar's friend. Whosoever maketh himself a king speaketh against Caesar."

* The following paraphrase uses the various Gospel accounts.

So Pilate brought him again before the people, saying "Behold, your king!"

"Away with him, away with him, crucify him," they cried.

"Shall I crucify your king?" said Pilate.

"We have no king but Caesar," said the chief priests. And finally Pilate delivered Jesus to them. The Romans, after all, had no great scruples about a human life. At the Saturnalia it was their custom to pay mock honor to a condemned man, then to execute him.

But this was not the end of it. For "Pilate wrote a title also, and put it on the cross. And there was written, JESUS OF NAZARETH, THE KING OF THE JEWS" in Hebrew, Latin and Greek. When the Jews tried to get him to change it, he said:

"What I have written I have written" (John 19:22).

So the suggestion of a political aspiration and revolt hangs over the last days, sharpening our picture of Jesus with a new edge both of possibility and of irony. Progressively we have been offered the divine babe, the sweet and knowledgeable child, the earnest youth, the obedient carpenter, the young man with a vision and a mission, the itinerant preacher, the lover of the inno-cent, the handicapped and the errant, the worker of miracles, the scourger of hypocrites and materialists, the visionary who sees the coming of the heavenly kingdom, the man who increasingly bears the world's burden as he sees that only through bearing it and suffering it can this kingdom come.

The tempo quickens as, leaving his beloved Galilee, he enters Jerusalem in triumph, curses the fig tree in what appears like a reaction of bitterness toward his fate, scourges the money chang-ers in the temple, holds a loving last supper with his disciples, and in the long discourse reported by John tries to impress upon them so firmly that they can never forget it his essential lesson of love. Then the agony of waiting, the betrayal, the trial and the dying. But in the scenes with Pilate there is the tantalizing view of a kingdom offered even as it is denied—an ironically bitter view of what might have been, rubbing abrasively against what must be.

Was he a pacifist?

"Blessed are the peacemakers," he said, "for they shall be called the children of God" (Matthew 5:9).

And again: "Ye have heard that it was said to them of old time, Thou shalt not kill; and whosoever shall kill shall be in danger of the judgement: but I say unto you, that every one who is angry with his brother . . . shall be in danger of the judgement" (Matthew 5:21–22).

"Ye have heard that it was said, Thou shalt love thy neighbor, and hate thine enemy: but I say unto you, Love your enemies, . . . and pray for them that persecute you; that ye may be sons of your Father which is in heaven" (Matthew 5:43–45).

"Have peace one with another," he said again, concluding another session of instructing his disciples, as if this were the highest goal (Mark 9:50).

As he prepares to send them out for the first time on their own missions, to preach that the kingdom of heaven is at hand, and to heal, cleanse, raise the dead and cast out devils, he advises them to inquire in each city what house is worthy, and to stay there.

"And when ye come into an house, salute it. And if the house be worthy, let your peace come upon it: but if it be not worthy, let your peace return to you" (Matthew 10:12–13).

Luke puts it a little differently:

"And into whatsoever house ye enter, first say, Peace be to this house. And if the son of peace be there, your peace shall rest upon it: if not, it shall turn to you again" (Luke 10:5–6).

This peace is clearly grounded on an old cultural pattern, for from ancient times the Jewish word of greeting has been Shalom, Peace.

When Jesus, about to enter Jerusalem, weeps for it, he says, according to Luke (19:42): "If thou hadst known, even thou, at least in this thy day, the things which belong unto thy peace!" The revised version puts it more clearly: "Would that even today you knew the things that make for peace!" He then goes on to predict that not one stone shall be left upon another, "because thou knewest not the time of thy visitation."

But what are the things that make for peace?

In the words, vibrating with that love which has ever since been the mark of true Christianity, spoken after the Last Supper, Jesus again brings peace to the center of his teaching.

"Peace I leave with you, my peace I give unto you: not as the world giveth, give I unto you. . . . I am the true vine, and my Father is the husbandman. . . . Abide in me, and I in you. As the branch cannot bear fruit of itself, except it abide in the vine; no more can ye, except ye abide in me" (John 14:27; 15:1, 4).

"These things I have spoken unto you, that in me ye might have peace. In the world ye shall have tribulation: but be of good cheer; I have overcome the world" (John 16:33).

The key to Jesus' concept of peace—the Jesus of John, at any rate—lies in these words: "I have overcome the world." We are turned back to his conviction of the world's transiency, and to the eternality of the world of spirit, of God.

If Jesus was in doubt about the imminent end of the world, he was not wrong about the victory of spiritual over material in the long view of history. All the material splendors of his own day, all the power of Rome and the fame of its great ones, have crumbled into dust, yet he endures. He has indeed overcome the world. Some 916,000,000 people consider themselves his followers, however poorly they measure up to his standards.

Peace, love, a quiet joy—these were the qualities Jesus promised his followers. To a remarkable extent the first Christians, and the best Christians ever since, have inherited them.

Yet how are we to reconcile his statement, "All they that take the sword shall perish by the sword" (Matthew 26:52) with "Think not that I am come to send peace on earth: I came not to send peace, but a sword" (Matthew 10:34)? Is not this a flat contradiction? How do we reconcile his violence of language against hypocrites, scribes and Pharisees, his physical violence against the money changers in the temple? Is this truly a man of peace?

I confess I see no way to resolve these contradictory sayings from Matthew. But it is clear that the prime message of Jesus was the force of love in human affairs, as the means—and the only means—by which God's kingdom would flourish.

This was not clear to his disciples. They expected more— much more. With the grand prophecies of the Old Testament ringing in their heads they had dreamed dreams of a Messiah, a new world, a last judgment, a political revolution, the restoration of the Jews to a cherished independence. But Jesus offered neither the seizure of political power dreamed of by the Zealots, nor the end of the world, nor the legalistic covenant with God that the Pharisees envisioned. He merely wanted to materialize the divine kingdom by changing men's hearts.

"Love one another." By simple stories of sheep and widows, of lost coins and returned sons, of weddings and vineyards, of masters and servants, he made his point as simply and as tellingly as he knew how. It was an old message—as old as the name of Jerusalem itself which means vision of peace. His was the peaceable kingdom—not the kingdom of Caesar or of the Apocalypse, of the Zealots or the Pharisees, but of plain men responding to a simple rule:

"Thou shalt love the Lord thy God with all thy heart and all thy mind and all thy soul. This is the first and great commandment, and the second is like unto it: thou shalt love thy neighbor as thyself."

What an amazing distillation of homely wisdom!

The life of Jesus only begins with his death. To say what it means would be to write a history of the world since then. We would have to repeat the heroic story of Saint Paul and the apostles, enduring persecution and martyrdom, carrying a despised religion beyond Palestine to the whole Roman world until almost miraculously it caught the imagination of men everywhere and ended as the official religion of the state which had once persecuted it.

As political power disintegrated, the church preserved the ancient learning, converted barbarian tribes, enforced some sort of order upon feudal nobles, and preserved enough of law and administration so that a political renovation could occur. Then came the great irony of the Crusades, as followers of the prince of peace made war upon the occupiers of the land where once he had lived. For a while, then, Europe was united from Spain to Sweden under the power of the church. Great cathedrals and monasteries gave testimony in stone to the power of the faith, great universities to the primacy of intellect in the Christian scheme.

But then renaissance and reformation began to erode the great monolith. New interpretations of what the Nazarene had meant opened new channels of belief to all sorts and conditions of men, and a pluralistic world began to emerge from the monistic. Not without bloodshed: in the name of the man of peace bloody wars were fought and frightful massacres and tortures invented. Out of all this came a nationalism which has ever since kept the world in turmoil, proving stronger in its appeal to men's emotions than the challenge to love and live peaceably. Then came Deism and the Enlightenment, then a new evangelism and awakening, then the social gospel and a new secularism in which the church when compared with national governments came to play a very minor role in shaping and dominating men's lives.

Disillusionment with a civilization which could produce so many wars, find God on the side of the battalions, speak peace and develop weapons of horror, profess a belief in the dignity of

man and drop atom bombs—disillusionment to the core once
again made men doubt the power of the faith to overcome evil.
Yet in our own time the struggle to find ways to world peace
and to intercommunication among sects and faiths, the apparent
rise in church attendance in the United States at least if not
elsewhere, the discovery that in a nuclear age the gospel of peace
and love of neighbor offer the only hope for human life—these
again testify to the vitality of the revolution begun by a carpenter's son and preached beside the warm waters of the Sea of
Galilee.

No other person in human history has had so vast and continuous an impact upon men's consciences, made them so uneasy
when they go wrong, stirred them to seek so many solutions,
upheld them when defeat seemed certain, and sent them back
so refreshed and determined into the arena. No one has exerted
so close and personal an influence upon so many people, whether
in the faith or outside it.

We feel as if we *know* him and he knows us. He is not a
remote abstraction but a friend, a person, a living presence. That
he has been this to millions is itself a miracle and a proof of
miracles. He comes to us from all directions and in many ways—
in the Gospels, in the history of the church, in church membership, in poetry and art, in hymnology and music. I find that I
can never separate him from the deeply moving chorales of Bach,
or from the joy and sweetness of Handel: "My yoke is easy and
my burden is light"; "Come unto me"; "I know that my Re-
deemer liveth." To this last I have learned to add, "in me."

That is the spirit and the genius of this godly man, that he has
known how to enter into us even when we are unwilling. No
religion can mean anything unless this happens. Its spirit must
come to dwell within, making the invaded person uneasy until
he does better—uneasy forever in response to that impossible
command, "Be ye therefore perfect." We know it to be impossible, yet the indwelling spirit—ours and his—requires it.

[94]

Now that we have in our days come face to face with the threat of human annihilation, we for the first time since Jesus uttered them can see the practical politics couched in the words of his central teaching:

"Love your enemies." "Blessed are the peacemakers." What other way is there, except utter destruction?

6. Saint Augustine
(354-430)

and Saint Francis
(1182?-1226)

The City of God and the City of Man

 The greatest of the four great fathers of the Roman Catholic Church, Augustine might seem to us too august to be human if he had not written the first great autobiography in Western literature. By that honest book we know him to have been very human indeed—a man captured by the delights of the flesh and keeping a mistress from a very early age, full of this-worldly ambition, resisting the authority of his father as most young men do, devoted to his mother even when the hot flesh impelled him to ignore her warnings "not to commit fornication, but especially never to defile another's wife."

Born in Algeria—the town was then Tagaste but is now Souk-Ahras—Augustine was therefore a provincial in a day when to be Roman was to be everything that mattered. In 354 when he was born his father, Patricius, was a provincial official—well enough off by comparison with the common people but still sufficiently hard-pressed so that he later found it difficult to pay for his son's education.

Patricius was a gentleman, a landowner, but unfortunately he belonged to the class of *curiales*—men whom Rome held responsible for collecting taxes. So at fifteen Augustine had to be snatched out of school, his father was so short of funds. Only by the greatest effort did Patricius finally scrape together enough money to let his son finish his education as a rhetorician.

Augustine was always closer to his mother, Monica—a devout Christian, a woman whose gentleness hid an iron will and whose patience hid, or perhaps confessed, an absolute certainty that her will since it conformed with God's would in the end prevail.

This patience must have been saintly, since year after year Augustine failed to gratify her by becoming a Christian. Instead he took a mistress, became a Manichaean, went off to Carthage to perfect himself as a rhetorician, and sired a boy whom he named, apparently without irony, Adeodatus—"the gift of God."

His father died, he returned to teach grammar at Tagaste, gained the friendship of the devoted Alypius, and again went to Carthage.

In the spring of 383, at the age of twenty-eight, he decided to make the great venture—a trip to Rome, the center of the civilized world, where he hoped to find a top job as a teacher of rhetoric.

In spite of his mother's secret prayers and tears, he still had not become a Christian, though he had grown disillusioned with Manichaeism. But in Rome the people he knew and had to rely upon for their influence were Manichaeans. It was not a happy situation for him.

So he grasped at the chance to go to Milan as a teacher of rhetoric when it came to him a year later. Milan was not Rome, but still it was a great city and the residence of the young Emperor Valentinian. It was also the seat of Bishop Ambrose— aristocrat, scholar, formerly a magistrate, and now a noted preacher.

"That man of God received me as a father," wrote Augustine, "and shewed me an Episcopal kindness on my coming. Thenceforth I began to love him, at first indeed not as a teacher of the truth (which I utterly despaired of in Thy Church), but as a person kind towards myself."

Augustine listened to his preaching with the trained ear of the rhetorician and was delighted with the sweetness of his discourse. At first he did not care what he said—only how he spoke. But by degrees he was drawn to the truth and cogency of the arguments. He abandoned Manichaeism and became a catechumen in the Catholic Church.

Monica soon came from Africa to live with him, full of joy when she learned of the step he had taken and certain that before she died she would see her son a Christian. Augustine's nameless woman and their son were already there.

Augustine kept visiting Ambrose, for anyone could enter without announcement at any time. He watched the great man eat or read but never talked with him, for there he sat in an aura of greatness which kept the visitors from him as if he had cast a spell over them.

"Those tides in me, to be poured out to him, required his full leisure, and never found it," said Augustine. Nevertheless, he persevered with his study of Christianity.

Meanwhile his mother seems to have arranged a rich marriage for him, and Augustine seems to have been agreeable to the idea of having a wife whose patrimony would make life easy for him. As he himself wrote, "By means of her ample patrimony, it were possible that all of those whom you wish to have living with you in one place could be comfortably supported, and that by this reason of her noble birth she could bring within your easy reach the honors necessary for a man to live a cultured existence." Was this to include his son Adeodatus?

When his wifely companion was sent away, he soon found it necessary to form another connection of the same kind. Then came a friend, Pontitian, from Africa with the story of two young men, betrothed like Augustine himself, who had turned their backs upon marriage and comforts to enter upon a monastic life.

There was something in Augustine that longed to be cared for, as Monica had always cared for him. The rich young wife was to do this. But now another possibility opened—mother church herself, and a community where "all of those whom you wish to have living with you in one place" could be gathered.

Torn between his love of women and a life of comfort, and the challenge of a monastic life, Augustine threw himself down one day under a fig tree and wept.

"Why is there not this hour an end to my uncleanness?" he cried.

And as he spoke, a child in a neighboring house began to chant: "Take up and read; take up and read." Taking it as a command from God, Augustine hurried to the place where his dearest friend Alypius was sitting with the volume of Paul which Augustine had just laid aside. Seizing the book, Augustine opened it at random and read to himself the words that first his eyes fell upon:

"Not in rioting and drunkenness, not in chambering and wantonness, not in strife and envying: but put ye on the Lord Jesus Christ, and make not provision for the flesh."

Now the sign had been given. Said Augustine: "Instantly at the end of this sentence, by a light as it were of serenity infused into my heart, all the darkness of doubt vanished away."

Together, he and Alypius went in to Monica. What she had seen in a vision years before had come to pass. It was now the summer of 386, and Augustine was nearly thirty-two.

Somehow peace was made with the family of the intended bride, the new mistress dismissed, and Augustine with his mother, brother, son and a few pupils removed to a country estate near Milan. Here Augustine taught, studied, wrote, and prepared himself for baptism.

On Easter Eve of the following year he kept a vigil, came to the altar after midnight, and was touched on the ears and nose by Bishop Ambrose in the ritual of opening; Alypius and Adeodatus too. Then, stripping naked, they were anointed in the baptistry and bidden to spit on Satan. Clergy and candidates then stepped down into the font which Ambrose had blessed.

Three times the converts were immersed, then sprinkled with oil and balsam and their feet washed. Then new robes of white were put on them, and candles placed in their hands. After the bishop had laid his hands upon them they went in procession into the basilica to make their first communion.

Augustine was now eager to return to Africa and establish a Christian community of his own, attended by those he loved. Political trouble had broken out in Italy. The usurper Maximus was already preparing to attack Milan as Augustine and his party left for Rome. But there, as they waited at Ostia for a ship, Monica died. Not, however, before she and Augustine had been caught up together in a mystical sense of divine being. At the end of it, Monica said:

"Son, for mine own part I have no further delight in anything in this life. One thing there was, for which I desired to linger for a while in this life, that I might see thee a Catholic Christian before I died. My God hath done this for me abundantly, that I should now see thee withal, despising earthly happiness, become his servant: what do I here?"

Five days later she fell sick of a fever. When friends, visiting her in her last illness, asked her whether she did not fear to leave her body so far from her own city, she answered simply: "Nothing is far to God." So at fifty-six she died, and Augustine returned sorrowing to his own city. But poor Adeodatus had lost the two women whose love had brought him up. We hear no more of his mother. He too soon died.

Back in Algeria in 388, Augustine settled his parents' estate, using his own share to found the first Augustinian monastery. There he spent almost three years—reading, writing, and conversing with a few devoted friends in the manner he had once planned to finance with a rich marriage; but now he had devoted himself to chastity and the church.

There word came to him of a high official in Hippo who had been heard to say that he too might renounce the world if only he could talk with Augustine. So to Hippo Augustine went.

[100]

It seems incredible to us nowadays, but in Augustine's time any man of promise might be snatched from whatever he was doing and forced by the congregation to become a bishop. Determined to maintain his quiet life of contemplation and writing, Augustine had kept away from towns in need of a bishop. But in Hippo he knew himself to be safe, for Hippo had a bishop, and no town was allowed two.

Nonetheless, when he went into the basilica there, the Christians literally seized him and dragged him to the altar. They could not make him bishop, so they made him their presbyter. Augustine protested and wept, but it did him no good. The congregation felt the need of a vigorous man, for their own bishop knew small Latin and less Punic and was of little use to them. Augustine was soon preaching daily. Now his skill as a rhetorician had full scope, his flair for the dramatic could reach an audience immediately instead of through the cooler medium of writing, and his personal magnetism and power got an immediate response.

His own abilities imprisoned him further, for he was the kind of man who cannot bear to see inefficiency flourish. Soon he was seeing to the church property and financial affairs, caring for the poor, mediating quarrels, and all this while preaching and writing voluminously.

Meanwhile he had founded another monastery at Hippo (now Bône). So valuable was Augustine to the congregation of that beautiful city that the Primate of Africa was persuaded to break the rule and give Hippo a second bishop.

A strange tension between love and strife characterizes Augustine's life from here on. Love was the central motive of his personal life, a love characterized by the relationship between child and parent and particularly between himself and his mother. Although normally concupiscent, he was not a taster, for he apparently remained true to his concubine for more than ten years. Clearly, he sought stability rather than novelty. His plans for a rich marriage indicate that, although women satisfied a natural urge, they were primarily mother figures.

This need for love and loving care Augustine sublimated in religious love, and he brought to the church a sense of God's love continually raising man up from his sinful state.

Yet while he taught love, his life was full of strife and controversy. For the latter half of his seventy-six-year span was largely spent in three great battles—against the Manichaeans, the Donatists and the Pelagians. These old theological controversies may seem unimportant to us now, but in their time they were as bitter as the struggle against communism. Augustine was particularly eloquent against the Pelagians, who felt that man was innately good where Augustine found him innately evil and therefore dependent at every moment upon God's grace and forgiveness. His struggle with the Donatists was even more important politically, since they outnumbered the orthodox Christians in Africa and had their own bishops in every important town. They held that only a priest whose personal life was blameless could administer valid sacraments.

But it is another work that fixes our attention on Augustine—his greatest, *The City of God.*

It is a strange work—written at odd moments over a period of thirteen years (413–426) and issued in several portions, full of disorder, of unholy glee over the imminent collapse of Rome and of blindness to its cultural beauties and its organizational genius.

Yet the central vision shines through. It is that of a city of God which would be within man's reach if only he would love God instead of himself and serve his fellows instead of his own selfish interests.

In his vision of such a city, Augustine naturally comes to grips with the problem of war and peace. What he had to say has affected our thoughts ever since.

It was Augustine who proposed the idea of just wars. But although he justifies, he does not approve them. "It is the wrong-doing of the opposing party which compels the wise man to wage just wars; and this wrong-doing, even though it gave rise to no war, would still be matter of grief to man because it is man's wrong-doing" (XIX. 7).

To Augustine, true peace was eternal peace, the peace which the just man would know in the afterworld where virtue no longer had to struggle against vice or evil. "And thus we may say of peace, as we have said of eternal life, that it is the end of our good. . . . For peace is a good so great, that even in this earthly and mortal life there is no word we hear with such pleasure, nothing we desire with such zest, or find to be more thoroughly gratifying" (XIX. 11).

Even those who make war, Augustine proceeds to argue, desire peace, and it is for this that wars are waged. "For every man seeks peace by waging war, but no man seeks war by making peace. For even they who intentionally interrupt the peace in which they are living have no hatred of peace, but only wish it changed into a peace that suits them better" (XIX. 12). Would he have believed this a few years later when the Vandals were at the gates of Hippo?

It is pride, he goes on to say, which leads men to impose their own will upon equals. "It abhors, that is to say, the just peace of God, and loves its own unjust peace; but it cannot help loving peace of one kind or another" (XIX. 12). Augustine thought no man could go so contrary to nature as to wipe out nature's traces. He did not see, as Freud has taught us, that some men love strife and contention and war because it satisfies the death-wish in them, or even because they are bored with the life they have, or see in war a chance to escape from a dull one or to win quick riches.

The object of a man's life is to make the best use of what is given him so that he may enjoy the peace of immortality. Peace therefore begins at home, in the life of the family. "Domestic peace has a relation to civic peace" (XIX. 16). It is the father's duty to frame his domestic rule in accordance with the law of the city, so that domestic and civic order may be in harmony.

The next step is toward a realization on earth of the heavenly city, which "calls citizens out of all nations and gathers together a society of pilgrims of all languages, not scrupling about diversities in the manners, laws, and institutions whereby earthly peace is secured and maintained, but recognizing that, however various these are, they all tend to one and the same earthly end of peace" (XIX. 17). Earthly peace depends upon "the perfectly ordered and harmonious enjoyment of God and of one another in God."

"When we shall have reached that peace," Augustine adds,

> this mortal life shall give place to one that is eternal. Perfect peace, in short, is not to be achieved on earth, where at best we can enjoy only an imperfect copy of the peace which belongs to the city of God. The strife between good and evil, in man and society, makes full peace impossible to man.
>
> Since, then, the supreme good of the city of God is perfect and eternal peace, not such as mortals pass into and out of by birth and death, but the peace of freedom from all evil, in which the immortals ever abide, who can deny that that future life is most blessed, or that, in comparison with it, this life which now we live is most wretched, be it filled with all blessings of body and soul and external things? (XIX. 20).

In that final peace of immortal life "it will not be necessary that reason should rule vices which no longer exist, but God shall rule the man, and the soul shall rule the body" into eternity (XIX. 27).

So finally the spirit of man shall be free of all vices and temptations, enjoying peace within itself (XXII. 24). "True peace shall be there, where no one shall suffer opposition either from himself or any other" (XXII. 30).

Powerful as Augustine was in his day and great as the shadow was that he cast across the Christian world into the Middle Ages and beyond, does he have anything to say to us? He takes for granted so many things we doubt or reject, what relevance has he to an age of overkill and fallout?

Well, I think his importance is in telling us that peace is a matter of the self-imposed reformation of the individual rather than a matter of techniques and strategies. You do not get disarmament by using an electronic computer to calculate the items each side shall discard. You get it by an internal reformation in which men recognize the greed and selfishness within themselves which create tensions, and then willingly give up private advantage for the more desirable and social and universally beneficial goal of peace.

Peace has to be paid for by self-sacrifice. It comes down to that. Specifically, it may mean paying higher taxes, allowing more imports, giving away surplus foods, opening one's home to overseas visitors, opening one's mind to new ideas, and taking one's professed religion seriously. These are all hard courses. Augustine shows us how, in the light of eternity, they may become easy. Sacrifices would be easier to make if we would only recognize the obvious fact that we must die—that our little space and trajectory upon earth are hardly perceptible in the grand scheme. Since we must die, what do we really profit by our greed? Since peace is the quality by which we measure what is good, why not purchase some of it while we can? Why not barter greed for peace? It will soon be too late. Why not now?

As for Augustine himself, he did not have too much of peace. At the end of his life the Vandals who had been pressing in upon the boundaries of the Roman empire came to the very gates of Hippo and laid siege to it. The Donatists whom Augustine had fought so bitterly slipped out to meet the enemy, eager to avenge themselves upon the church and the state which Augustine had made them hate. Unable to stand against this double threat, the Roman legions were defeated. Augustine died on August 28, 430, while the siege was going on. So he failed to see the Vandals pour in through the gates, their victory by a bitter irony made possible by his own stand against the Donatists.

Two saints less alike than Augustine and Francis could hardly be contained within the category of sainthood. Augustine was a scholar, a man of words, an administrator, a controversialist, a performer. Francis was a mystic, eloquent out of feeling rather than intellect, no administrator, a healer, a visionary, an idealist determined to put his ideals to work. Francis poured out his love of God upon the sick and the poor; Augustine looked for a full return of the love he gave to friend, mother or mistress. Francis' outgoing love was a bond that bound him to Christ and to God; Augustine needed such love to sustain him and bring out the gifts he could then exercise for others.

The thing that makes them in the end not so very different is an endearing humanness. Augustine so tied and bound in his early years to the love of woman, Francis in his to revels and gaiety and song; Augustine overwhelmed at last by an awareness of his sinfulness, Francis by the misery of the poor and their need of his loving care. Augustine planning to marry a rich woman so that he could live in ease, Francis angered with his brothers for turning murderous robbers from the door. Augustine coming to the bishop's study to see the great man and going away without a word, Francis turning away from the loathsome sores of the leper, then running back in contrition to kiss the rotting hand.

These were men. They let us see what a glory mankind is despite all its meanness—not because they were perfect but because they took the imperfections they had and built something better. Augustine sublimated his sexual drive into battling for the church, his desire for a comfortable home and circle of friends into a monastery, his rhetoric into the defense of the church. Francis turned his love of fun and music and comradeship into joyful service, into poems of praise, into a unique brotherhood.

What they have to say to us, therefore, is not so much what we find in their spoken or written words, but in their lives. Each contributed mightily to man's dream of peace and his conception of it. Yet both, ironically, nearly drowned in strife and controversy.

More than eight hundred years lie between the birth of Augustine and the birth of Francesco Bernardone at Assisi about 1182. The Roman empire had been swept away, and the rough strong tribes from the north had chopped up the remains among themselves. In the midst of carnage and disorder the Church had preserved the ancient learning and provided a rock for men to cling to. Gradually the barbarian had been tamed, the knight had rallied to the standard of chivalry, courtly love had become an intricate game, the great universities were being born, chanson and romance were in the air, troubadours sang their songs, castles perched on defensible hills, and soon the mighty gathering up of creative forces was to burst out in the structures and paintings of Giotto and the poems of Dante.

Francesco's father, Pietro Bernardone, a well-to-do cloth merchant, spent much of his time away from home. Therefore Francis, like Augustine, was much with his mother and was devoted to her. Pica Bernardone, daughter of the Count of Boulement in Provence, was a lady of culture. From her, no doubt, Francis learned to love singing, and French, and gentleness.

Yet at twenty he had to leave all this when, as one result of the struggle between emperor and pope, the powerful city of Perugia attacked Assisi. Joining all the rest of the men from eighteen to sixty, Francis trotted off on his own horse, fought, was captured, and had to spend a year in prison. Yet even in prison he kept that sweet temper and gay manner which had already become his hallmark.

He kept it up until he was released. Then, back in his comfortable home and with his mother to tend him, he fell terribly ill. But as soon as he recovered, or thought he had, he volunteered to fight for the pope in the south. It was characteristic of him that he gave the splendid military equipment his family had provided to one who had already won knighthood but had only a shabby outfit.

At the first night's stop, according to Saint Bonaventure, Francis heard a voice saying, "Francis, who can do better for you, the lord or the servant?" The lord, Francis answered.

"Why, then, do you leave the lord for the servant?" said the voice.

"Lord, what would'st Thou have me to do?" Francis asked.

"Return to your own country and you will be told what to do."

So Francis, dressed in the second new military outfit his no doubt exasperated father had provided at great cost, turned back home and did not use it at all. Other accounts say he was too sick to continue.

In any case, he was soon the leader of a gay band of young men who spent their nights parading the streets in handsome clothes, singing as they went, led on by torches to feast and drink their fill. On one such night Francis had treated his friends to a banquet and, as often, had been master of the revels. As they sallied out into the streets, Francis fell behind, tired of all the fun and finding it suddenly meaningless. Was it for this that the voice had sent him home?

When his companions turned back to look for him, they found him in a trance and began teasing him about being in love.

"Yes," Francis said, "I am in love with a bride nobler and richer and fairer than you have ever seen."

The bride was poverty. He had seen it always about him, for every city had its poor and its lepers, and he had flung coins to these loathsome people, a breed so different from himself that he had never had to think about them. But now he knew that they had something to do with him, though he did not yet know what.

To begin his new life, he went on a pilgrimage to Rome. He was now twenty-four.

Entering the great basilica of Saint Peter, he knelt at the altar while other pilgrims cast their small coins through the grating to the apostle's tomb below. In one of those sudden acts that was typical of him, he drew out his purse and flung its whole contents through the grating.

Penniless in a strange city, he came blinking out into the sun, grabbed hold of a ragged beggar, and persuaded him to exchange clothes. Then he went back to the church steps and begged— begged out of real need. Now he knew his lady poverty at first hand. Now he understood what poverty did to the poor, and why Jesus had blessed them. Perhaps he began to have an intimation of how he would make of poverty a rule of life. He was ready now to return to Assisi.

Soon after his return, he was riding near the lepers' hospital one day when he met a leper. Always before he had flung a coin to the ground and made off as fast as he could. But now a new understanding was growing in him. He got down from his horse, took the leper's loathsome hand in his, placed the coin in it and kissed it, though fully believing that such contact would give him the disease. Instead, the contact with suffering gave purpose to his whole life.

Now he made a point of visiting the lepers. He laid aside his fine clothes and went in rags. His former friends threw mud at him when they met him in the street.

One day he went to pray at the dilapidated little church of San Damiano. He went in, knelt at the altar, and prayed:

"Great and glorious God, and Thou, Lord Jesus, I pray Ye, shed abroad Thy light in the darkness of my mind. . . . Be found of me, Lord, so that in all things I may act in accordance with Thy Holy Will."

And a voice answered: "Francis, go and repair My church which as thou seest is wholly in ruin."

So he went to work. But he gained the wrath of his father by taking a valuable bale of cloth from the warehouse, carrying it to Foligno, and selling it for far less than its value, in order to get materials for the church. When his father took him before the

Bishop to disinherit him, Francis, without waiting for the papers to be drawn up, threw off his clothes and returned the money, saying:

"My Lord Bishop, I will give back unto him with a light heart not only the money that belongeth unto him, but my clothes also."

Weeping, Bishop Guido got up and flung his own cloak over the hair shirt.

Francis was now free to live the life of poverty toward which he had been groping.

Begging stones at Assisi, he bore them on his own frail shoulders to San Damiano. He begged for his food from door to door. To one who had always been accustomed to the best, these scraps must have been nauseating. Yet he ate them. He worked at the leper hospital, and he did not shrink from washing the disgusting sores, the rotting flesh.

He found another little church to rebuild—Santa Maria degli Angeli, an ancient building whose foundation went back to pagan times. Saint Benedict had loved it, taken possession, and built a monastery nearby; the ruins were still there. For six hundred years the monastery had operated, then in dangerous times a hundred years back been abandoned. Portiuncula, the little portion, it was called.

On Saint Matthias' day in 1209 Francis came to the newly restored church to serve a mass which the old priest from San Damiano was saying. When he began to read the gospel for the day, Francis knew that it spoke to him:

"Heal the sick, cleanse the lepers, raise the dead, cast out devils. . . . Provide neither gold, nor silver, nor brass in your purses, nor scrip for your journey, neither two coats, neither shoes, nor yet staves. . . ."

Francis, in that forthright way of his, pulled off his sandals, threw aside his wallet, made himself a garment shaped like a cross, and replaced his belt with a length of common rope. The next morning he went barefoot on the stones to Assisi and began immediately to preach in the streets.

"The Lord give thee peace," he would begin. And then he would speak of the love Jesus had commanded. Soon disciples came to him—Bernard the wealthy businessman and Peter the lawyer, Giles the farmer and Sylvester, an old priest. Bernard gave away all his wealth to the poor, standing in the Piazza San Giorgio with Francis to help him.

When the number had grown to the apostolic twelve, Francis said:

"Let us go to our Mother, the holy Roman Church, and tell the pope what the Lord has begun to do through us, and carry it out with his sanction."

Barefoot, carrying only the rule of their order, they set out to visit Innocent III—statesman, theologian, aristocrat, and scourge of heretics. Out of pure innocence, Francis walked into the Lateran Palace, by pure good luck found the section of it where the pope lived and where by another stroke of luck he happened to be pacing the corridor. Francis sank to his knees, dirty and shoeless as he was, and began to speak. As soon as the pope could find a voice, he ordered him out.

Discouraged, Francis and his friends slipped out to the street where, by another stroke of luck, they met Bishop Guido from Assisi. The bishop found them a place to stay and introduced Francis to one of the pope's advisers, Cardinal John of Saint Paul. Francis so impressed the cardinal that he persuaded the pope to see him. Into this splendid presence of princes of the church in their rich robes came the twelve barefoot men, begging only for permission to follow literally the commandments of Jesus. The pope kindly suggested that the men join some other order instead of founding their own.

But Cardinal John persisted for them. Francis was asking for permission to do what the Savior had commanded. Could a pope refuse him that?

[111]

The pope deferred his decision, asking Francis to pray for guidance.

That night the pope dreamed a dream. A church was about to collapse into ruins when a little man in a habit girded with a rope ran and shored it up. When Francis returned, the pope blessed him and his companions and sent them happily on their way. Now their work could begin.

But war broke out again between Guelph and Ghibelline claimants to the imperial throne. Assisi had shut her gates against an expected attack from Perugia. Francis, whose whole way of life was based upon the self-denying love that brings peace, now begged the factions within Assisi to end their quarrels. On November 9, 1210, as a result of his urging, the citizens signed a Treaty of Concord, promising to love God and to work together for the common welfare. It was a testimony to the power Francis, still a young man, had earned for himself.

Francis' happiness was complete when the Benedictines gave him the use of Portiuncula as the headquarters for his order.

Within a year Francis had another convert and another problem on his hands, when the lovely eighteen-year-old daughter of Favorino Scofi, the Lord of Sasso Rosso, begged to be taken into the order. The end of it all was that the Benedictines gave Francis his beloved San Damiano for a convent. The second order began with Clare and her fifteen-year-old sister Agnes, who could not bear to be parted from her.

Strangely, the rule of poverty strongly attracted many wealthy people. The example Francis gave them was stronger than sermons, stronger than prayers. Many gave away their wealth and entered the order.

To meet the great longing of people who wanted to follow a Franciscan life without entering a monastery, Francis founded his third order for worldlings who, though remaining in their homes, would practice charity and humility and live abstemiously. Here, too, Francis was able to impose his rule of peace. The men did not carry arms, were pledged to maintain peace, and were excused from oaths that forced them to fight whether the cause was just or not. In an Italy torn apart by quarrels among cities, they threw their influence on the side of peace.

Before long this influence was felt throughout Europe, for the third order increased as rapidly as the other two. It still lives today. Its members have included Christopher Columbus, Petrarch, Giotto, Dante, the mystic Angela of Foligno, Roger Bacon and a great many more. Through Giotto and Dante, Francis inspired a whole new era in the arts.

Everyone knows the charming legends of Saint Francis and the birds, or knows at least the pictures in which they surround him.

It was on a preaching tour that he came to some trees full of birds and decided that he should preach to them. When he began to speak, the birds flew down to him and remained quiet until he had finished. What he told them was that as God cared for them, "So, my little sisters, keep yourselves from the sin of ingratitude, and always strive to praise God."

And the birds opened their beaks, stretched their necks, and bowed their heads to the ground. And when he dismissed them with the sign of the cross, they rose into the air with a wonderful song, formed themselves in the shape of a cross, and flew off in four flocks to the four main compass points.

On another occasion when he was traveling to La Varna and had stopped to rest under an oak tree, a great flock of birds came winging to him, showing their joy by singing and flapping their wings, some settling on his head, some on his shoulders and arms and knees.

"My dearest brothers," he said to his companions, "I believe it to be the pleasure of our Lord Jesus Christ that we should dwell in this lonely mountain, because our sisters and brothers the birds show such joy at our coming."

About 1214 Francis joyfully set out for Spain to preach to the Moors, but he reached Spain weakened with illness and had to return home. In 1219 he set out once again, headed this time for Egypt where the crusaders were besieging the sultan at Damietta. They had been at it for a year and a half with little success. Man of peace that he was, Francis still thrilled to the sight of the bright-colored pavilions, the knights in armor, the brilliant banners, the singing and the blare of trumpets. They brought back a sharp yet tender memory of the days not so long ago when he had dreamed of becoming a knight and had sung the troubadour's songs with his friends. But he had seen war. He knew that along with bravery it brought greed; along with fraternity, brutality.

On August 29 the great army moved to attack and was thoroughly beaten. After Francis had done what he could for the anguished and the dying, he went to the papal legate and begged permission to cross the lines and preach to the sultan. The legate reminded him that the sultan had offered his men a golden ducat for each Christian head they brought him. But martyrdom was to Francis a goal rather than a fear. Choosing Illuminato for his companion, he set out.

Two lambs scampered across the path in front of them.

"Put thy trust in the Lord, brother," he told Illuminato, "for in us that saying is fulfilled: Behold, I send you forth as sheep in the midst of wolves."

Somehow they succeeded in being taken before the sultan in his great pavilion. Gorgeously dressed, he was surrounded by his court in their rich and colorful attire.

The sultan had ordered a carpet woven with crosses to be spread before him. When Francis walked upon it, the sultan delightedly pointed to what he had done.

"We Christians have the true cross," Francis said. "The crosses of the thieves we have left to you, and these I am not ashamed to tread upon."

The quick answer so delighted the sultan that he was willing to listen to a sermon. Francis stayed for several days and had several talks with the sultan but was unable to convert him, even when he proposed to walk into a fire and if necessary give up his life so that peace might come to the world through a common allegiance to the prince of peace.

The sultan declined. Francis had to return, unharmed and unsuccessful, to the Christian camp.

The crusaders attacked again, broke through, and devastated the city. Sickened by what he saw, Francis went on to visit the Holy Land before returning home.

By the time he reached home in 1220 his order had grown so large that some kind of organization and administration were needed. Francis had kept to the strict vow of poverty. The brothers were to work for their food whenever that was possible, and at whatever task offered. But as the order grew, other brothers wanted to make it a learned order and to this Francis was opposed. He was a man who knew God intuitively, directly, with all his being and without need of theology, philosophy, metaphysics. He feared that book learning would interfere with the life of service; let other orders be learned, be teachers.

All this came to a head through the person of Brother Elias, a man who loved power and who wanted to build up the order by erecting proper buildings in place of the miserable huts Francis preferred, who wanted the order to hold property, provide libraries for the intellectually inclined, infirmaries for sick and elderly brothers, and all the administration that would be required.

In 1220 Francis, opposed to any such changes but unable to cope with a kind of work he was not fitted for, resigned his office of minister-general, saying:

"Lord, I give Thee back this family which Thou didst entrust to me. Thou knowest, most sweet Jesus, that I have no more the power and the qualities to continue to take care of it. I entrust it, therefore, to the ministers. Let them be responsible before Thee at the Day of Judgment, if any brother by their negligence, or their bad example, or by a too severe punishment, shall go astray."

It is a fine statement—so honestly humble and practical, so full of love.

Elias became minister-general. After the death of Francis he became even more strict and overbearing, scourging and imprisoning brothers whom Francis had loved and letting his violent temper loose upon all. At last he was forced out. But meanwhile the order had split in two, the strict Franciscans and the men who wanted to build up a strong order. The split remains. Yet down through the years the spirit of Francis has lived on in men who have cared for lepers and orphans, walked fearlessly into plague-stricken cities to nurse the infected, and gone wherever disaster struck and human need was desperate.

As for Francis, he withdrew more and more into the silent places, to the mountain retreats his admirers had provided for him. Yet he was not left in peace, for Elias kept at him to modify the old rule of poverty. In 1223 Francis wrote out a new order and walked all the way to Rome with it to get the pope's approval. He had changed nothing essential. Elias had to bow to the pope's authority.

Back in his mountain retreat, Francis devoted himself to prayer and fasting. Refreshed, though his health was failing, he again walked barefoot through the world, preaching and healing and renewing men with his love.

By 1224, when he again left his holy mountain of Alvernia (La Verna), he had to use the donkey a loving friend had sent him, for he could no longer walk. Wherever he went, the people crowded around him to see him and receive his blessing—this man who had become a saint in his own lifetime.

It was clear that he could not live long. Yet he traveled from place to place, was treated by famous doctors whom his friends wanted him to see, still giving away his only cloak when confronted by poverty and he had nothing else to give.

As Francis' health weakened, Assisi began to fear that he would die on his travels and they would never get his body back.

[116]

To possess the bones of a saint was, in those days, no small matter for a city. So Assisi sent an armed guard to escort him while he rode in a litter. They brought him safely back, though he was in pain now, suffering because of the long neglect of his body.

He died when only forty-five in his beloved Portiuncula, close to the church of Santa Maria degli Angeli which he had himself restored.

No one had ever come so close to imitating the life of Jesus; no one had ever taken with such engaging and wholehearted literalness the commands of the Gospels: Go and sell all that thou hast and give to the poor. Take no thought for your life, what ye shall eat, or what ye shall drink. Blessed are the poor. Blessed are the peacemakers, for they shall be called the children of God.

"God give thee His peace." This was his greeting, the greeting of all Franciscans, wherever he went.

The peace Francis preached and practiced was an internal thing—a gift of God, available to all men who would practice love of God and neighbor, humility, and compassion for all suffering, all poverty.

But true compassion meant entering into that very suffering and poverty. And this means self-mastery, conquering of self— the very lesson Buddha taught.

"Above all graces and gifts of the Holy Spirit that Christ gives to His friends is the grace to conquer self, and willingly to bear any pain, injury, insult and hardship for love of Christ."

Strangely enough, such power comes only with humility.

"God could not find a viler creature on earth to employ for the marvellous work He intends to accomplish," Francis told Brother Masseo. "He has therefore chosen me to confound the nobility, the greatness, the power, the beauty, and the wisdom of the world. He has chosen me so that men may understand that every virtue and every good thing proceeds from Him alone, and not from any creature."

The worthiness or otherwise of the needy never troubled Saint

Francis; this was not for him to judge. So when a young brother one day turned away from the door three desperate and hungry men, known to be robbers and murderers, and then told Francis what he had done, he was shocked to find that instead of being praised for his courage he was blamed for turning away the needy. Francis sent him off with bread and wine to overtake the men, to kneel before them and beg their forgiveness, and to say that Francis begged them never to do evil any more but to fear God. If they would do this, Francis would look after them.

As they ate, looking at the young brother humbly kneeling, it happened to them as to the thief on the cross. Their own crimes suddenly came into focus. Penitent, they went to Francis, promising to do whatever he ordered.

Within a short time Francis accepted them into his order.

"They are truly peace makers," wrote Francis, "who amidst all they suffer in this world maintain peace in soul and body for the love of our Lord Jesus Christ."

It was his wisdom to see that peace cannot come of man alone. For men must believe in a power beyond themselves, a power whose motive and object is peace, so that they will be willing to conquer their own greed and passion. Only through this internal reformation can peace ever come.

It is all there in that beautiful prayer of his:

"Lord, make me an instrument of Your peace. Where there is hatred, let me sow love; where there is injury, pardon; where there is doubt, faith; where there is despair, hope; where there is darkness, light; and where there is sadness, joy.

"Divine Master, grant that I may not so much seek to be consoled as to console; to be understood as to understand; to be loved as to love, for it is in giving that we receive; it is in pardoning that we are pardoned; and it is in dying that we are born to eternal life."

Augustine laid down the foundation for peace based upon God's will for man. He made it the highest goal, as Jesus had in making the common greeting of the Middle East, "Shalom," a goal to be striven for by a life of self-denial.

Francis took Jesus, took Augustine literally. He lived that life of self-denial to the fullest. He went himself and sent his disciples into the world as Jesus had, saying, "May God bring you His peace," living in such a way that if men had been able to follow him, peace would have been achieved.

Between Saint Francis and ourselves there stretches a turbulent sea of events in which much of the storm has been stirred up in the name of religion. There is no need to review here the dismal history of Europe—the struggles between pope and emperor, the inquisition, the brutal massacres in the name of putting down heresy. It cannot be wiped out or glossed over. It is a permanent part of the human record. Its value for us is to make us wary of witch hunts.

For a long time the church of Saint Augustine and Saint Francis seemed wrapped up in itself and not much concerned with the fate of man in the workaday world. But in his great Encyclical Letter, *Pacem in Terris*, Pope John XXIII brought the church back to the ground on which its founder had stood, which Augustine had expounded and Francis had practiced. It has been made clear now, both to the faithful and to all men everywhere, that the church stands for peace based upon social justice, and that it believes in the forgetfulness of self that Francis practiced, following in the steps of his Master.

"How strongly does the turmoil of individual men and peoples contrast with the perfect order of the universe!" His Holiness observed that the proper ordering of human affairs in our time requires "the establishment of a world community of peoples."

Gently calling attention to the excesses of nationalism, the pope reminded us:

"The fact that one is a citizen of a particular State does not detract in any way from his membership in the world community. . . . All political communities are of equal natural dignity.

[119]

"The advantages and conveniences which nations strive to acquire for themselves become objects of contention; nevertheless, the resulting disagreements must be settled . . . by an equitable reconciliation of differences of opinion."

His Holiness quoted Pius XII to show that "Violence has always achieved only destruction, not construction; the kindling of passions, not their pacification; the accumulation of hate and ruin, not the reconciliation of the contending parties."

The attack on war must therefore be two-pronged: we must overcome the inequities and injustices which breed war, and we must put an end to the arms race, ban nuclear weapons, and move toward complete disarmament.

"Today the universal common good poses problems of worldwide dimensions, which cannot be adequately tackled or solved except by the efforts of public authorities . . . in a position to operate in an effective manner on a world-wide basis." Pope John therefore earnestly hoped that the United Nations may become ever more equal to the magnitude and nobility of its tasks. "May the day soon come when every human being will find therein an effective safeguard for the rights which derive directly from his dignity as a person, and which are therefore universal, inviolate and inalienable rights."

Then at the end he came back to the one basis for peace that Buddha and Jesus had emphasized:

In fact, there can be no peace between men unless there is peace within each one of them; unless, that is, each one builds up within himself the order wished by God.

Hence St. Augustine asks: Does your soul desire to overcome your lower inclinations? Let it be subject to Him who is on high and it will conquer the lower self: there will be peace in you; true, secure and well-ordered peace. In what does that order consist? God commands the soul; the soul commands the body; and there is nothing more orderly than this.

However, peace will be but an empty-sounding word unless it is founded on the order which this present Encyclical has out-

*lined in confident hope: an order founded on truth, built accord-
ing to justice, vivified and integrated by charity, and put into
practice in freedom.*

It is a matter for pride and hope that the firm foundations of
peace based upon love as Jesus taught them, on which Augustine
built his City of God, and which Francis carried into his every-
day life and spread around the world through his three orders,
should in our day have been clearly and courageously reiterated
by the head of the Catholic Church. It would be a mighty force
for peace if Catholics would take the lessons of this great
Encyclical to their hearts and practice them in their lives, thus
encouraging the rest of us to follow.

The Church has once again taken leadership in the unending
quest for peace and provided a chart to steer by.

But how shall we achieve peace, when we have to face opponents who deny the message?

Who could have guessed, two thousand years ago, that Jesus
would be remembered more than a few months after his crucifixion? If miracles of faith were not interwoven into human
history, we might have ceased to exist as a species long ago.

7. William Penn and the Quakers
(1644-1718)

The Way of Love

 The hundred and seventy years of our co-
lonial history were full of remarkable men, but none more attractive and truly prophetic of the American dream at its best than
William Penn.

His life is like a stormy Elizabethan drama—full of turn and
counterturn, of plots, stratagems, treasons, familiarity with kings,
violent arguments with a loving father, even more violent pam-
phleteering, ruination and recovery, the gift and loss of a princely
territory.

We think of Penn as the peaceful Quaker and paternalistic
founder of Pennsylvania. We see him stand there in Benjamin
West's familiar painting of Penn and the Indians, firm and fleshy
and rather stodgy, forever dispensing a justice which too rarely
entered into our relations with the Indian.

Such moments came but rarely to Penn. Most of his life this
lover of concord was in the midst of a controversy, a fight for
justice, or a struggle to preserve his fortune.

Penn's father, the admiral, could afford the best for him. To
the house on Tower Hill in London came tutors to shape the
young mind. At sixteen Penn entered Oxford. But he stayed

only a year and a half. No one knows for certain why he left, but he was already getting ideas about freedom of religion and objecting to compulsory chapel, and this may have been a factor.

Clearly his father thought he had come under the wrong influences for one destined to a great place at court, so he packed him off to the Continent on a tour which lasted two years. William bought modish French clothes, wore a sword, and was attacked one night for failing to see and return the hat salute of a perfect stranger who chose to consider himself insulted. Although he managed to defend himself, the young Penn was struck with the stupidity of forms. Why should a man be willing to kill over "hat, knee, or title"?

Penn left Paris to study at Saumur with Moïse Amyraut, a great scholar and liberal Calvinist. It was here, no doubt, that he became familiar with many of the authors whom he was to quote so liberally and impressively in his own works. Amyraut, a champion of the personal liberty made possible by Christ's gift to man, was exactly the sort of influence to which Penn was open in his young search for significance, challenge and promise. It was from Amyraut that he learned the doctrine of morality based upon free will, guided by that of God in every man.

When Amyraut died, Penn continued his wanderings until he was called home just as he was about to become twenty. The war with Holland was coming on, and his father needed him at home when he went off with the fleet. William even served a few days at sea with his father, bringing back dispatches which he delivered personally to King Charles. The king came out in nothing but his nightgown, greeted the young man, and kept inquiring for his father.

William now had about a year and a half at Lincoln's Inn. Since much of his life was involved in court fights and controversy, the law he learned there was of great value to him. But then came the Great Plague, which drove his family out of London.

In 1666 his father sent him to manage his estate in Ireland, where his title was being disputed. He also counted on contact with society there to wean the young man from his religious leanings. An old friend, the Duke of Ormond, presided as Lord Lieutenant over a court that was brilliant without being full of the immorality prevailing at Whitehall.

When a mutiny broke out at Carrickfergus, Penn volunteered for service and gave a good account of himself. Ormond then offered him a small command, but the admiral sent off a gracious objection and the matter was dropped. Perhaps he had higher ambitions for his son. In any case, Penn had his portrait painted in armor at this time. It shows a handsome, rather serious, and perhaps proud young man with flowing hair. He looks out at us frankly, even boldly, a man whose convictions are not easily changed.

In Ireland, William came again in contact with the Quaker Thomas Loe whom he is said to have met first in his own home as a boy. Loe's eloquent and sincere preaching moved him deeply, and Penn began to attend Quaker Meetings.

He was attending Meeting in 1667 when a soldier came noisily in and did his best to break it up. Penn jumped up, grabbed him by the collar, and was ready to throw him down the stairs when several Friends restrained him, reminding him that they were a peaceable people and did not settle things by force. The soldier meanwhile went off to the magistrate who sent officers to break up the Meeting. They took Penn and several others prisoner.

Penn got his release by writing to Lord Orrery, president of nearby Munster. The letter made that claim for freedom of conscience to which Penn was to devote much of his life.

His father, having got wind of the event, sent for William to come home at once. There were bitter scenes between them, for William would not give up his religious ideas or his allegiance to Friends.

William's use of the Quaker thee and thou enraged his father. "Thee and thou whom you please except the King, the Duke of York and myself," he said. But William, answering him with that look we see in the portrait, said that he must speak in the singular to all alike.

The poor father tried anger, pleas and prayers, and ended by ordering him out of the house. The son left with a small bundle of clothes, but was soon sent after and brought back. Not long after he was turned out a second time. But when his father saw that there was no changing him, he "winked at his Return to, and Continuance in his Family."

Penn now devoted most of his time to speaking and writing in behalf of the Quakers and their radical ideas. His early tracts, full of the fire and excess of youth, were violently controversial. For writing "The Sandy Foundation Shaken," with its attack on orthodox religious views, he was sent to the Tower and held there nearly nine months. No doubt he managed to do a good deal of writing there, too, for the output of tracts and books continued, as it did throughout his life—157 titles in all.

Released in 1669, Penn began a period of visiting Friends Meetings, preaching first in England, then on the Continent. He was now well known to older Quaker leaders—to the founder, George Fox, to Isaac Penington the Quaker mystic, and to his family. Isaac's wife had first married Sir William Springett, who died of a wound suffered in the Civil War while he was commander of Arundel Castle. A few weeks after his death his daughter had been born and named, after him, Guilielma. That was in 1644, the year of Penn's birth.

Isaac, son of a lord mayor of London, was often imprisoned for being a Quaker and had much of his estate confiscated, yet he persisted in his faith. That Penn should have admired this man for his courage and endurance is not surprising, nor that he should have fallen in love with his age-mate, the charming, sweet-tempered and intelligent Guilielma. Penn adored her— "the most beloved, as well as the most worthy of all my earthly comforts." They were married in 1672.

The admiral had died in September, 1670, so young William

had at his disposal a fortune of about £1500 a year—a handsome sum.

"Son William," the admiral is supposed to have said at his death, "if you and your friends keep your plain way of preaching, and keep to your plain way of living, you will make an end of the priests to the end of the world. . . . Live all in love."

William had meanwhile been twice again in jail. One of these occasions led to a trial of historic importance, for with Penn's encouragement the jury refused to be bullied into bringing in the verdict the court wanted, ultimately finding Penn not guilty.

"You are Englishmen," Penn called to them from the bar, "mind your privilege, give not away your right."

"Nor will we ever do it," the foreman promised.

A higher court sustained their finding and censured the lower court for fining and imprisoning jurors.

With his bride, Penn now settled down at a home in Hertfordshire and continued his controversial writing. His latest imprisonment had been for six months, so the change to country life must have seemed idyllic. Often Guilielma would go with him when he traveled about the country attending Meetings and speaking, even when she was pregnant and the travel on rough country roads must have been harrowing. But many things are possible to young lovers in their twenties.

We know Penn as the founder of Pennsylvania. But if he had never done this work, he would still be famous as one of the great battlers for religious toleration. With his position, his fortune, his ready store of learning, his enthusiasm and stubborn determination and perseverance, he hammered away continuously by writing, by court action, by using his influence in high places all the way up to the throne.

When the king sent an emissary to him in the Tower to win him over, he sent back the message:

"Those who use force for religion never could be in the right."

England's ancient liberties, he argued in "England's Present

Interest Discovered," 1675, had nothing to do with the church, which had now begun to meddle in matters that should be none of its concern. "Church Government is no real Part of the old English Government." To preserve these liberties, government must observe "a balance toward the several religious interests." It should promote general and practical religion, not a single church. For conscience cannot be coerced. Since each man must believe as experience and understanding lead him, a nation of one church would be a nation of liars.

Penn was ahead of his time and had to suffer for it. Finally, in 1688, his long efforts bore fruit in the passage of the Toleration Act. But the sufferings Quakers had to endure before the Act was passed, and were willing to endure for their convictions, almost pass belief.

"The Widdows Mite hath not escaped their Hands," wrote Penn; "They have made her Cow the forfeit of her Conscience, not leaving her a Bed to lie on, nor a Blanket to cover her."

During the twelve years of the Commonwealth 3000 Quakers were imprisoned and 32 died in jail. During the quarter century of Charles II's reign, another 15,000 were jailed and 450 died there. Penn felt sure that more than 5000 had died from punishment and harassment. They were fined over and over again until their estates melted away. They were driven out of the land, flogged from street to street and parish to parish, invaded in their homes without warrants, tried and bullied and sentenced illegally. Parents were hailed away and children left helpless. In one case at least, when every adult in a Quaker Meeting had been carted away to jail, the children gathered on Sunday and held Meeting all the same.

This is a part of the price once paid for the freedom we now enjoy—and so often count as nothing, by failing to use it.

In 1677 Penn went to the Continent with George Fox, Robert Barclay, and other Quaker leaders to encourage and extend Quakerism in Holland and Germany. He also wrote letters of encouragement to Friends in the West Indies, Maryland and New England where George Fox had traveled.

In 1675 Penn almost by chance became involved in America. John Fenwick, a Quaker, had bought one of two equal shares into which New Jersey had been divided after Charles II had given it to his brother James. The purchase was in trust for another Friend, Edward Byllinge. When differences arose between the two Friends, Penn was chosen arbitrator. In the course of his work, he drew up the Concessions and Agreements which amounted to a constitution for West Jersey.

"We put the power in the people," stated the proprietors. Religious freedom was guaranteed, and life, liberty and estate were protected by jury trial. Thanks to the liberal constitution, many Quakers went over and settled there in order to be free from the constant harassment in England, and to establish communities where they could live in the peace they valued so highly.

The prospects for Jersey set Penn to thinking about a colony of his own in the new world, so in 1680 he asked the king to grant him a tract of about 300 by 160 miles between Maryland and Jersey, as a return for the large sums his father the admiral had expended in his Majesty's service.

Charles, himself a secret Catholic, had some sympathy for the sufferings of the Quakers, and no doubt thought it would end wrangling if large numbers of them left the country. The grant was signed in 1681. Charles insisted on naming the grant Pennsylvania in honor of the admiral, though William made every effort to get the name changed to Sylvania—partly out of modesty and partly, no doubt, because he was already under some criticism from Quakers who feared that his wealth and position would lure him away from plainness.

Penn, determined that his "holy experiment" as he called it would succeed in providing a just government and prosperous society for all believers, drew up a "Frame of Government" which was several times revised but which provided a council and popular assembly, religious liberty, fair trial, and prison reform.

"Government seems to me a part of religion itself," he wrote, "a thing sacred in its institution and end." Pennsylvania, if he could succeed, would be an example to the world of sound government, full justice, freedom of conscience, and peace.

It was essential to his plan that he start off on a very different footing with the Indians than had other Englishmen. So with the first settlers he sent them a message which included these words:

> I have great love and regard towards you, and I desire to win and gain your love and friendship, by a kind, just and peaceable life; and the people I send are of the same mind, and shall in all things behave themselves accordingly; and if in any thing any shall offend you or your people, you shall have a full and speedy satisfaction for the same, by an equal number of just men on both sides that by no means you may have just occasion of being offended against them.

On the first of September, 1682, Penn sailed for America on the *Welcome* with a hundred people, leaving behind his beloved Guilielma and their children. Her mother's illness prevented her from leaving, but she planned to join him there—a plan that was not to be fulfilled.

Penn did meet with the Indians (though the details have often been disputed) and he did make with them that treaty of which Voltaire said:

"It was the only treaty between those nations and the Christians which was never sworn to and never broken." Quakers refused to take judicial oaths.

Penn had a sympathetic understanding of the Indians, perhaps because his Quaker faith that there is that of God in every man let him see them as men, not savages. Too, the Indians were natural mystics, and their sense of the divine and its pervading quality was congenial. Like the Quakers, Indians met and deliberated as a group, listening patiently to all opinions and reaching a consensus. Although it may never have occurred to Penn, they also had the kind of stolid endurance Quakers had shown throughout the years of their persecution in England.

Delighted with his new land, Penn wrote an enthusiastic letter to the Free Society of Traders back home, full of happy descriptions of the climate, the soil, the prospects for agriculture. He described the Indians and their ways with obvious interest and praised the grandeur of their language which he was trying to learn. And he reported that he had agreed with them that in any dispute, "six of each side shall end the matter."

Returning to England in 1684, he was able to report, "Not one soldier, or arms borne, or militia man seen, since I was first in Pennsylvania." The Quaker ideal of a peaceable kingdom, he felt, could be realized.

Shortly thereafter Charles II died and James II came to the throne. With James, Penn had so much influence that he was able to get a pardon for the philosopher John Locke, and then a general pardon for all the Quakers then in prison. Thirteen hundred of them walked out to freedom from the indescribably filthy jails of the time. With the Declaration of Indulgence in 1687 and the Act of Toleration in 1689, Penn's long fight for liberty seemed rewarded.

It was Penn's effort to establish freedom of conscience and to get relief for the religiously persecuted which brought him to court. He and James II were personal friends. James respected his judgment though he did not always take his advice—advice which Penn knew to be unpopular when he gave it. As a Catholic, James was glad to have Penn's support for freedom of conscience for Catholics as well as dissenters. This was further than Milton had gone before Penn, or than Locke went after.

Biographers have found it hard to understand how Penn and James could have been friends. Yet the basis for that friendship is if anything too apparent. Only the hostility of historians to James has obscured it. Both men wanted religious toleration in England, and both wanted traditional English liberties preserved.

James made his stand clear in the Declaration of Indulgence of 1687, which for the first time separated religion from nationality. If he had followed Penn's advice the following year and released the seven bishops he had thrown in the Tower for refusing to do his will—this as an act of grace on the birth of his son—he might have saved his throne and preserved the toleration he believed in. Instead, the bishops won acquittal and James disappeared in the Glorious Revolution. Penn boldly remained in London, was twice examined by the council, and truthfully declared his friendship for the king as well as his loyalty to the new government. In 1690 Queen Mary, still not trusting him, proclaimed him a dangerous person. Still he remained in London instead of fleeing to the country.

Pennsylvania, meanwhile, was having troubles of its own, chiefly as a result of friction between the province proper and the territory (Delaware) granted Penn by the Duke of York, all now under one government but having different interests. Another source of conflict was the Quaker determination to live peaceably and without a militia. With European conflicts at the boil, England wanted a firm colonial defense.

So in 1692 the governorship was taken from Penn and given to the governor of New York. The next year Pennsylvania was annexed by the crown. At the same time Penn was accused of treasonable correspondence with the exiled James II, but friends at court went to work and won for him the assurance that no further steps would be taken against him.

This was not enough for Penn. He had been publicly accused; he must be publicly exonerated. He won his point.

Then came the hardest blow when early in 1694 his beloved Guilielma died in his arms, leaving him three children to raise.

Six months later his governorship was restored to him, when he promised to see that his frontiers were defended. In 1696 he married Hannah Callowhill, a Quaker of Bristol whom he had long known. She was twenty years younger, but a woman with great firmness and powers of management. In the disasters that lay ahead for Penn, she was the one who saved him from complete ruin.

The trouble had begun in 1690 when Penn, since he expected to be tried for treason, conveyed all of Pennsylvania to his steward, Philip Ford, adjuring the right to have the deed rendered void! Over the years Penn had grown careless in examining the various accounts Ford rendered and the papers brought for his signature. Ford saw that he could build a fortune for himself upon Penn's negligence.

Penn was also concerned over the peace of Europe. War had been going on here and there throughout the century, and steadily since 1688. Many of the nations had aligned themselves against France, whose fleet the English and Dutch defeated in 1692, though the next year the French defeated the British. Watching the folly of all this seesawing, Penn wrote his "Essay towards the Present and Future Peace of Europe" in 1693.

It boils down to a simple proposal that all states be prepared to unite against any aggressor. A European parliament would be set up, with votes allotted to each state according to its size and strength, up to a total of about ninety delegates. Meetings should be held every year or two, and all points of dispute raised and voted upon by ballot. The meeting room should be round with lots of doors to enter by so that there need be no dispute for precedence!

Such a parliament would not diminish sovereignty at home, nor would the states have sovereignty one over another.

"If this be called a lessening of their power, it must be only because the great fish can no longer eat up the little ones, and that each sovereignty is equally defended from injuries, and disabled from committing them."

All he asked, said Penn, was that the same rules of justice and prudence by which families and cities and nations are governed be extended to all of Europe, so that peace may prevail.

As for extending it to men of different nations, he had already done that in Pennsylvania, where English, Swedes, Germans, Hollanders and Indians were living amicably together. Why not in Europe?

It seems eminently sensible. Such proposals always do. Only they assume that men are willing to grant equality to those of other nations, whereas for some reason or other a nation always seems impelled to regard itself as more equal than any other! For brother, for neighbor, for fellow citizen we are willing to curb our greed, but the man beyond the border is the stranger from whom we must recapture all that we have given in fellowship to those nearer by. How else can one account for the failure of such proposals as Penn's?

Penn's pacifism, of course, was deeply rooted in his religion. Government to him was part of religion because through government man subjected what was brutish in his nature to reason, to law, to good order. And peace was the test of good order, the test of good and successful government.

"What sort of Christians must they be," he asked, "that can hate in His name, who bids us love; and kill for His sake, that forbids killing, and commands love, even to enemies? O, that we could see some men as eager to turn people to God, as they are to blow them up, and set them against one another."

Again: "A good end cannot sanctify evil means; nor must we ever do evil, that good may come of it. . . . Let us then try what Love will do: for if men did once see we love them, we should soon find they would not harm us. Force may subdue, but Love gains; and he that forgives first, wins the laurel" (*Some Fruits of Solitude*).

"Governments, like clocks," he reasoned, "go from the motion men give them; and as governments are made and moved by men, so by them they are ruined too. Wherefore governments rather depend upon men, than men upon governments. . . . If men be bad, let the government be never so good, they will endeavor to warp and spoil it to their turn."

So, like all those great teachers who had thought about the problem before, he too came to the conclusion:

"Those who would mend the world must first mend themselves."

It was the rock on which the hope of peace kept foundering, and still does.

Practical politics have a way of mocking men's best thoughts. As a result of Louis XIV's aggressive warfare, what we know as King William's War broke out in America. When the Lords of Trade proposed to William that all the American colonies be placed under a military dictator, Penn in 1697 offered instead a "Plan for a Union of the Colonies." Each colony was to send two representatives to a permanent congress, with power to adjust complaints, to consider means of maintaining the safety of the colonies against the public enemies, to set quotas of men and charges. But the plan was not realized.

In 1699 Penn, now fifty-five, returned to his beloved Pennsylvania. A good many problems awaited him—the suppression of piracy, how to deal with slavery, relations with the Indians. As before, he got on well with the Indians, making a treaty with them which bound them not to help any enemy of England or of Pennsylvania, nor to trade with any persons not approved by Penn or his representative.

After eighteen years Pennsylvania still had no militia or stockades. Its peaceful understanding with the Indians had endured while massacres and continuing friction had occurred elsewhere, so that its advice on dealing with the Indians was often sought after.

"If men did once see we love them, we should soon find they would not harm us." Penn's whole method boiled down to that. It reminds us of what John Woolman, a New Jersey Quaker (1720–1772), wrote about his desire to visit the Indians:

"Love was the first motion and then a concern arose to spend some time with the Indians, that I might feel and understand

[134]

their life and the spirit they live in, if haply I might receive some instruction from them, or they might in any degree be helped forward by my following the leadings of truth among them."

How rarely had any European approached the Indian in that spirit!

In October, 1701, after making some requested changes in the charter, Penn left for England where the king was pressing Pennsylvania to unite with the other colonies for defense and to build fortifications. Quaker pacifism and power politics had come face to face.

As a matter of fact, the period from 1700 to 1740 was a sort of golden age of Quakerism in America. Pennsylvania had a predominantly Quaker assembly, and Philadelphia was the cultural center of the whole seaboard. In Rhode Island half the population was Quaker and for over a century the governors had been Friends. In North Carolina at one time the governor and half the assembly were Quakers, while Friends owned most of New Jersey and maintained a strong influence even after surrendering their control in 1702. In Quaker towns throughout these colonies the Meeting was the spiritual, intellectual and economic center of the community. If disputes arose, they were settled there and not allowed to infect the whole community. So far as human nature would permit, love and mutual concern guided behavior.

The government Penn set up, commemorated by the Liberty Bell, survived until the Revolution when colony gave way to state, although Quakers withdrew from government in 1756 when the governor declared war on the Indians.

Was the holy experiment a success, then, or a failure?

Penn did manage to establish religious liberty, a home for the persecuted of Europe, prisons that were to reform not punish, a society free of aristocracy, and a prosperous economy. The democratic quality of the Society of Friends, with its management of affairs through the Meeting where all have equal voice, and its peaceful way of coming to a common agreement instead of accenting the disagreement of Yea and Nay—these entered into

[135]

the bloodstream of American democracy. Friends believe in social reform, in education, and in moral commitment. All these things had their effect.

In the end, Penn's effort to maintain peace failed, but through no fault of his own. He had demonstrated that peace could be had with the Indians, but he lacked the power to keep Europe's imperial conflicts outside his borders.

Pennsylvania ultimately compromised its principles by making some contribution toward the expense of defending the colony from the French and Indians, but then for fifty years it refused to erect defenses or fight for the empire.

The final period of Penn's life was far from easy. His son William became the ringleader of a band of dissolute roisterers in Philadelphia. Pennsylvania continued to provide him with difficult problems including a reluctance to pay him what was his due. The steward to whom he had entrusted all his affairs for many years, Philip Ford, turned out to be a villain. By manipulating accounts and getting Penn's signature on various documents, he built up a claim to the monstrous sum of £14,000. He then died, leaving the claim to his wife and son. Penn was able to locate accounts he had never bothered to examine before, showing that Ford had actually received £17,859 and paid out for him £16,200, and had then juggled this balance of £1,659 in Penn's favor into the huge debt.

Rather than pay it, Penn went to Fleet Prison for nine months. In the end, he settled for £6,800 which he had to borrow from his father-in-law and other friends. The settlement restored Pennsylvania to him.

Finally in 1712, worn down with his problems, he agreed to sell Pennsylvania back to the crown for £12,000 with the clear understanding that the laws and privileges he had won for the colonists should be honored. The Penn family retained some lands, but William's desire to end his life in America was not fulfilled.

[136]

"I purpose to see you, if God give me life, this fall," he wrote to friends there in 1712, "but I grow old and infirm, yet would gladly see you once more before I die, and my young sons and daughters also settled upon good tracts of land, for them and their heirs after them, to clear and settle upon, as Jacob's sons did."

But in this same year he began to have a series of strokes which affected his memory. Still he attended Meeting, enjoyed his children and grandchildren, and took pleasure in the country-side and in the beautiful home at Ruscombe where he now lived.

He gradually grew weaker, so that he needed help in walking, and it became harder for him to talk. He died in 1718 in his seventy-fourth year and was buried beside his first wife and two of their children at Jordans Meeting House (Buckinghamshire).

Surely no other pacifist has lived as stormy a life as William Penn—railed at by mobs for his preaching, clapped into jail over and again, fighting with the pen he seems to have grasped all the more firmly after giving up his sword.

As for the sword, everyone knows how, when he asked George Fox's advice whether to continue wearing it, the Founder had replied, "Friend Penn, wear it as long as thou canst." He did not wear it long.

Jefferson thought Penn "the greatest lawgiver the world has produced; the first, either in ancient or modern times, who has laid the foundation of government in the pure and unadulterated principles of peace, of reason and right."

Charles Sumner said, "To William Penn belongs the distinction of first, in human history, establishing the law of love as a rule of conduct for the intercourse of nations."

Penn had felt in his own life that change that let him know men could "mend themselves." Well-born, well-to-do, with all sorts of favorable worldly prospects in front of him if he followed the usual course, he had chosen instead to join the despised Quakers and thus to stand in danger of losing all. When silence

[137]

would have served his own interests, he spoke out—for religious toleration, for fair trials, for the liberty of Englishmen.

With wealth assured, Penn risked it all at the hands of a government which fined him cruelly in an effort to batter down his resistance. Over and again he left a comfortable home to stay for months at a time in unheated jails, giving up liberty in the fight for liberty. He made long and uncomfortable journeys for nothing but to visit and encourage fellow Quakers throughout England. And he created through his own effort a vast and fruitful and hospitable refuge overseas where men could get away from the persecution of government and the badgering of a spiteful and ignorant public.

Yes, men can "mend themselves." The proud young man in armor had become all this—lawgiver, preacher, writer, champion of human freedom and conscience—by no external agency, but through what Quakers call the Inner Light. And it has remained a Quaker conviction that men can and must go on mending themselves—that this is the meaning of life, the meaning of Christianity, of all religion.

In 1660 when the Commonwealth ended and Charles II came to the throne, and when England was still binding up the wounds of civil war, a small group of people having neither power nor influence presented a statement to the new king. "A Declaration from the Harmless and Innocent People of God, called Quakers," they called it. And this is what it said:

"We utterly deny all outward wars and strife, and fightings with outward weapons, for any end, or under any pretence whatever; this is our testimony to the whole world. The Spirit of Christ by which we are guided, is not changeable, so as once to command us from a thing as evil, and again to move us unto it; and we certainly know and testify to the world, that the Spirit of Christ, which leads us unto all truth, will never move us to fight and war against any man with outward weapons, neither

for the Kingdom of Christ, nor for the kingdoms of this world.
. . . Therefore we cannot learn war any more."

That is the famous peace testimony of Friends, and though
some have departed from it, yet it still remains at the heart of
the Quaker view of life and has many times been reiterated and
explained.

> The relationship of nation to nation, of race to race, of class
> to class [said the Philadelphia Yearly Meeting in 1934] must be
> based on this divine law of love, if peace and progress are to be
> achieved. We believe in those principles, not as mere ideals for
> some future time, but as part of the eternal moral order and as a
> way of life to be lived here and now. War is a colossal violation of
> this way of life. If we are true to our faith we can have no part
> in it. . . .
> We reject as false that philosophy which sets the state above
> moral law and demands from the individual unquestioning obedi-
> ence to every state command. On the contrary, we assert that
> every individual, while owing loyalty to the state, owes a more
> binding loyalty to a higher authority—the authority of God and
> conscience.

The Philadelphia Yearly Meeting Faith and Practice, 1955,
explains:

> We base our peace testimony on a fundamental conviction
> that war is wrong in itself, wrong in the sight of God. We desire
> to apply pacifism constructively to concrete situations in the
> service of mankind as well as to remove economic and political
> causes of the outbreak of war; but we are clear that actions in
> this regard must be attempts to give concrete expression to love
> and must flow from a sense of religious responsibility and from a
> deep reverence for the will of God as revealed in Jesus Christ. . . .
> In proportion as individuals feel and obey the obligation to
> respect the Divine Light of truth in every person, and to recog-
> nize the brotherhood, the essential unity, of all mankind, it
> becomes possible to raise conflicts from the level of combat, re-
> sulting in victory and defeat, to the level of problems that can
> be solved.

Nowhere is the combination of high idealism and practical common sense better illustrated than in this remark. Combining the practical with the ideal has always been a hallmark of Quakers, who have insisted on translating their faith immediately and practically into this-world results, as in the case of their Declaration to King Charles. To how many a persecuted minority would it have occurred to tell a powerful ruler that the faith they professed was going to cost him soldiers?

"Problems that can be solved." Perhaps that is the key and the secret of the way Quakers work.

Instead of looking only at the negative side—refusal to serve in the armed forces—Friends turn the thing around to find what they can do.

"He who works to improve the civic, economic, social and moral condition of his country and the world is more truly patriotic than he who exalts his own nation at the expense of others or supports and justifies its action irrespective of right or justice," continues *Faith and Practice*.

"God is not alone the God of things as they are but the God of things as they are meant to be" (All Friends Conference, London, 1920).

In their three-hundred-year preoccupation with conflict and their effort to do something about it, Friends have made some discoveries likely to be overlooked by those intent merely on asserting their own privileges.

"It is the Quaker ideal to comprehend the ethical and spiritual significance of the whole situation and to deal with it above the storm of controversy and propaganda. Such an attitude brings into view the transcendent or eternal aspect which should be the aim of the religious body" (New England Yearly Meeting *Faith and Practice*, 1950).

Sometimes the whole vision steps on toes, as in the case of John Woolman's:

"O that we do declare against wars, and acknowledge our trust to be in God only, may walk in the light, and therein examine our foundation and motives in holding great estates! May we look upon our treasures, the furniture of our houses, and our garments, and try whether the seeds of war have nourishment in these our possessions" (*Journal*).

But Friends have never been afraid to step on toes—nonviolently, of course!

One thing that has kept Quakers on their own toes through these three hundred years is a form of organization so simple, yet so demanding and so effective, that it has rarely degenerated into pure wheel-turning for its own sake.

Meeting for Worship and Meeting for Business are interrelated. Friends gather weekly for worship, and in addition for a monthly Meeting for Business which also begins in silent worship. A clerk introduces items to be considered. Everyone has a chance to speak. Differences are recognized but not accented. If they appear to be growing hot, a period of silence is called for. If the mind of the group is obviously divided, the subject is tabled for another day. Ultimately a solution will be found which satisfies everyone and which is usually better than the one originally proposed. When the clerk senses that the group has reached agreement, he drafts and reads a minute. Friends then say, "I unite with that," "I agree," or "That meets my mind." If, after silence, no dissents are heard, the act is taken to represent the sense of the Meeting. No voting. No division. No stressing of differences. The method, as well as the goal, is peace.

It is an effective method which combines order with flexibility, making the most of each individual insight while gathering all together in a way which not only expresses the group mind but makes every member conscious of being fused into it.

Working in this way, Friends have set up their Service Committees to pursue practical ways of carrying the peace testimony to all parts of the world without regard to races, religions or political alignment.

In Germany after World War I Friends served a million meals

a day to children and students. They are now working with Algerian and African refugees. Wherever conflict threatens, they send missions or set up centers where opponents can meet each other and discuss differences in a spirit of reconciliation, or live together in fellowship. Work camps gather the young of many nations to tackle projects that will wipe out or alleviate the wounds of war or poverty. College students assemble in international seminars to discuss world problems and to experience the frictions and the necessary self-discipline involved in living together at close quarters. Conferences for diplomats bring young and rising officials together to explore ways of bridging the gaps which separate nations and make for conflict. Always the effort is to hear all sides without prejudice and passion, to understand rather than to judge, and to seek that higher consensus which rises above race, nation or political persuasion.

Nobel Peace prizes have been awarded to Emily Balch and Philip Noel-Baker, both Quakers, and in 1947 to the two service groups, English and American.

Friends are not easily discouraged. They are not blind to human imperfections, but neither are they defeated by them. For their own history proves that progress has been made. Quakers are no longer hanged, imprisoned, dispossessed for what they believe.

"The rise of the people called Quakers," wrote the historian George Bancroft, "is one of the memorable events in the history of man. It marks the moment when intellectual freedom was claimed unconditionally by the people as an inalienable right."

Penn had as much to do with that victory as any individual. But the victory and the benefit have come to us all.

It is not accidental that pacifism is an inseparable part of this victory. Fox and Penn and Friends ever since their time have seen that peace and freedom are really inseparable, for freedom disappears in wartime. The victory over arbitrary imprisonment and persecution for belief or conscience was a great one. But if it is to be fully enjoyed, there has to be peace. Peace will come when men are willing, even as Woolman, to face the fault in themselves which breeds war and give up privileges that breed conflict.

If we doubt that men will do so much, we should think of Penn.

If we seek a guide for ourselves, we can hardly do better than these cheerful words of George Fox:

"Be patterns, be examples in all countries, places, islands, nations, wherever you come; that your carriage and life may preach among all sorts of people, and to them; then you will come to walk cheerfully over the world, answering that of God in every man."

8. Thoreau
(1817-1862)

Civil Disobedience

 He liked to call himself an inspector of snow-storms and a companion to woodchucks, yet his thoughts, though published obscurely for the most part in his lifetime, came to influence decisively the thinking of Gandhi and Tolstoy.

Around Concord, his home town, he was regarded either with tolerant amusement or Puritan indignation as a young man who succeeded at nothing, who couldn't earn his keep, or in any case not in a manner befitting any self-respecting and provident New Englander. That experiment by Walden Pond, made up of beans and moonshine, his neighbors mostly regarded with contempt. What did it prove, that a man should build a cabin about the size of an outhouse for $28.12½ and then live on beans, rice and molasses?

If Henry Thoreau had been a moron or an idealist, they could have assimilated him, for a New England town like Concord had learned how to deal with both. But Henry, with a Harvard education and a family business he might have made prosper if he put his mind to it, was another matter.

The worst of it was, he knew how to succeed in business without really trying. His father's little lead pencil and graphite firm, for example. When stereotyping sparked a sudden demand for graphite, it was Henry who took enough time off from doing nothing—his regular occupation—to devise a new method of preparing the stuff which greatly lowered costs and raised profits.

Did he then stick to it—enlarge his premises, increase his output, and provide a steady family income so that his mother could stop scrimping and taking in boarders?

He did not. He wandered back to his woods and fields again and let the business go hang. Concord could understand failure— even the failure of a dreamer like Bronson Alcott of the many daughters. It could never understand a man who succeeded at failure by really trying, by making failure his goal.

Oh, he had written a few things. Who in Concord hadn't? He lectured now and then at the Lyceums, but not consistently and with a steady income as his friend Emerson did.

And there was another thing. What ailed a young man, that he was content to be just a handyman—even to a philosopher? Living with the Emersons—strange enough in itself when his own family had a home right in town, or on the edge of it— didn't justify a Harvard graduate in looking no higher.

Of course he didn't stick to it—no longer than two years. He didn't stick to anything, though he did move back to live with Lidian and her children when Mr. Emerson went off to Europe. Strange that such an arrangement hadn't raised eyebrows in Concord. But Henry had made such a failure of everything, it seemed the town didn't even have to worry about his succeeding with other men's wives. On this score, everyone had to admit that whatever you said of Henry, you had to acknowledge his purity. Aside from a few young letters exchanged with Ellen Sewall and Lucy Brown, he hardly noticed the other sex. In the end, such a virtue would tend to be regarded as just another failure.

No, he didn't stick to anything—not even to living near Walden Pond in a ten-by-fifteen hut that wasn't big enough to swing a cat in. Not that he'd have swung one. He loved cats, they were

[145]

so cussed independent and self-centered. Like him. For a fellow who'd never amounted to anything, he seemed downright conceited.

Graphite manufacturer, handyman, schoolteacher, tutor to Emerson's brother's family on Staten Island, Lyceum lecturer, bean farmer and weeder of other people's gardens, carpenter—and what a pair he and Bronson Alcott made, building Emerson a summer house, with Bronson always getting new ideas and tearing down as fast as Henry could put up—and surveyor. There was a job you might have expected him to keep. Good clean outdoor work, taking him through field and forest, out among the trees and the creatures he loved as if they were his own kin. When the town had to do some planning about dams and bridges, Henry turned in as pretty a job of surveying as anyone could ask for and signed himself Civil Engineer down in the corner. Looked like a good beginning. But as usual, a good beginning in Henry's case turned out to be the grand finale.

Take his writing. Oh, he published a poem or two here and there, and Horace Greeley down in New York thought well enough of his stuff to peddle it some to editors—what little he could get from Henry's pen. Horace even managed to get a few fees for him by badgering the editors till it was easier to pay than duck. But what did it come to, either in money or in print?

His first book, for instance, the one about his boat trip on the Concord and Merrimack Rivers. Couldn't get a publisher to risk bringing it out, not even with Mr. Emerson's backing. So he paid for the printing himself. Never sold more than a couple hundred. Ended with the printer turning it all back on his hands. The books, it seems, had been wrapped in packages marked H. D. THOREAU'S CONCORD RIVER. All the printer had to do was cross out RIVER and hand the packages to the expressman.

Said Henry, after getting them: "I have now a library of nearly nine hundred volumes, over seven hundred of which I wrote myself."

The only other book he ever brought out in his lifetime was

the one about living down by the pond, and no one ever heard he made much on that either.

Too bad. Because the funny thing is, Henry Thoreau was one of the nicest men God ever created. Ugly as a mud fence, of course. But full of fun. When he'd get to talking and his eyes sparkling, you'd forget that big nose that made him look as if he would pitch over on his face. They say he left a pile of writing in his journals. But what good's that after a man's dead? Just clutter up the attic till the house burns down some day, and there's an end of it.

Yes, Henry was a real nice man. Dead at forty-four. Probably if Concord had to spare a man, it could get along without Henry Thoreau about as easy as anybody, and not miss him. He just never made himself essential. He didn't have a niche of his own where you could find him when you needed him, like the cobbler or the blacksmith or Sam Staples the jailer.

What was it made Henry go to jail, now—make it so Sam had no choice but to lock him up? Some crazy notion about not paying taxes to support a government he didn't believe in. First time it was on account of the church tax, and you can understand a man's reason for that. Selectmen let him off when he wrote out something like this:

"Know all men by these presents, that I, Henry Thoreau, do not wish to be regarded as a member of any incorporated society which I have not joined."

Doesn't that sound like him, though? But the second time, that was as much as to say any man can stop paying his taxes any time he doesn't happen to agree with what the government's doing. That way we'd have anarchy. Never met a New Englander yet who wasn't agin' the government some of the time—or most of it. But Henry was mostly anarchist, though he died as peaceful and easy as a man could. Funny thing, but Concord does miss him. You can usually find another cobbler or jailer. But where are you going to get another Henry Thoreau?

Something like this, if the manner may be forgiven, is the way Concord folk looked at Henry David Thoreau, who had been christened David Henry by Dr. Ripley but with typical cantankerousness had turned it upside down.

The mystery is that he wouldn't stay dead. His inconsequential writings, still-born or first uttered in periodicals that were soon buried, kept breaking through the soil with the willful sturdiness of those beans he had planted at Walden Pond. His sister Sophia arranged for new editions and new works culled from his manuscripts. His friends Ellery Channing and Franklin Sanborn, with their praiseful accounts, kept his work alive. Yet his reputation faltered and flickered. Then instead of dying, it began to increase. Finally in 1962, on the hundredth anniversary of his death, his bust was placed in the Hall of Fame.

What is the vital juice in this failure of a man that not only keeps him alive but has spread his name and his influence over the whole world?

All those who love nature and solitude and wild things naturally love Thoreau. They respond to his bold assertion that "all good things are wild and free." Through him, they make their escape to the pond, the ten-by-fifteen hut, the long mornings of basking in the sun, the afternoons of sauntering southwestward in search of the elusive conelike red flower on the topmost branches of the white pine, or stalking a fox and giving him a good run for his money.

Yet Thoreau's world reputation, by a strange paradox, rests more upon his demand for social reform—a concern which is minor when measured by the bulk of his voluminous journals or even by its proportionate space in his best-known works.

Thoreau was more anarchist than reformer, more individualist than social man, yet the reformers claim him too.

How could he be both the lover of wild things who had signed off from all incorporated societies and yet the inspiration of such reformers as Tolstoy and Gandhi?

The heart of Thoreau's faith is in man as individual. Men

[148]

make institutions; institutions do not make men—not at least to begin with. But institutions can get a grip on a man which will warp him from his natural bent, and that is why Henry was willing not only to sign off but to go to jail rather than support them.

He would have had no use for the assumption Freud and Marx have implanted in us that a man is not responsible for what he is. Freud excuses us on the ground that we are victims of psychic crosswinds we cannot control; Marx lays the blame on a society which exploits all its working members. By a curious irony, the Marxist dialectic as applied by an autocratic government ended by making all men servants of the state.

To Thoreau it would have appeared like madness to argue that you had to build a powerful state so that, *magnum mysterium,* it could then wither away and leave everybody happy. Why not be happy now, he would ask? This was the answer he had given in the case of the man who had devoted his life to growing rich so that he might ultimately have the leisure to write poetry. "He should," remarked Thoreau, "have gone up to the garret at once."

Thoreau found men wrong-headed in most of their assumptions about values. Why work six days and rest one? Why not the other way about? Why make life miserable by drudging to get things that would only make you more miserable by making you more burdened?

Thoreau's answer to Marx was simple: the economic system is not the cause of man's misery; it is merely the sign of what is wrong with him. Let a man learn to live for something better.

More, Thoreau was willing to take the responsibility for himself. He didn't want government, or the church, or abolition and temperance societies, or anyone else to take it. The position is one we can hardly understand today, with our social security and federal commissions and foreign aid and our genius for organizing voluntary associations.

Thoreau was a reformer, and a radical one. But he believed

with all his heart that if men were going to be saved, they had to do it for themselves, from within. Perhaps societies cannot be built on his model. His answer would be: When has it ever been tried?

The last words he whispered were "Moose" and "Indians." Perhaps they came closest to his dream of living in nature, sustained by her bounty.

The idea that man must reform himself from within is essentially religious. "Be ye therefore perfect, even as your father in heaven is perfect." "Love thy neighbor as thyself." All the great edicts of conduct are based on the faith that men have within them the power to change, to grow, to be good. The great religious leaders have proved this in their own persons. But they have never proved it for the mass of mankind.

Thoreau proved it to his own satisfaction—at Walden, on the Concord, in the Maine woods. A practical, down-to-earth man in his ability to do any sort of chore and to be at home outdoors, he was enough a Transcendentalist to feel in the depths of his being that through nature man came in touch with a truth beyond particular phenomena—a truth that was somehow directly communicated.

Thus believing, Thoreau was mostly content to work upon himself. Yet when he saw his country making up a war with Mexico—in order, he felt, to extend slavery—when he saw Texas brazenly annexed and Polk elected on a frankly imperialist platform, and this only seventy years after the colonists had declared the right of a people to govern themselves, then he had to explode. He exploded first in his journal, that bank in which he thriftily deposited all his thoughts with as keen an eye to building up capital and accumulating interest as any Concord merchant.

Ultimately he gathered his indignations together and in 1848 made a lecture of them. "Civil Disobedience," he called it. It appeared in the first number of *Aesthetic Papers*, hopefully edited by Elizabeth Peabody. Further numbers were promised if the public responded. Fifty subscribers could hardly be called popular demand: *Aesthetic Papers* died with the first issue. So, it would seem, did "Civil Disobedience."

On the contrary, it went on germinating underground like those beans, until years later it bore fruit in Russia, South Africa, India, and our own South.

And what, essentially, did it say?

That when the state does wrong, it is the duty of the individual to resist it—to withhold his tax, go to jail if necessary, make a protest, and refuse by all means to cooperate in an unjust action.

"There will never be a really free and enlightened State until the State comes to recognize the individual as a higher and independent power, from which all its own power and authority are derived, and treats him accordingly."

Most men, Thoreau argued, serve the state like machines— some chiefly with their bodies, some with their minds.

A very few, as heroes, patriots, martyrs, reformers in the great sense, and men, serve the state with their consciences also, and so necessarily resist it for the most part; and they are commonly treated as enemies by it.

If ten honest men only,—ay, if one HONEST *man, in this State of Massachusetts, ceasing to hold slaves, were actually to withdraw from this copartnership, and be locked up in the county jail [for not paying taxes], it would be the abolition of slavery in America.*

If men would respond to the voice of conscience, standing up for what they knew to be right, reform would be instantaneous.

A minority is powerless while it conforms to the majority; it is not even a minority then; but it is irresistible when it clogs by its whole weight. If the alternative is to keep all just men in prison, or give up war and slavery, the State will not hesitate which to choose.

Yet no one really proved this proposition until Gandhi began filling the jails of South Africa and then of India.

The trouble with government as Thoreau viewed it is that it easily becomes the tool of a few people seeking their own advantage. "The standing army is only an arm of the standing government. . . . Witness the present Mexican war, the work of comparatively a few individuals using their standing government as their tool; for, in the outset, the people would not have consented to this measure."

Thoreau's program was simple. Let each man consult his own conscience and live by it. "The only obligation which I have a right to assume is to do at any time what I think right."

An admirer of the Hindu sacred books, Thoreau heartily agreed with the Bhagavad-Gita: "The man consists of his faith; he is verily what his faith is. . . . He who does the duty born of his own nature incurs no sin."

Civil disobedience thus turns out to be a higher form of obedience to the truth that lies within the self, out of which all social virtue must in the end be built.

The issue in Thoreau's day was slavery—a palpable evil, supported by the Fugitive Slave Law which he despised. When Massachusetts judges sent an escaped Negro back into slavery in 1851, Henry exploded again in his journal. But it was another three years before he got up enough steam to do a lecture about it. The immediate occasion was the capture of another fugitive, Anthony Burns, sent back to slavery in a cutter provided by government.

Speaking at Framingham on the Fourth of July, 1854, Thoreau first paid his compliments to the judges who had sent the man back.

Such judges as these are merely the inspectors of a pick-lock and murderer's tools, to tell him whether they are in working order or not, and there they think their responsibility ends. . . . The law will never make men free; it is men who have got to make the law free. They are the lovers of law and order who ob-

*serve the law when the government breaks it. . . . Whoever can
discern truth has received his commission from a higher source
than the chiefest justice in the world who can discern only law.*

The judges and lawyers, he said, "consider, not whether the
Fugitive Slave Law is right, but whether it is what they call constitutional. Is virtue constitutional, or vice? Is equity constitutional, or iniquity? In important moral and vital questions, like
this, it is just as impertinent to ask whether a law is constitutional
or not, as to ask whether it is profitable or not."

It is not enough to be law-abiding. A man has a right to demand of the law that it be just, and to break it if it is not.

"As I love my life, I would side with the light, and let the dark
earth roll from under me."

If we object that by this method we would fall into anarchy,
Thoreau would say: Why not? "Whatever the human law may
be, neither an individual nor a nation can ever commit the least
act of injustice against the obscurest individual without having
to pay the penalty for it."

Another five years passed before he found an occasion big
enough to call him back to the same theme.

John Brown had made the raid on Harper's Ferry, had fought
his battle at the arsenal, and having been arrested on October
16, 1859, was awaiting death.

Two years before, he had been a guest in Thoreau's home,
and only a few months back he had spoken in Concord Town
Hall before leaving for Virginia.

On October 19 Thoreau spilled out his feelings in his journal
to the extent of about two thousand words. Two days later, the
same. The next day, six thousand angry, emotion-charged words.

Finally on October 30 he was ready. He sent a boy about town
to give notice that he would speak in the vestry of the church.
His friend Sanborn, who had introduced him to Brown, sent
back word that he had better wait until public feelings had
cooled.

"Tell Mr. Sanborn," said Henry, "that he has misunderstood

the announcement, that there is to be a meeting in the vestry, and that Mr. Thoreau will speak."

He spoke.

It was an ideal subject for him. In John Brown he saw the sort of man who by a single act could change history, forcing government itself to change.

"He had the courage to face his country herself when she was in the wrong." This was his theme and really his whole defense of that man who had been the cause of so much bloodshed.

"Though you may not approve of his method or his principles, recognize his magnanimity," Thoreau pleaded. "No man in America has ever stood up so persistently and effectively for the dignity of human nature, knowing himself for a man, and the equal of any and all governments."

He went further:

"I hear many condemn these men because they were so few. When were the good and the brave ever in the majority? It was his peculiar doctrine that a man has a perfect right to interfere by force with the slaveholder, in order to rescue the slave. I agree with him. I think that for once the Sharps rifles were employed in a righteous cause."

With this plea for John Brown, Thoreau takes the extreme step in civil disobedience—violent resistance to government itself. Where the state has failed to recognize basic human rights, he argues, passive resistance is no longer adequate.

His position was not popular, but it was arresting. Worcester, then Boston invited him to repeat his talk. But no Boston printer would bring it out.

From the civil disobedience of 1849—refusal to pay taxes as a protest against slavery and imperialism—Thoreau had moved by 1854 to the position that when the law itself failed to live up to principles of justice, an individual should break it. By 1859 he had come to believe that violent opposition to a government which enforced laws clearly opposed to basic human rights was not only excusable but the moral duty of concerned citizens.

This seems a long way from peace. It was, in fact, a cry of defiance from an individualist who was more anarchist than reformer and who believed that every good act must come out of an inner conviction and commitment. Thoreau's strategy of civil disobedience, though swept under by the tragedy of civil war, stayed alive in the seed in a way that would have delighted this lover of nature.

With Gandhi, it sprang to full growth. With the new struggle for civil rights it has returned by way of Martin Luther King and others to its own country.

Thoreau's contribution to a peaceable world is a moral one: individual man must resist evil, whether it appear as discrimination or in the law itself. If every man would do this, war would be unnecessary, for evil would be attacked at the root, before it could grow into war.

He thought the Mexican War an indefensible aggression, and said so. In the same year (1845) that he built his hut at Walden, the United States had annexed Texas, already had its eye on New Mexico and California, and was disputing the Oregon territory with Great Britain. By 1848 when the Mexican War ended (at a cost of nearly one hundred million dollars and the loss of 13,000 lives on our side, most of them from disease), it was clear that a vast new territory stretching from Oregon to Texas was ours—but by what right? This was Thoreau's question. He refused to support it. Yet a few years later he defended John Brown's use of force against slavery. Force, he argued, can be used justly only to make men free.

"It is men who have got to make the law free." Thoreau's words apply very strongly to our case today. We have the law, but the weight of social custom and attitudes makes the law a helpless prisoner of prejudice. Not until the law operates in the hearts of all our citizens can we get on with our work of aiding freedom abroad, where our moral support is needed but is now in a deep freeze because of our failures at home.

In "Civil Disobedience" Thoreau shows us what we can do as

individuals to bring justice and equity and peace into the world. He shows us that resistance—civil disobedience—is an instrument of peace available at any moment to any man who is sick of injustice or evil, and that true peace comes by individual acts of resistance. When enough men feel this way, the dam will break and the waters will spread out to cover and nourish the dry earth.

9. Tolstoy
(1828-1910)

Christian Pacifism

 The Tolstoy everyone knows and admires is
the novelist, the creator of unforgettable scenes and people—of
Anna Karenina and the relentless and crushing effects of her
passion, of Kitty whose innocence and trust are bruised by
Levin's diaries, of the battlefield of Borodino or the burning of
Moscow, or of old General Kutuzov, whose brilliance consisted
in being able to sit quietly and wait while a vast battle unfolded
itself along the lines of its own destiny, since he had the wisdom
to know that no man could truly direct such an undertaking.

Tolstoy himself came to reject and disown his greatest works.
They seemed to him frivolous, even harmful. His own spiritual
pilgrimage led him beyond his novels and into a world where
they would no longer be necessary.

None of the people Lev Tolstoy invented is as interesting as
himself. A master of fiction, he was still greater as a man.
Wherever you touch Tolstoy—through his own diaries or his
many books on the meaning of life, in the memoirs of those who
knew him, in his correspondence, or in the many public events
which grew out of his teachings and actions—you know you are
in the presence of a vital personality.

How can we capture his essence: the full, manly, vigorous involvement in life, the deep gift of transmitting life itself to his pages, the sincere, intense grappling with things as they are, the religion both warm and practical?

Religion came to be the central concern in his life, a religion both unorthodox and universal in its applicability. Of course the Church could not afford to have within its ranks a man who took religion so seriously, so it excommunicated him—the greatest religious teacher and the clearest expounder of the teachings of Jesus ever to come out of Russia. Sadly endearing to us is his failure to work out this religious vision in his own life. In the place of that universal spirit of love which he sought, he lived in a very hell of dispute and discord with his wife.

He was a lonely, contradictory, impulsive, reasonable, understandable yet inexplicable human being—in short, a perfect Tolstoyan character.

The thing to which Tolstoy devoted the larger part of his life was a search for life's true meaning and the conduct which that meaning laid upon the believer. Peace was inseparably intertwined with Tolstoy's discovery of life's meaning. But the path by which he came to eventual understanding was a long one. When he had traversed it he found, looking back, that it was too steep for many to follow—found, too, that those who had tried to follow by founding Tolstoyan communities all ended by falling over steep precipices. And when he looked ahead, he saw that the summit was not to be his after all. Yet he saw it up there, shining in the sun like the sharp, crimsoned peak of Jungfrau.

The excitement of entering into Tolstoy's life is the feeling he gives of living always on the frontier of a discovery which will renew and light up all of life, making poetry, love, faith and living synonymous—of a promise always about to be fulfilled.

Even as a boy, Lev was a seeker after truth. He was obsessed by dreams of goodness, wanting to sell his carriage and give the proceeds to the poor, happy to be loving someone or something even when he was not loved. In this, perhaps, he was behaving like many who believe themselves to be ugly and so do not expect much return of love.

He did indeed present an almost simian ugliness. Two huge ears held his long, brutish face in the grip of a great parenthesis. His hairline plunged far down his forehead toward small, deep-set gray eyes. As if to make up for the brief forehead and beady eyes, a large nose spread across his face above a pair of thick lips. These features, of course, became more pronounced as he grew older.

Even before he could know how he looked to others, life was piling on the blows that would heighten sensitivity. Before he was two, his mother died. When he was nine, his handsome, high-spirited father followed. Three years later the aunt who had taken charge of him also died, so that he had to be sent off to another. Even a child less thoughtful than Lev might have been hammered down by such a beginning.

When he was only five his older brother had invented a game called "Muravian Brethren." He had apparently heard vaguely of the Moravians. The game consisted of crowding in under chairs and blankets, pressed close together in the dark. Brother Serezha also announced that he had a secret which, once he revealed it, would make everyone happy. Then all would become Muravian Brethren together and would love one another. As for the secret, he had written it on a green stick and buried it in the forest.

"The ideal of the Muravian Brethren," Tolstoy wrote years later, "bound to each other by love . . . including all human beings under the wide vault of heaven, has always remained with me."

When he went to live with his Aunt Paulina in Kazan at the age of thirteen, a different sort of world opened up. Kazan was a gay, sociable place and his aunt a gay, sociable woman.

"With all my heart I wanted to be good," he wrote of this time in his *Confession*, "but I was young, I was filled with passions, and I was alone, utterly alone, in my search for good. Each time I tried to express my most intimate yearning—to be morally good—I met with contempt and derision; and whenever I gave in to disgusting passions, I was praised and encouraged."

So at fourteen he made his first trip to a house of prostitution with his brothers, then wept bitterly beside the bed when it was over.

But at fifteen he made friends with a boy who like himself was seeking the meaning of life. It seemed now to young Lev that man's destiny was to strive for moral perfection. Yet it was to be many years before Tolstoy, after what he regarded as loose and depraved conduct, was to find his way back to the path of perfection. Women, drinking, gambling all took their toll of him. Although he entered the University of Kazan, he found no course of study that appealed deeply enough to draw him away from his life of pleasure. Finally he gave it up and at the age of twenty-three joined his brother in the army. He was sent first to the Caucasus, then to Bulgaria, and then at his own request to Sebastopol where the Russians were undergoing a siege in connection with the Crimean War. Bravery and good cheer under trying conditions made him popular.

Along with his military career, Tolstoy had also taken up writing. His very first effort, *Childhood*, a clearly autobiographical narrative, was eagerly accepted by one of the best periodicals. *Boyhood* and *Youth* soon followed. But when his tales from Sebastopol began to appear he became so much of a celebrity that Czar Nicholas had him removed from danger. When he reached St. Petersburg, he found himself a sensation. Turgenev and other famous literary men welcomed him as one of themselves, and everywhere parties were given in his honor. What every author dreams of, Tolstoy had achieved, apparently with little effort and at the age of twenty-six.

He "swept around St. Petersburg like a hurricane," said his daughter, Alexandra, "reveling in his position of a recognized author, delighting in intelligent conversation, alternately shy, embarrassed, hurt, and throwing the proper denizens of St. Petersburg into a state of alarm by the sharpness, the daring of his unexpected views, contravening as they did the truths generally accepted."

It all failed to satisfy him. The army had brought him face to face with death, and therefore had made him ask the meaning of life. His religious mysticism, his thirst for goodness, had revived.

Between 1857 and 1861 he made three trips out of Russia to the countries of western Europe. Thereafter he never left Russia. The strongest recollection of these journeys was the guillotining he attended in Paris. As he saw the head part from the body and the two parts fall with a thud, he felt a sickening realization that nothing could justify such an act. He began to question the basis of all governmental powers.

"There is within us only one infallible guide: the universal Spirit which whispers to us to draw closer to one another." This was what the guillotine had taught him.

Back home at the family estate, Yasnaya Polyana, he threw himself into working with and for his serfs, whom he had already freed in advance of emancipation. He opened a free school, did some of the teaching himself, and proved to his own satisfaction that peasant children could learn quickly if only the teacher would present knowledge in such a form that the student would eagerly snatch at it. Compulsion, he was sure, killed the desire to learn. In ways that strikingly resemble the progressive movement in this country, Tolstoy engaged the interest and awakened the curiosity of his pupils. The schools could not have been an unmitigated success, however, for after two years he closed them and went off to the steppes for a period of loafing and drinking kumiss.

When the serfs were emancipated in 1861, Tolstoy took on a new job. The new law required explaining and adjudicating wherever reluctant or bewildered landlords came into conflict

[161]

with the peasants. As mediator, Tolstoy worked hard to settle these cases in his district. He held the job for a year, then gladly gave it up. His decisions were generally regarded as just, but his office was a shambles, for Tolstoy had no gift for tidy administration.

In 1862 he not only resigned as mediator but also married Sophia Behrs, the daughter of a physician whose practice was among Moscow's social elite. Tolstoy upset the parents by falling in love with the second daughter instead of the eldest, but he persisted, got his way, and just before the marriage showed her the diary of his many lustful loves, just as Levin was to do in *Anna Karenina*. It was a great shock to her.

"I think I shall never be reconciled to it," she wrote in her diary.

Tolstoy found himself head over heels in love. "I lived to be thirty-four without ever knowing that one could love so much or be so happy," he wrote.

Since she was a city girl, while he belonged to the country and could not long be happy away from it, difficulties were bound to erupt. Yet, despite quarrels, the early years were happy ones. As the babies began to come along with startling regularity, however—thirteen in all—Sophia became mired in maternity and resentful of all the burdens she had to bear. She tried to interest herself in country affairs, but they bored her. She doggedly copied Tolstoy's manuscripts, although he was a particularly difficult writer to work for. He scratched out, wrote in, filled the margins, and then wrote on top of other words until much of the sheet was nearly indecipherable. The measure of Sophia's devotion might be taken by her work on one manuscript alone, *War and Peace*, a book of some fifteen hundred pages. She copied the whole thing seven times!

This book and *Anna Karenina* were the chief products of the years from his marriage until 1877.

Meanwhile the children kept coming. Tolstoy was a delightful father when not engrossed in something else. Several of the little ones died in their early years, however, leading Tolstoy back to his speculations about the meaning of life. As the surviving children grew older, their mother felt that they must live in Moscow in order to get a proper education and social life, and this became a source of continuous friction since Tolstoy could not long stand city life. So for long periods they were in Moscow and he in the country.

About the time he finished *Anna Karenina* he suddenly, in the midst of all his good fortune, felt that life had come to a standstill.

"I, a fortunate and healthy man, felt that I could not go on living," he said. He thought of suicide when he saw a piece of cord. He gave up hunting for fear that he might shoot himself.

Then suddenly it came to him that he had felt fully alive only when he believed in God.

"Everything around me grew full of life; everything received a meaning. . . . To know God and to live—it is the same thing!"

When the government called for volunteers to help with the census in 1880, Tolstoy asked to be sent into the slums. What he saw made him so miserable that he wanted to give up all his property. Men and women, he found, were crowded together into flophouses so foul that it sickened him to go into them. In an agony of sympathy he bought hot drinks for them and handed out money, the chief effect of which was to start a near riot. The situation was too much for him; he felt helpless.

Already he had tried to simplify his own life in the country, dressing like the peasants and working with them in the fields. Now he told his wife that he could no longer hold property. He turned everything over to her and the children. Still the quest went on.

His wife could not understand his religious ideas, his preoccupation with religion, his stubborn determination to mow, plough, reap and cobble like a common peasant, his distaste for property, his refusal to write more novels, his dislike of Moscow and refusal to live there with the family.

"It can only sadden me," she wrote, "that such intellectual energies should spend themselves in chopping wood, heating the samovar, and cobbling boots."

Here was a man who had won—apparently with no great difficulty—all the things she valued: fame, literary reputation, friends in high places, money. That he persisted in throwing all these away, that he was willing to throw upon her the burden of copying manuscripts, bearing children, managing a large household, tending to the property, and looking out for all the needs of servants, children, and visitors—that he could do this indicated to her that he had neither love nor regard for her.

Said Sophia: "That old feeling of grief because of the little love Lyovochka bears me in exchange for my great love for him—all this rose in me with terrible desperation."

Matters grew worse as the years wore on, exacerbated no doubt by Tolstoy's giving up sexual intercourse on the theory that it was somehow impure. Wits pointed out that he gave it up only after the fire of youth had left him and he wouldn't miss it very much. Still, the renunciation must have seemed to Sophia like something intended as a personal affront to her.

Her jealousy of Tolstoy's amanuensis, Vladimir Chertkov, was another item. Chertkov, a somewhat pompous man, became the agent for the publication of Tolstoy's works abroad. Relations between the two men were so intimate as to disgust Sophia—she could not stand it when they kissed. Chertkov, moreover, seemed to be imprisoning Tolstoy within the cage of his own thoughts. Tolstoy, like any man who is full of original ideas, was constantly changing them. Chertkov, quoting himself to him, tried to make him an orthodox Tolstoyan. This Tolstoy never could be!

Besides, he brought people to the house whom Sophia heartily disliked—"the dark people," as the family came to call all the Tolstoyan cultists who came trooping to meet the famous writer.

When Sophia became convinced that Chertkov was getting hold of manuscripts she should have had for the edition of Tolstoy's works she was bringing out, she became uncontrollable.

Stormy scenes rent the family. She took to snooping amongst Tolstoy's papers. Even in the night he would awake and find a light in his study and Sophia rummaging among his things. The situation became unendurable to both. When Sophia began reading his diaries, she found many accounts of their quarreling. When she forced him to expunge them, he took to keeping a secret diary and she discovered that. She wrote her own diary after first reading his to see what he said about her. If it had not been tragic, it would have been very funny.

So life, to this man who had discovered the secret of peace and harmony, became a living hell from which he longed to flee. He made plans but could not execute them for fear of what it would do to Sophia. She had become really deranged, given to fits of fury, screaming, weeping, rushing off to commit suicide and being pursued and brought back. What could a man do?

Every step Tolstoy took toward a fuller realization of the good life as he saw it, every book he wrote to explain his discoveries, seemed to trigger a further step into the depths for Sophia.

In *My Confession*, 1882, which his biographer Ernest Simmons calls one of the noblest utterances of man, Tolstoy took the unpopular position that religion offers the only explanation of life's meaning but that faith in the dogmas of the church is erroneous. In this way he managed to alienate both the freethinkers and the churchgoers.

When he came to consider what meaning there was in life that was not destroyed by death, he had to admit that in addition to the reasoning knowledge on which he had hitherto relied there was also in every living man "another kind of knowledge, an unreasoning one—faith, which gives a possibility of living."

"Reasoning knowledge brought me to the conclusion that life was meaningless. . . . Faith gave a meaning to life and a possibility of living."

Dramatically, as only he could do it, Tolstoy describes his

dark night of the soul and the stages by which he came through hopelessness to that sudden awakening:

"A voice seemed to cry within me, 'This is He, He without whom there is no life. To know God and to live are one. God is life!

"Live to seek God, and life will not be without God.' "

The effect of this discovery, Tolstoy tells us, was as if he had suddenly found himself sitting in a boat which had pushed off from an unknown shore. He had oars, but all around him he saw boats floating downstream. Those in the boats assured him that this was the way to go. He let himself go with them until he saw that rapids lay ahead and that boats were breaking up in them. Then he began to row hard upstream, toward the shore that had been pointed out to him before he was set adrift.

"That shore was God, that course was tradition, those oars were the free will given me to make for the shore to seek union with the Deity."

Then he looked about to see what was being done in the name of religion.

"At this time Russia was engaged in war, and, in the name of Christian love, Russians were engaged in slaying their brethren. . . . I looked round on all that was done by men who professed to be Christians, and I was horrified."

In "What I Believe," published the following year, he argued that while life is a misfortune to the one who seeks only the personal welfare that death will destroy, it is a blessing to the one who seeks to establish the Kingdom of God here and now. The essence of Christianity is to love God and neighbor as thyself, a law preached also by the sages of other faiths.

In submitting our animal natures to the law of reason we truly live. Reason, which we receive from God, is the only means by which truth can be known. The activity of reason is love, which impels man to sacrifice himself for others.

In "What Then Must We Do?" Tolstoy describes the shock of working in the slums and his effort to understand why people

[166]

live in such degradation. His conclusion is that the rich are to blame, that the only solution is for everyone to labor usefully, and that this would then not only take the rich off the backs of the poor but would actually benefit the rich by improving their health and taking up time which otherwise is spent upon idle and harmful and expensive pleasures. To consume the labor of others is destructive; to eat and not work is dangerous as well as immoral.

Do your own dirty work, Tolstoy concludes, and serve the needs of others. Only by changing our attitudes toward property and work can we end conflict and war.

"The Kingdom of God," published in 1893 but begun in 1890, carried his thoughts a step further. All governments are immoral because they exist for the rich and powerful. The only escape from oppressive government is to live according to the precepts of Jesus. Christian teaching is based upon the individual human soul, and the salvation of that soul lies in service to others, not in the advantage to self upon which communism and socialism are based.

What occupies Tolstoy throughout most of the pages of this book is the insanity of war. The book was inspired by letters he received from American Quakers who had read "My Religion." The news of their pacifism and their efforts to follow the original teachings of Jesus aroused his enthusiastic interest, as did news of the nonresistance movement in America sparked by William Lloyd Garrison and Adin Ballou.

There are, Tolstoy argues, three life conceptions in man's history—the personal or animal, the social or pagan, and the universal or divine. "According to the third life conception, man's life is contained neither in his personality, nor in the aggregate and sequence of personalities, but in the beginning and source of life, in God.

"We are all brothers, and yet I live by receiving a salary for arraigning, judging and punishing a thief or a prostitute, whose existence is conditioned by the whole composition of my life."

Government favors the powerful and punishes the weak. Military might enslaves us all to the system which produces it, whether it be communist or capitalist. Militarism claims to preserve the system at the very moment when its own tyranny is bringing about a change in the system we give our allegiance to. So we are forced to oppress ourselves.

"The power of the state, far from saving us from the attacks of our neighbors, on the contrary causes the danger of the attacks." Each nation, while professing its devotion to freedom, arms against its neighbors, thus making war inevitable.

"The bad always rule over the good and always do violence to them," says Tolstoy. "The violence of the state, by allowing the bad to rule over the good, is the very evil which it is desirable to destroy." That is, the power which men seek corrupts them, and once they have seized it they will keep it by any means. So violence and government are interlocked.

The first step, says Tolstoy, is to recognize that the kingdom of God is within. To realize it, we must give up the lies and hypocrisy on which society is based. No matter what we do, we cannot escape death and the impermanency of all our acts, except through being part of the kingdom of God.

The essential message of the book is nonresistance, an idea which became the core of his thinking about government and society.

But life, as Tolstoy showed in the work piece called simply "On Life," is based upon struggle.

"However much religious and scientific superstitions may assure men of some future golden age, in which everybody will have enough of everything, the rational man sees and knows that the law of this temporal existence in space is the struggle of all against each, and of each against each and against all."

Even love of the "animal" variety (one has to remember Tolstoy's threefold analysis of life) is but an aspect of this struggle, since it seeks pleasure at the expense of others.

[168]

True love, then, becomes possible, only on the renunciation of happiness for the animal personality. . . . Love is the preference of other beings to one's self, to one's animal personality. . . . And there is no other love than this, that a man should lay down his life for his friend. Love is love only when it is the sacrifice of one's self. . . .

[The body will be annihilated], but that which cannot be annihilated is my peculiar relation to the world, which constitutes my peculiar ego, from which has been created for me all that is. It cannot be annihilated, because it alone has existence.

For the man who knows himself, not by his reflection in an existence defined by time and space, but by his growth in a loving relation toward the world, the destruction of the shadow of the conditions of time and space is merely the token of a greater degree of light.

Remembering his beloved brother led him to the insight that "the force of his life after his death in the flesh has the same action as before his death, or an even more powerful one, and acts like every truly living thing. . . . I cannot deny his life, because I am conscious of its power upon me." So Jesus lives in millions of men and women today. From this evident fact Tolstoy had to conclude that "he who lives by love now, in this present, becomes, through the common life of all men, at one with the Father, the source, the foundation of life." This conviction was the necessary basis of his peace testimony.

He saw suffering as an inescapable part of life. But he also saw in it an opportunity.

Activity directed to the immediate loving service of the suffering and to the diminution of the general cause of suffering—error—is the only joyful labor which lies before a man, and gives him that inalienable happiness in which his life consists.

This concept of service is basically religious. So, in "What Is Religion?" Tolstoy tried to say why religion is necessary to man. With that special charm of earnestness and stubborn seeking which runs through all his work, Tolstoy decided that "a rational man cannot live without religion, because religion alone gives the rational man the necessary guidance as to what he should do, and what he should do first and what next. A rational man cannot live without religion precisely because reason is an element of his nature."

But true religion does not consist in accepting a creed and making certain prayers and offerings at certain times.

"God is a Spirit whose image lives in us, the power of which we can increase by our conduct." If only we would teach this to our children, instead of abstruse and questionable and unprovable doctrines:

> . . . then, instead of irrational strife and separation, very soon, without the help of diplomatists, international law, peace congresses, political economists, and socialists of all sections, a peaceful, friendly, happy life would come about for humanity, directed by this sole religion.

But we have been so accustomed to organizing our lives by violence—bayonets, bullets, prisons, gallows—that we suppose this to be the only way society can endure.

> By means of the army, the clergy, the police, and of the threat of bayonets, bullets, prisons, workhouses, gallows [the rulers] compel the enslaved people to continue to live in their stupefaction and slavery without ousting the rulers from their positions of privilege.
>
> In proportion as the habit of violence and crimes practised under the guise of law by the custodians of order and morality themselves becomes more frequent and cruel, and is justified in greater measure by the inculcation of falsehood uttered as religion, people become more and more firmly established in the idea that the law of their life is not love and mutual service, but struggle and the devouring of each other.

If instead of military drill and rewards for military exploits, governments would distribute prizes for exploits of love, man's better nature might gradually take control.

But Governments have not only never and nowhere taken this duty upon themselves, but on the contrary have always and everywhere defended with the greatest jealousy the existing false and outlived religious teaching, and persecuted by every means those who have attempted to transmit to the people the foundations of true religion.

Tolstoy himself was constantly being frustrated by a government which refused him permission to print his controversial writings (they consequently circulated by the thousands in duplicated copies), kept him under surveillance, jailed his followers though it did not dare imprison him, and ultimately had him excommunicated—he, the most religious man in all Russia! In the truly noble profession of faith written on that occasion, he closed by quoting Coleridge to the effect that he who begins by loving his Christianity above truth will soon love his church or sect above Christianity and will end by loving himself above all else.

"Religion is not a faith established once for all in supernatural events," he argued. "Religion is the relation of man to eternal life, to God, in accordance with reason and contemporary knowledge, which alone moves man forward toward the end for which he is intended."

"On Reason, Faith and Prayer" (1901) returned to familiar themes.

"Reason unites us," Tolstoy argued here, "not only with our contemporaries, but with men who lived two thousand years before us, and with those who will live after us."

Since reason is given to all men, it unites all ages, races, sages. And what men of reason teach is essentially the same:

Act toward others as thou wouldst wish them to act toward thee; do not revenge thyself against those who do evil unto thee, but return good for evil; be abstinent, chaste; not only refraining from killing people, but be not angry against them; keep peace with all.

So, from the time he was fifty until the end of his long life, Tolstoy kept seeking and probing for that green stick which would make all men good and happy, meanwhile living a marriage which illustrated how discordant life could be for a man who had worked hard to find the truth and follow it.

Since Tolstoy's convictions about peace stem from his religion, we need to be clear about his convictions.

God, for Tolstoy, was "He without whom there is no life. To know God and to live are one. God is life. . . .

"If we seek God, we shall find goodness. If we seek true goodness, we shall find God," he wrote in his diary only a month or so before he died. "Love is only the striving toward the good. . . .

"To live in God's sight does not mean to live in the sight of some God in heaven, but it means to evoke the God who is within you and live in His sight." This only a few weeks before his death.

To Tolstoy, as to all mystics, the God within and the God that was universal was one and the same, because the nature of God was his inwardness, his indwelling presence.

"I believe that the only meaning of my life is that I should live it only by the light within me, and should hold that light on high before men that they may see it," he wrote. And again, in a late diary entry: "One must be like a lamp, closed to outside influences, such as wind or insects, and also be clean, transparent, and brightly burning."

Just a few days before his death he wrote in his secret diary:

> God is the unlimited Whole, of which man acknowledges himself to be a limited part. . . . The more the manifestation of God in man (life) unites with the manifestations (lives) of other beings, the more he exists. The union of this life of one's own with the lives of others is accomplished through love.
>
> God is not love, but the more love there is, the more man reveals God, the more truly he exists. . . . We recognize God only by being conscious that He is manifested in us.

A few months earlier he had written:

Love is one's awareness that one is a manifestation of the Whole, the union of oneself with the Whole, and love for God and one's neighbor.

And:

Thought how essential it was to preach to people an equal love for ALL, for Negroes, savages, and one's enemies, because if we do not preach this, there will not and cannot be any liberation from evil, there will only be what is most natural: one's fatherland, one's people, its defense, armies and war. And if there are armies and war, there will be no end to evil.

Tolstoy was far from blind to the evils and errors that stood in the way of true religion and its fruit, peace. We live, he saw, in an insane world where the insanity is general, organized, social and even intelligent. Property, he believed, was the pivot on which all evil turned, because it allowed some men to enjoy the labor of others without themselves making a fair return. Marxism was no answer, because it would merely change the make-up of the ruling class. Its anti-spiritual, anti-religious basis was a warning that it could not correct what was wrong with society, for the life of man must grow not from a material base but from a higher one.

Tolstoy was certain that society could be renovated by observing the teachings of Jesus. He knew from his own experience that he had suffered as much by following the doctrine of the world as many a martyr endured by following Christian teachings. So why not choose the better way? That way was not to be found either in quietism, a religious detour which he despised, nor in revolution, since the revolutionists completely failed to understand the basis of happiness and man's destiny. It was in that universal law of behavior that sages of whatever time and place had taught.

So he devoted the last years of his life to assembling *Thoughts of the Sages,* an anthology of what was basic to all religions and to the thought of the great teachers. Since true religion was truly

[173]

universal, perhaps a book which all could accept would form the foundation for one religion which in turn would usher in that wonderful world of the green stick.

If God is within all men, they must as brothers do to all men as they would be done by. Where they fail, evil enters in. But we must not resist evil by force, since this generates more evil. This principle of nonresistance to evil became a central item of faith.

> *I do not believe [an American visitor, Dr. Alice Stockham, reported him as saying] that violent resistance to evil is ever justifiable under any circumstances. Violence . . . is . . . an aggravation of the original evil, since it is in the nature of violence to multiply and reproduce itself in all directions.*
>
> *As soon as I admit my right to property, I necessarily will try to keep it from others and to increase it, and therefore will deviate very far from the true teaching of Christ.*
>
> *An adversary will not continue to strike a man who neither resists nor tries to defend himself. It is by those who have suffered, not by those who have inflicted suffering, that the world has been advanced.*

In a book which he called *Power and Liberty* Tolstoy spelled out his feelings about the way power led to violence.

"Power, then, is the united will of the masses, avowedly or tacitly transmitted to rulers chosen by the masses," he argued.

His military experience had taught him that the men who gave the most orders were least involved in the action. So he concluded that the men who are most directly concerned in events have the least responsibility for them. Men think that their rulers make the decisions which determine events. But actuality is much more complicated than this, and it is a product of so many forces that we can never know and evaluate them all.

"So in history, what we know we call necessity; what we do not know, we conceal under the name of liberty!

"To history, liberty is what we do not know about the life of humanity."

Provoked by the sentimental effusions that accompanied the

visit of a Russian squadron to France in 1893, he burst out in "Christianity and Patriotism" with an attack on the whole basis of these military establishments, visits, and expenditures. The real cause of all this affection, he says, is that France and Russia are getting ready to attack Germany. When sentiment has been properly whipped up, the order will be given "by God's grace" in the emperor's name.

"The bells will be rung, and long-haired men will throw gold-embroidered bags over themselves and will begin to pray for the slaughter." As for the men who must do the fighting, "They will go to freeze, to starve, to be sick, to die from diseases, and finally they will arrive at the place where they will be killed by the thousand, themselves not knowing why, men whom they have never seen and who have done them and can do them no harm."

Deutschland über alles expresses both the philosophy and the fallacy of patriotism.

> *This sentiment is not at all exalted, but, on the contrary, very stupid and very immoral: stupid, because, if every state will consider itself better than any other, it is obvious that they will all be in the wrong; and immoral, because it inevitably leads every man who experiences the feeling to try to obtain advantages for his own state and nation, at the expense of other states and nations—a tendency which is directly opposed to the fundamental moral law recognized by all men: not to do unto another what we do not wish to have done to ourselves.*

Patriotism goes clean against the principles of equality and brotherhood we profess. No matter how we have tried to conceal the teaching of Christianity, it has nevertheless trickled through to us so that we cannot help but see how incompatible patriotism is with its basic principles.

"Patriotism is slavery," says Tolstoy. It makes us promise in advance to do whatever the state demands of us, without knowing whether or not this will square with conscience.

"There does not exist, and there has not existed, a case of aggregate violence committed by one set of men against another which has not been committed in the name of patriotism." From ruler to journalist, banker to teacher, "these persons consciously and unconsciously spread the deception of patriotism, which is indispensable to them for the maintenance of their advantageous position."

So the parades, the triumphal arches, the fireworks, the uniforms, the visits of state all create the pretense that something grand and necessary is being done, when in fact everyone would be better off if nothing of the kind were going on.

"Patriotism now presents to men nothing but the most terrible future; but the brotherhood of the nations forms that ideal which more and more grows to be comprehensible and desirable for humanity." Tolstoy thought the change as inevitable as the falling of autumn leaves, for he assumed that men would be guided by reason rather than by their passions.

If men would only be bold to express the truth of the brotherhood of nations and the criminality of exclusive membership in one nation, says Tolstoy, a new and vital public opinion would develop, and we would escape from the death cell in which we now live.

"If only!" It has always seemed such a small "if" to men who could see the truth clearly. The truth they have not seen is that men praise reason but are moved by their passions and frustrations.

Writing to an American correspondent in 1896, Tolstoy said:

> It is as impossible to unite patriotism with peace, as at the same time to go out driving and stay at home. ["Patriotism or Peace."] What produces war is the desire for an exclusive good for one's own nation—what is called patriotism. And so to abolish war, it is necessary to abolish patriotism.

Everyone knows that war is bad, but no one dares admit that patriotism is the cause of it, or that it is a survival from barbarous times entirely inconsistent with Christianity.

When a conquering prince asked Confucius how to increase his army so as to overcome a stubborn tribe, the sage replied:

"Destroy all thy army, and use the money, which thou art

wasting now on the army, on the enlightenment of thy people and on the improvement of agriculture, and the southern tribe will drive away its prince and will submit to thy rule without war." This might serve as a parable of aid versus war.

Tolstoy took the extreme position that violence is never justified. He took literally the command of Jesus, "Resist not evil." He had little faith in organized efforts for peace, for he felt that nothing but the widespread refusal of individuals to take part in wars could end them. So he refused to serve on the committee of the Tenth International Peace Congress held in Paris in 1900.

When the Russian government in 1898 proposed a conference to limit armaments and preserve peace, he told the *New York World:* "The consequences of the proposal will be words. Universal peace may be achieved only by manifesting self-respect and disobedience to governments that demand taxes and army service for organized violence and murder."

Disarmament by conference is impossible, he wrote in a letter on the peace conference, because the strong will never abdicate, and "the thing that has to be checked is to be the instrument by which it is to be checked"—an impossibility.

Men in a democratic or constitutional state are even worse off than those in a despotic one, he argued, because while the latter may be free even in the midst of violence, the former are slaves who accept the legality of the violence done to them.

Condemning both czarism and revolution, he still refused to lend his support to the constitutional reformers within Russia who were agitating for representative government. His instinct was against organization; he was really a Christian anarchist who believed that the only way society could mend itself was through a change of heart in the individuals who made it up.

When his Social Democrat friends asked him if there wasn't a difference between killing as the revolutionist did it and as the policeman did, he answered in strong peasant language:

"There is as much difference as between cat-shit and dog-shit. But I don't like the smell of either."

He was in touch with people throughout the world who believed as he did that one must not resist evil by force—with William Lloyd Garrison's son, with Gandhi, with the American Quakers. He read Adin Ballou's *Christian Non-Resistance* and was delighted with it. William Jennings Bryan came with his son, impressing Tolstoy so much that he gave up his morning occupations for a long talk which included the topic of passive resistance. Bryan in turn was so fascinated that he sent off a wire to cancel his audience with the czar and stayed on to talk. When he asked Tolstoy whether he would use force against a monster who tortured a child, Tolstoy said:

"I have lived in this world for seventy-five years, and I have never yet seen such a monster. Yet I see how millions of people, women, children, are being destroyed as the result of the wickedness of governments."

He went on writing against violence, governments, and patriotism, and the Russian government went on banning his works. But it could not prevent their circulation, either in Russia or throughout the world. When war came with Japan, he wrote another blast against the evil of war which he called "Bethink Yourselves." The *London Daily News* called it a great epistle to humanity.

On a May morning in 1905 he was going through his mail and reading his paper, when, according to his daughter, he burst out:

"No, this is impossible! One cannot live like this!" And he began to dictate "I Cannot Be Silent."

"Nowadays they talk about executions, hangings, murders, bombs the way they used to speak of the weather. . . . It is impossible to live like this." Once again he spoke out against all the palpable evils. Once again the government banned his writing, which spread out nevertheless across Russia and across the world.

In 1909 Tolstoy was invited to attend the eighteenth Peace Congress in Stockholm. For such a congress to meet without the world's staunchest spokesman for peace seemed impossible. When he spoke to his wife about it, she screamed and wept and said she would not let him go. Then she threatened to kill herself. This went on until he promised not to go.

Meanwhile he had become the world's most famous writer. While the Russian government continued to harass those who followed his ideas, especially those refusing military service, it dared not touch him; his fame was too great. He begged them to jail him, for he felt guilty that others who followed his ideals should suffer while he went free. He was deeply moved when a young disciple, E. N. Drozhzhin, who refused the soldiers oath was placed in solitary confinement for a whole year, then sent into a disciplinary battalion where he got tuberculosis and died in prison.

Tolstoy did his best to protect the Dukhobors, who had long subscribed to principles like his own. When the Cossacks entered their community, killed four, and scattered four thousand after imprisoning their leaders, Tolstoy investigated, sent a report to the *London Times,* and helped with the arrangements by which British Quakers resettled them in Canada.

Unfortunately the communities established on Tolstoyan principles—land held in common, everyone working, simple diet—all failed. In place of love there was recrimination, while disputes over who might own what seemed more acute than in a property-holding society. The trouble was, they could not check their cantankerous human natures at the gate.

But Tolstoy's fame kept on growing. His seventieth birthday had brought public celebrations and greetings from all over the world. When he heard that great plans were being made for his eightieth, he begged that they be given up. Wherever he went, word spread that Tolstoy was coming. Everyone wanted to see him—this man who defied church and government, whose ideas were said to be destructive of all order and which yet appealed to every heart, they were so direct and simple and true. On one occasion at Kursk the crowd grew so vast that he and his family were in danger of being crushed by it.

Sophia Tolstoy was becoming more and more unstable in these latter years, the scenes more violent, the threats of suicide more frequent. One of the hundreds of such incidents occurred just after the crush at Kursk. Tolstoy fainted after getting into the train. When they got him home he was unable to speak lucidly. Yet all Sophia could think of was to demand his keys.

"I don't understand. . . . What for?"

"The keys, the keys to the drawer with the manuscripts!"

If he was going to die, she wanted to make certain that the manuscripts were in her hands.

Thus while he was revered and honored throughout the world, he had to live in a hell at home. Doctors could do nothing for her hysteria. Yet Lev could or would do little or nothing to remove the irritant which kept setting her off—the giving over of his literary works to the public instead of leaving them to her. The battle kept coming to a head between Sophia and Vladimir Chertkov, who was handling certain of Tolstoy's literary works. This Sophia could not bear. Certain that Tolstoy had made a will (he had) which would deprive her of full rights to his works and that Chertkov was to blame, she kept frantically spying, eavesdropping, and rummaging through his papers until he could stand it no more.

In the middle of the night of October 27, 1910, and at the age of eighty-two he sneaked out of his own house and went off in search of that peace which had become the main quest of his life, both philosophical and personal. In a letter to his wife which remained unsent, he explained that he wanted to go away like the Hindus, consecrating his last years to God.

But there were no years remaining. He died a few days later in a room which the station master of Astapovo let him use, after writing these last words in his diary:

"All is for the good of others and chiefly for me."

At the end of his life it still bothered him that he had not lived up to his ideals. "Every day I go out on the road and there stand five tattered beggars," he wrote, "while I ride a horse and after me a coachman."

That pathos of promise versus performance, of maturity's failure to realize the dreams of youth which he caught so beautifully in his novels, also caught up with him in his own life. He saw the magnificence of human possibility and the degradation of its actuality, and he kept pointing the true way fearlessly. Yet he could not achieve it himself.

To have peace, you must change society. To change society, you must first change men. But can you? When he tried to change himself—giving up his property, surrendering the rights to his writings—he succeeded only in making a hell of his own household.

Tolstoy's is the noble tragedy of a great man who saw the truth but could not live it. His struggle to understand is heartening, his courage to say what he found inspiring. His failure is deeply tragic because it involves us all. For we all fail in precisely the same way. He knew what the good life was and how to achieve it through self-denial, suffering and love. He was ready to make all these sacrifices. But those who claimed to love him best prevented him—his wife, his family, and the pressures of society. So we all succumb to the eroding temptations of society, not to save ourselves or even out of a selfish thirsting after pleasures, but in order to conform, in order to do what we think good for our children though it may only ruin them.

Tolstoy's Christian anarchism may not be a workable answer to our problems, but it is a noble protest against what is, and a bright prediction of what might be.

They buried him, as he had requested, among the oaks near the edge of the ravine, in the place where long ago his brother had buried the green stick—that magic, wonderful stick with the secret message which revealed how all men might live happily together forever.

10. Nobel
(1833-1896)

The Best Minds

 If there is one name, aside from that of Jesus, that has been associated in our time with the word peace more than any other, it is that of the developer of those prime aids to destruction, nitroglycerine and dynamite, and the kingpin in the world-wide munitions trusts which long bore his name.

The popular image of Alfred Nobel is that he spent his life devising ways to kill men, then left his fortune for the granting of prizes which would by encouraging positive contributions to peace, literature and science, balance his account. Like all simplifications, this one contains a little truth mixed in with a great deal of error.

Alfred Nobel was a genius in the field of explosives, but his scientific interests reached out into many fields. It was only because men wanted dynamite more than aerial photography or pipelines or artificial silk that his many other inventions did not grow in importance until after his death.

But as the years go by, we tend to forget the dynamite and remember the prizes, which would have pleased Alfred Nobel—that lonely little man who never had a friend in any real sense except his mother, who failed to catch the one woman who might have been a match for his sensitive, rather morose but tender spirit, who fought with his father and wrote a play exalting father-murder and torture, and who wasted a fortune on a pretty little gold digger whose shortcomings were perfectly obvious to him and who gave him only a few fleeting glimpses of joy and eighteen years of misery.

In the year of Alfred's birth, his father—who had seemed to be prospering as an architect and builder in Stockholm—suddenly went bankrupt. So Alfred was born to real poverty as well as to physical frailties which pursued him throughout his life.

To recover his fortunes, Immanuel Nobel went off to Finland and then to Russia, leaving wife and children in Stockholm, where her relatives helped to keep the little family alive.

Alfred's mother taught him to read and write, and when he was eight Alfred went off to school. He stayed only a little over a year, and that was all the formal schooling Europe's foremost inventor ever had.

In 1842 he, his mother, and his brother Ludvig joined Immanuel in St. Petersburg, while brother Robert went off to sea for a while. Immanuel, having sold the Russian government his invention of submarine mines and having set up a workshop and foundry, was now able to house his family in luxury. They had a big house, a staff of servants, tutors for the boys—even a hot water heating system which Immanuel had invented to combat the Russian winters.

At sixteen Alfred, now considered old enough to join his father and two older brothers in the growing business, was packed off alone to visit Europe and the United States, carrying out some commissions for the firm while he grew up by being on his own. In New York he attached himself to another Swede, John Ericsson, inventor of the improved steamship, who would one day build the ironclad *Monitor* and sink the Confederate *Merrimac*.

Alfred returned to Russia in 1852 as the war fever was rising again in Europe. When the Crimean War broke out in 1854, Russia was short of everything mechanical and diabolical. For many of its needs it turned to Nobel et Fils, who overnight became manufacturers of steam engines. They also turned out submarine mines, cannon, and other war essentials. Immanuel had to put every possible cent back into the business in order to meet the demands. But the government promised to keep his expanding factory busy when peace was restored. It failed to do so. Once again Immanuel was caught short. He turned the big plant over to his creditors and left for Sweden.

Still wedded to the industry that had ruined him, he began experimenting with nitroglycerine. He wrote Alfred to inform the Russian army chiefs about these new experiments, and then to hurry home. But Alfred found that as usual his father's enthusiasm had run ahead of his success. So he began experimenting himself. What he ultimately came up with was a compound of nitroglycerine and gunpowder suited to industrial uses but not to military. This made Alfred happy but disgusted his father, who still thought of explosives as something for armies.

It was not only a disinclination to blowing up people that led Alfred in this direction but an honest desire for a steady income. He had seen his father's war business fall apart. But he knew that the need for an explosive to open mines, build roads and tunnels and railroads, and improve quarrying operations would be a boon to the bursting industrial revolution.

So, with a sample of his wares in a lead cartridge case, he made his first business call at a granite quarry in Huvudsta, Sweden. The results astonished the old hands who had been using simple gunpowder. Alfred took out his first patent on his explosive in 1863. He then went on to develop the primary charge—a tube of gunpowder set inside a container of nitroglycerine and set off with a fuse. Nothing happened until he made a tightly sealed package of his charge, whereupon a beautiful explosion ensued. He went on improving his new device—

perhaps the most important in its field since the discovery of gunpowder.

In 1864 he began the regular manufacture and sale of his explosive, and word of its efficiency soon spread throughout Europe. Orders poured in. A wealthy Stockholm businessman, J. W. Smitt, appeared interested in investing the capital the young industry needed.

Then, on September 3 while Alfred was in the city to discuss the formation of the new company, something went wrong. The shop blew up, killing five people. One of them was his younger brother Emil, home on vacation from Uppsala University.

What had happened? No one ever knew. The Nobels were well acquainted with the nature of nitroglycerine and of the cautions to be observed in making it. Had Emil tried a shortcut or failed to maintain the proper temperature?

His father, blaming himself for not being on hand to supervise, soon suffered a stroke, and then another from which he never fully recovered, remaining an invalid until his death eight years later.

But so far as the investors were concerned, the explosion only whetted their appetite for so effective a product, and the company was capitalized at 125,000 kroner and 125 shares, sixty-two of which went to Alfred.

But when he tried to find a place to make the stuff, he was hounded from one location to another, until he finally fitted out a floating workshop which he moved about as angry complainants appeared.

The next year he set up a company in Germany and sold off the Norwegian rights in order to send his parents off to a water cure. Traveling throughout Europe, he formed alliances with local businessmen, supervised the building of factories, trained workmen and supervisors, and gave public demonstrations to prove how effective his product was.

This last activity was shortly taken off his hands by accidents large and small. From the German plant at Krümmel not far from Hamburg, nitroglycerine was shipped to all corners of the world. Often the acid was incompletely neutralized. So it began to eat its way through the zinc can in which it was sealed, soaking the sawdust in the surrounding crate. It leaked onto rusty wagon wheels, into ship's holds, and out of the baggage rooms where enterprising salesmen or consignees left it. Although instructions went with it, the stuff looked so innocent that many failed to take it seriously until it was too late.

In New York a porter who found a leaking case that had begun to give off a pinkish vapor, carried it out and dumped it into the street. He shattered all the windows in sight, but was miraculously unhurt. There was a terrible explosion in San Francisco (14 killed), then in Panama (47 killed). In May, 1866, the Krümmel plant blew up, and then the one in Norway. A man who wanted to collect insurance on some overinsured cargo blew up the steamer *Mosel* at Bremerhaven. He killed 28 people, including himself, and injured 184, but before dying he confessed to the first nitroglycerine crime.

Nobel still insisted that the explosive was safe when properly handled, but the number who had learned this art apparently did not include all of those who worked for Alfred Nobel.

Then he found in diatomaceous earth a material that would absorb and stabilize nitroglycerine. He called the new product dynamite. Or "Nobel's Safety Powder," depending on whether the customer valued safety or impact most. In any case it was the same product. And the business prospered.

Nobel's share in the American explosives industry is much too complicated to get into here. He ran afoul of sharpers, Congress, freebooting competition, rival companies, the du Ponts, and other hazards either unknown or less virulent in the Old World. He left the United States after his second visit with a sharp distaste for the country. It is a strange irony that this rip-roaring country which immersed Alfred Nobel in so much conflict was later to supply far more winners of the peace prize than any other land. Nobel never did realize much money on his American affiliations, despite the vast amount of dynamite made and sold here.

Each country where he operated was a special case, calling for its own sort of business arrangement. How had Nobel, with only a year's schooling and some tutoring, learned to be a master financier and manager as well as salesman and inventor? How had he learned half a dozen languages so that he spoke them all with ease? How had he managed in so short a time to set up so many establishments? What sort of man was he?

He was brilliant. He was a worrier. He had an easily forgettable face, most of it covered by brown beard but the visible part showing rather sad and kindly eyes, under heavy brows, and a high forehead. Short and nearsighted, he moved with short quick steps as if he were in a hurry. He kept a careful diet, did not smoke or drink or play cards or dance, and still was in poor health. Heart trouble and severe headaches often made him restless and sarcastic. Yet he was a charming conversationalist, he gave elegant little dinners when in the mood, and with all his preoccupations he carried on a tremendous correspondence, always answering the writer by hand in his own language. He often tried keeping a secretary, but for one reason or another—they were often young men who got promoted into the business—he never held one long.

When his brother Ludvig asked for a biography, Alfred wrote:

"Greatest merits: Keeps his nails clean and is never a burden to anyone. Greatest faults: Lacks family, cheerful spirits, and strong stomach. Greatest and only petition: Not to be buried alive. Greatest sin: Does not worship Mammon. Important events in his life: None."

In France Nobel formed a partnership with Paul Barbe and his father, steelmakers. Both Nobel and young Barbe were in their thirties when the agreement was made. It held for twenty-two years. Nobel, as he liked to do, left all details to his colleague. Barbe not only built an industry in France but formed a huge cartel of all the Latin countries. But in the end he nearly carried Nobel down with him in a grand disaster.

In England Nobel again had to fight opposition, for interests there wanted to push guncotton instead of dynamite. But eventually he got permission to go ahead, formed a company with some well-to-do Scots, and chose the site for a factory at Ardeer in Ayrshire. By dispersing the various processes in separate buildings, he set up the only big dynamite factory that never had a major accident.

When he built a factory in Italy, in 1873, he remembered Ascanio Sobrero, the man who had discovered nitroglycerine in 1847, gave him a comfortable job as consultant, and used him as a sort of trademark or trade mascot.

The companies multiplied until they had to be combined into trusts in order to keep some sort of order and prevent competition amongst themselves. This piling up continued until all the subsidiaries and parent companies of the German and British companies merged in 1886.

In 1873 Alfred Nobel began to use a Paris address on his patents. Since leaving Sweden eight years before he had been traveling much of the time. Now he bought a fine house in a fashionable part of town near the Arc de Triomphe and had it stylishly decorated while refusing to help the decorator with even a hint of his preferences. But he did see to it that a room next to his study was turned into a well-equipped laboratory. And there, one night when he could not sleep because of a cut finger which he had treated with collodion, he wondered what would happen if instead of dissolving guncotton in ether to make collodion he should dissolve it in nitroglycerine. After a little experimenting he produced what he called blasting gelatine, which became the world's most powerful explosive. It made possible the great Swiss railroad tunnels.

Nobel grew richer, more powerful, and lonelier.

"I have no family to furnish the only kind of survival that

[188]

concerns us," he wrote to his brother's wife in St. Petersburg, "no friends for my affections or enemies for my malice."

He was about to make friends—both of them women, each charming in her way, but neither destined to bring him the love and family life he craved.

In 1876, rich, lonely, overwhelmed with work, this forty-three-year-old genius put a rather pathetic advertisement in a Vienna newspaper. Although he still lived mainly in Paris when not traveling, he apparently thought that the item he was looking for could best be found in the Austrian city.

"Elderly, cultured gentleman, very wealthy, resident of Paris, seeks equally mature lady, linguist, as secretary and supervisor of household," read the ad.

It was seen by a young lady of thirty-three, the Countess Bertha Kinsky, who had come to a crisis in her life from which there seemed to be no escape.

Child of a titled but impoverished family, she had gone to work as governess to four daughters of the von Suttner family. The von Suttners, also titled, were her social inferiors, but they still had their money. This was what in the end made all the difference.

Bertha had come to the von Suttners in mourning for a fiancé, Prince Adolf von Sayn-Wittgenstein-Hohenstein, who had sailed off to the United States to open a career as a singer but had instead caught a fatal disease. When the von Suttners' son Arthur came home for the summer, he found it hard to keep his eyes off Bertha, if indeed he tried at all, for she was a very beautiful woman. Thirty-three—seven years older than Arthur—she had a handsome oval face which was only enhanced by its imperfections: the right eye more widely open than the left; brows that arched, then straightened out. The overall effect of the straight nose, good forehead and full lips was almost if not quite queenly. And Arthur was captured.

Then his mother saw them in the garden together. The next

morning Bertha agreed that it would be best for her to leave. She answered the advertisement, went to Paris, and there she discovered that Alfred was far from "elderly." She thought his features neither ugly nor handsome, his expression rather gloomy but modified by kindly blue eyes.

Alfred was delighted with her. He put her up at one of the best hotels, since the apartment he intended for her in his house was not ready. He took her on drives through Paris, proud of the horses and carriage which were one of his few luxuries. He even showed her the long autobiographical poem he had written long ago in English; she thought it "splendid." Clearly, Alfred was hoping that at last his loneliness might end.

"Are you fancy free?" he finally asked her one day.

"No," she said. And when he urged her, she told him the whole story.

"Let a little time pass," he wisely counseled her. "A new life, new impressions—and you will both forget—he perhaps even sooner than you." Clearly, he hoped so. A new life opened before him. Bertha was not only a lady and a linguist. She was a fine pianist, sang beautifully, had read widely—in short, she was everything that the poet, the idealist, the spirit in Alfred Nobel needed to make life rich and rewarding.

After a week of this enticing companionship, he had to go to Stockholm on business. When he returned, she would move into her apartment, become his secretary and hostess and—who could tell what more?

Two days later he wired her: ARRIVED SAFELY SHALL BE BACK IN PARIS IN A WEEK.

But at the same time came another telegram, from Vienna: CANNOT LIVE WITHOUT YOU.

A woman of Bertha's quality could not hesitate. She sold her only heirloom, paid the hotel bill so that Alfred need not, and without waiting for him to return took the train for Vienna with only a little small change left over.

If only Alfred had been in Paris, or if a few more weeks had

[190]

passed, the whole story might have been different. Despite the displeasure of the von Suttners, Bertha and Arthur married, went to the Caucasus, made a precarious living as tutors, but ended by becoming famous as writers, she more so than he. She did not meet Alfred again for eleven years, by which time she was well known. But they exchanged letters occasionally, and it was she who led him to the peace movement.

Several months after Bertha's departure, Alfred stepped into a flowershop at the health resort of Baden-bei-Wien while he was on a business trip in Austria. An arrestingly pretty girl of twenty waited on him. He took note of her blue-gray eyes set off by heavy lashes and arched brows, her black hair parted in the middle, her small lithe body. She had no education or culture—he detected that immediately—only a thirst for life and pleasure. She was the child of a poor Jewish family in Vienna and her name was Sofie Hess.

He invited her to go for a ride, was flabbergasted by the shallowness and naïveté of her talk, but fascinated by her femininity and her obvious way of using it. Perhaps it was her transparency that intrigued him. She quite obviously longed for the things he could give her.

During the next two years he came calling when he could, no doubt with gifts. He gave her enough money so that she could quit work, live comfortably in Vienna, and improve herself. There was something in her, he thought, worth bringing out. He ended by taking her off to Paris and setting her up in a comfortable apartment on the Avenue Hugo near his own home. He hired a maid and a cook for her and told her to engage a companion who could teach her French. Perhaps it was not until she found herself mistress of all this luxury after an impoverished childhood that she gave herself to him out of a gratitude which, in her code, he now deserved.

But it was a hopeless alliance. There may have been for Alfred moments of forgetfulness, of relaxation, of comfort. But there was no meeting of minds or spirits, and a long dreary way ahead.

Sofie, idle, spoiled, unable or unwilling to learn anything, grew more and more demanding, made senseless expenditures, spent money by the handful and demanded more. Restless, fancying herself in ill health, she wandered from one spa to another. She complained that Alfred spent too little time with her, but when he came they fought. The more he granted her outrageous requests, the more demanding she became. Her family, too, made demands upon him.

His letters to her when they were separated show the efforts of a kindly uncle to guide a wayward child. He urged her to leave him, to find someone younger, "a simple upright man" to whom she could be a good wife.

But luxury had spoiled Sofie. She was seen with other men. Finally in 1884 she persuaded Alfred to buy the villa in Ischl, near Vienna, that they had been renting. Because it was in a good neighborhood, he thought they should pretend to be married. He sent letters and telegrams to her as Mrs. Sofie Nobel. Soon of course the word got out. When Bertha wrote to inquire, Alfred replied quite honestly that he was not married, but he had to stretch the truth to say that there was no young lady.

Not long after he had spent $100,000 on the Ischl place and another huge sum to put it in shape, Sofie was traveling again and Alfred was complaining:

"This insanity has been going on for seven years now, useless for you and exacting for me. It has embittered and wasted my life. I wish to devote my time to my work, to science, and I look upon women, all and sundry, young and old, as encroachers who steal my time."

And a little later, when she was smothering him with errands in Paris on behalf of the new house:

"Everyone my age has the need to have someone around him to live for and to love. It was up to you to be that person, but you have done everything imaginable to make it impossible."

The thing could only go from bad to worse. Ultimately Sofie found herself pregnant by an Austrian cavalry officer, who was forced to marry her and to resign his commission. After the wedding he walked out of the church and out of her life. Then he too began asking Nobel for money!

Alfred saw less and less of Sofie but kept on paying her a generous allowance. After his death she threatened to publish his letters, but was bought off by the executors who promised to pay her the allowance as long as she lived. She died in 1919.

Alfred went on with his inventions and his mergers, but the apartment he had prepared for Bertha was never occupied. The right woman never appeared, and Alfred's loneliness was never filled.

More and more he tried to free himself of business so that he might devote himself to the scientific work on which his firms were based. He never limited himself to explosives. In the laboratory he established at Sévran near Paris he went into electrochemistry, optics and biology as well as chemistry. He worked on synthetic rubber and leather and silk, on methods of extruding synthetic fibers, on improvements in the phonograph, telephone, electric battery and lamp, and on light metal alloys. The work continued, in the final years of his life, at laboratories in San Remo on the Riviera and at Bofors in Sweden, many of his ideas proving their fruitfulness to his companies long after his death. He worked on improved paints, shellacs and lacquers, on cables and wires, on aerial photography by means of rockets and parachutes, on oil pipelines, and the production of sodium and potassium by electrolysis.

The work on weapons and explosives continued too. He developed new propellants for projectiles and rockets, the hot and cold drilling of gun barrels, explosives and fuses for artillery shells, and the high explosive combining nitroglycerine and nitrocellulose (guncotton) which he called ballistite.

This last discovery led him into difficulties in England where

Frederick Abel, the government's expert on explosives, asked for and received full information about the new product, then devised a simple substitution which was made possible by one faulty word in the patent, and himself patented cordite. Nobel sued, lost, and had to pay heavy court costs. The only satisfaction he got was the judge's comment that the moral right was with Nobel.

The removal of his laboratory to San Remo came about as the result of his French colleague Barbe's complicity in various financial-political scandals which rocked the Nobel companies to their roots. Nobel again had to step in, reorganize, get rid of men implicated with Barbe, pour in capital. For a while he thought he was ruined and planned to get a job as chemist with his German firm. The French forbade him to go on with his work at Sévran.

Sickened by the whole experience—he had trusted Barbe implicitly all these years—in 1890 he bought a villa just over the border in Italy on the Riviera at San Remo, built a far better laboratory than he had had in Paris, and built a pier out to sea for ballistic experiments. The neighbors were not happy about having an explosives laboratory move in. Nobel's explosives had, especially in the early years, had an irritating habit of blowing innocent people without warning into the next world. He bought out one especially fearful neighbor. Time, and the spaciousness of his estate, quieted the rest.

Nobel's fame as king of destruction had been brought to notice two years earlier, in 1888, when his brother Ludvig died. Careless reporters assumed the dead man was Alfred, who therefore had the satisfaction of picking up his Paris paper one morning to read his own obituary. There he saw how posterity would regard him: as the dynamite man, the wealthy destroyer of lives. Was this to be the meaning of his life?

Loneliness gripped tighter the next year when his beloved mother died. To no one else had he ever come so close. From the years of sickly childhoood when she had petted and encouraged him to the final years when he delightedly kept her in luxury, with funds to spend as she would on the less fortunate, he had adored her. Now, of all the family, only brother Robert remained.

Once the French companies were reorganized, Alfred resigned all his board memberships and presidencies, settling down at San Remo to devote himself as fully as possible to science, the one love which had not forsaken him.

Meanwhile Bertha von Suttner had become famous as the author of *Die Waffen Nieder* (*Lay Down Arms*), the *Uncle Tom's Cabin* of war and armaments, which appeared in 1889. Editor after editor had refused to serialize it, though they had been delighted to publish her before. Her German publisher, who had to bring it out in accordance with her contract, moaned that it would ruin him. It was an immediate success, made a fortune for him, and was soon in a dozen languages.

Alfred Nobel, who more than any other man had made modern armaments possible, read the book and wrote her a graceful note of praise.

The peace societies quickly made her their heroine. She founded a peace society in Austria, was promptly elected president and chairman of its delegation to the imminent Third World Peace Congress in Rome. And there on the site of the Capitol where Cicero and Mark Antony had spoken, she spoke so eloquently and feelingly out of a warm heart and a love for humanity firmly based in her own richly fulfilled life that the delegates leaped to their feet to give her a thrilling ovation. Bertha von Suttner, who might almost have been Mrs. Alfred Nobel, from that time on until her death in 1914, when all she had worked for fell apart, was the first lady of pacifism.

She was one of those at the Fourth World Peace Congress, Berne, 1892, to write a reply to the exciting news that Benjamin Harrison, President of the United States, was inviting all nations to enter into permanent arbitration agreements. The reply went a big step further, proposing a league of nations. It was to take twenty-nine years and another war to achieve this result.

Bertha had invited Nobel to attend the congress and had even raised a small contribution from him. With the £80 he sent her, he also wrote:

"To demand disarmament is almost to make oneself ridiculous to no profit. To demand the immediate establishment of a court of arbitration is to come into collision with a thousand prejudices and to make every ambitious man an obstructor."

Instead, he had an idea of his own:

"Would it be too much to ask, for example, that for one year the European governments should engage to refer to a tribunal, formed for this purpose, any difference arising between them; or if they should refuse to take this step, to defer every act of hostility until the expiration of the period stipulated?"

This way, he argued, nations could gradually be drawn into ways of peace, since they could hardly object to such short-term undertakings. Then they would readily renew for another year.

"Thus, without a shock and almost without realizing the fact, they will come to a period of prolonged peace."

The idea was much too mild for Bertha, but at least she had engaged his interest. She asked him to come to the congress in August but failed to get his promise.

One day while she rested on the hotel veranda after a round of conferences, a waiter came to announce a visitor. It was Alfred Nobel. He begged her not to give him away—did he fear that the papers would ridicule the dynamite king for turning up at a peace congress?—confessing that he had already attended a session in the gallery and had heard her speak. He was still skeptical. She begged him to stay and hear more. He countered with an invitation that she and her husband be his guests in Zurich when the conference ended.

The von Suttners found a suite waiting for them at the Hotel Baur au Lac at the tip of Lake Zurich, one of the world's beauty spots. Alfred sharply criticized the windbags and the grandiose ideas of the congress. But then he said:

"Inform me, convince me; then I will do something great for the movement."

Did he, unconsciously, want to be wooed by this still lovely woman who might have been his wife, though through the innocent channel of peace? Was it her arguments or her overflowing womanliness, her eager eyes and the animation of her fine features, that drew him along? Was he thinking about world peace as he heard her, or of the peace and joy he might have had with her all these years if only that other telegram had gone astray?

For several days her persuasions went on, while he raised every objection he could think of and enjoyed every sally with which she renewed the attack and pressed her assault on him.

He took her and her husband out on the luxurious all-aluminum motor launch he kept on the lake, and while the grand scenery changed and opened before them the talk went on. Finally he said:

"Perhaps my factories will end war sooner than your congresses. On the day when two army corps will be able to annihilate each other in one second, all civilized nations will recoil from war in horror and disband their forces."

The reunion with Bertha—it was the last time he was to see her—had immediate results. He hired an ex-diplomat to go into the whole matter of peace, leaving him completely free to work as he liked. But the effort fizzled like a pre-Nobel fuse and nothing came of it.

Nobel, who kept working at the problem in his own mind, came to the conclusion that only collective security could prevent war, and that such a plan might lead to partial disarmament. All countries need only pledge to unite against any initial aggressor; it was as simple as that.

By 1893 he had decided to leave a part of his fortune for peace prizes. Women, he felt, thinking no doubt of Bertha, could play a major role.

"Every worthwhile step in the direction of peace will bear fruit, and a message of really great progress in this direction will awaken in all good and sincere women feelings and trains of thought which will be implanted in coming generations."

In 1893 the University of Uppsala gave him an honorary doctoral degree, much to his delight. It was the school from which his beloved young brother Emil was vacationing at the time of the fatal explosion, and the school one of his ancestors had attended, marrying the daughter of a great professor, Olaf Rudbeck. What meant most to him, however, was recognition as a scientist.

The next year he bought one of Sweden's largest armament works at Bofors, poured in capital, and with the help of his nephew Hjalmar (son of Robert) made it so efficient that it captured a good share of the armaments business which was soon flourishing under the stimulus of three wars.

Near Bofors he also established a summertime home and a laboratory. The home was not ready until 1895, when King Oscar of Sweden was among the first to use the modest guest-rooms. By the next summer, his last, Alfred was too ill to take much pleasure in it. But the neighbors loved to see him speed through the countryside behind his stallions in a carriage shod with rubber and therefore noiseless. As night came on, electric lamps run by the turning wheels made an unaccustomed blaze. To the country folk the king of dynamite must have looked like Satan himself.

His heart was giving him more trouble these days, and he did not miss the irony of it when the doctors ordered him to take nitroglycerine. During the winter of 1895–96 he was ill a good deal of the time. In August of the latter year his brother Robert died. So the weakling of the Tribe had survived them all. But not for long. In November he sent his last letter to Bertha, who had written him an account of the Seventh World Peace Conference. A few days later he was sitting at his desk in San Remo when a massive stroke crumpled him. Servants found him, carried him to his room, and called the doctor. Alfred could speak nothing but Swedish now, and no one around him knew the language.

He died alone on December 10 with no friend or relative near him—a lonely, tired man, famous yet truly known to few, brilliant, yet honored for the wrong things. It is hard to think of another man who so perfectly combined inventive skill with the ability to organize it into fruitful industrial production, or who offers such a strange contrast between the public reputation of munitions maker and the inner determination to advance the cause of peace.

Poor man, he had not had much of it in his life. Perhaps that was why he knew how to value it.

As soon as his will became known to his brothers' children, and that he had left everything but minor legacies to establish his prizes in peace, literature and science, a movement began to break it.

It would not have been difficult to do. He had not consulted a lawyer. He had failed to specify how the money was to be vested —legally, he had even failed to name an heir. With all his grim experience with courts and lawyers, it is hard to understand how he could have risked his whole fortune so casually. True, he was against inherited fortunes, and he thought a man should have only what he earned, aside from a provision for his education. All the more reason, then, that he should have drawn a tight will so that his family could not break it.

There were other difficulties. He had no legal residence. He had never acted as a citizen of any country and was rather proud of it. His country was science, which knew no boundaries. But until it could be determined where he belonged, the will could not be probated. If France succeeded in claiming him, difficulties would be greatly compounded.

The effect of liquidating Nobel's holdings in his many companies presented dangers, and to the surviving members of the Nobel family, particularly in the case of the Nobel Brothers Naphtha Company—the Russian oil business.

But gradually, with the help of Ludvig's sympathetic son Emanuel, the two executors, Ragnar Sohlman (Nobel's young Swedish assistant) and Rudolf Lilleqvist (a Swedish industrialist), began to make headway.

Sofie was promised her allowance for life if she would turn over all Nobel's letters and their envelopes. The Nobels were granted a substantial but undisclosed sum—perhaps the income from all of Alfred's holdings for a year and a half—in exchange for not contesting the will. Large quantities of bonds were secretly withdrawn from the banks in Paris and gotten out of the country to prevent the French from seizing them and claiming a heavy tax.

But it was a long time before all the objections died down. As late as February, 1898, King Oscar himself summoned Emanuel and tried to get him to contest the will.

"Your uncle has been influenced by peace fanatics," he said, "and particularly by women." He was angry with Nobel for having made Norway responsible for awarding the Peace Prize. But Emanuel insisted that his uncle's will must be carried out to the fullest and the proceeds devoted as he had planned to the benefit of all mankind.

The Statutes of the Nobel Foundation were finally approved, its board appointed, the Nobel Institutes set up which would assist the Swedish Academy and the other designated bodies in awarding the prizes. Meanwhile in Norway the Storting established the method by which it would appoint the selection committee for the Peace Prize and drew up its rules, establishing an institute which would assist the committee in its work and promote fellowship between nations.

Alfred Nobel had stated the purpose of his Peace Prize very simply:

"To the person who shall have done the most or best work for fraternity among nations, for the abolition or reduction of standing armies and for the holding and promotion of peace congresses."

Clearly, he thought of Bertha when he included the last phrase. But Bertha was passed over when the first award was made in 1901.

By the time the judges were ready to act, Nobel's financial affairs had been settled and about eight million dollars made available to the Foundation. And on the fifth anniversary of his death the first prizes were awarded. The Peace Prize, awarded at a ceremony in the Norwegian Storting, was split between Jean Henri Dunant, father of the Red Cross, and Frédéric Passy, president of the French Society for Arbitration between Nations. They were distinguished gentlemen, indefatigable workers, and they deserved recognition. But they were not the "dreamers who find it hard to get on in life" whom Nobel had hoped he might help. Throughout its sixty-year history, the prize has continued to be given to the well-established and well-known.

Finally, with some urging from Emanuel Nobel who told the writer Björnson, a member of the prize committee, that he knew his uncle had intended the prize for Bertha, it was awarded to her in 1905.

From 1901 through 1963 the Nobel Peace Prize has been awarded to fifty-one individuals and seven institutions. In seventeen of those years there has been no award at all.

To sketch the contributions of all these winners is impossible here. They have included pioneers in the pacifist movement like Bertha and Passy. They have included specialists in the field of international law (Louis Renault, Auguste Beernaert), and in arbitration (Elihu Root). They have embraced the men who brought the League of Nations to life—Wilson, Léon Bourgeois, Lord Robert Cecil. Then there were the men who tried to ease tensions by the signing of treaties and international agreements—Dawes, Briand, Stresemann, Kellogg, and sturdy pacifists like the German Ludwig Quidde who fearlessly attacked militarism in his own country. John R. Mott's contribution was primarily through the international work of the YMCA. Jane Addams and Emily Balch made their contribution through the Women's International League for Peace and Freedom. Norman Angell was primarily a popularizer of ideas, with a gift for appealing to a wide public. Cordell Hull was one of the important early architects of the United Nations, Lord Boyd Orr a leader in promoting peace through adequate food supplies, Ralph Bunche an example of the way peace can be preserved through UN mediation, Léon Jouhaux a founder of the International Labor Organization.

Albert Schweitzer is unique—the sort of individual Alfred Nobel had in mind, with a commitment to a way of life which makes for peace. He seems a man apart from most of the others, yet not so far away from men like Fridtjof Nansen and Georges Pire, honored for their work with refugees.

Strangest bedfellow was Theodore Roosevelt, shuffled in as one of those responsible for the First International Court of Arbitration at the Hague and for helping to end the Russo-Japanese War, and known for remarks such as: "No triumph of peace is quite so great as the supreme triumphs of war." He was later to help plan the strategy to defeat the League of Nations.

Albert Luthuli, when he received the award for 1960, became the first winner who was neither European nor American. (Americans, incidentally, have received more peace prizes than any other nationality.) A champion of racial equality and the ending of apartheid, he was chairman of the African National Congress and therefore constantly harassed by the government—which, however, allowed him to make the trip to Oslo to receive his prize.

Dag Hammarskjöld (Chapter 15) and Linus Pauling, the only man to receive two complete and separate Nobel prizes, bring the list down to date.

As for the institutions, they include the International Committee of the Red Cross, the Nansen International Office for Refugees, the UN High Commission for Refugees, and the British and American Friends Service Committees (Quakers).

Well, what does it all add up to? Did Alfred Nobel's magnificent gift bring us any closer to the end of war? Is there not something dreary in the very record of all these good men and women working valiantly to end war while each generation brings on a more horrible and destructive conflict? What have all these peace congresses, arbitration tribunals, disarmament plans, and condemnations of munitions makers achieved? Except to prove, over and again, that none of the schemes man has been able to devise has had any real effect in stopping a war that people really wanted to fight? Has Nobel's instinctive skepticism not proven right, his reluctant but hopeful idealism wrong?

But perhaps these are the wrong questions, or not the only ones. What would be the difference to us if there had been no Nobel Peace Prize?

For one thing, the prizes have to a degree made peace respectable by attaching a large sum of money to it. No longer can peace workers be dismissed as crackpots when more than $30,000 may suddenly fall into their laps. For another, they force the world to think about peace each December tenth if at no other time. They have even elevated peace to an equal place with chemistry, physics and medicine—the highest kind of tribute our science-struck era can pay.

Sixty years of prizes have not proven Nobel's thesis that a cooling-off period and automatic common action against an aggressor will end war—nor even his odd guess that a weapon of absolute destruction would do so.

The fifth column, guerrilla warfare, internal subversion, genocide, and virulent forms of totalitarianism have all erupted to make the problem of peace more subtle and difficult than it was in Nobel's day.

[203]

Yet essentially the work of the United Nations has followed his two tracks—arbitration during a cooling-off period, and bringing weight to bear against the aggressor.

It would have pleased Alfred Nobel that the supreme negotiator of our time, Dag Hammarskjöld, was a Swede with close ties to the University of Uppsala and uncannily skillful in the art of gathering forces and consensus for peace. In Hammarskjöld, at last, idealism and hard practicality merged again as they had in Alfred Nobel. Hammarskjöld, too, was an incredibly hard worker, a poet—and lonely. He was the sort of man Nobel had in mind and never found in his lifetime. That the Nobel prize found him, though not until after his death, completes the pattern—two men from one sturdy little country, each in his own way a grappler with giants and bending those giant wills to order and law. Nobel worked his miracles with industry, business, and the forces of nature; Hammarskjöld with the giant states which threaten peace in our time.

Nobel went to nature and found dynamite; he went to industry and found wealth. Hammarskjöld went into the arena of national power and enforced some sort of law upon the chaos of brute strength.

Nobel explosions still rock the earth, but they are mostly peaceful ones now, for the military uses of his explosives have been superseded. His peace prizes meanwhile have brought him an immortality beyond anything he expected. Perhaps they will still prove a mightier charge than his dynamite.

II. Carnegie
(1835-1919)

Peace Through Philanthropy

If the art of hand weaving in Dunfermline, Scotland, had remained a profitable activity for the hundreds of men who practiced it in their homes, we should probably never have heard of Andrew Carnegie. But with the coming of the power loom, his father's beautiful damasks no longer found a market. Desperate, the Carnegies in 1848 came to America where relatives had already opened the way. And Andrew followed a course to unimagined riches so logical and so prompt that his biography reads like the most banal of Horatio Alger's tales. Alger, indeed, would never have imagined a career so rapid and so fantastic—he would have thought it too excessive to be instructively moral.

In many ways Carnegie looks like another Nobel. He too was undersize. He never had much formal schooling. Though not a sickly child, he suffered a sunstroke in early manhood which made heat intolerable, providing him as soon as he was able to afford it with the excuse to spend half of each year in Scotland. He was devoted to his mother and never thought of marriage until after her death. His rise was early and dramatic. He enjoyed a genius for organization, though always leaving details to his assistants. He made his huge fortune in an industry that was as basic to warfare as munitions. A charming talker, he enjoyed meeting and knowing practically all the great men of his day. And while his fortune was vastly greater than Nobel's, he too devoted most of it to the welfare of mankind, and a generous portion of it specifically to peace.

There is something humanly appealing about Carnegie, however, from the very moment of his birth in the weaver's cottage of Dunfermline to his death eighty-three years later in the Berkshires that is different from the worried, wandering, worn-out Nobel. Carnegie was always full of bounce and enthusiasm, always confident, canny, alert, alive.

So when he was twelve his parents brought him to America and settled in Allegheny next to Pittsburgh. What, one wonders, would have happened if the parents had happened to settle, say, in New Haven or Louisville?

Although Andrew's father, William, seemed unable to cope with the new environment, Andrew and his mother Margaret responded to it from the first—she perhaps as much as anything because it reunited her with beloved twin sisters. Andrew immediately got a job as bobbin boy—$1.20 a week for working twelve hours a day, six days a week. He soon changed to tending a cantankerous steam engine in a dark cellar because the job paid forty-five cents more.

Then after a year of this, his Uncle Thomas Hogan found him a job as a messenger boy at the telegraph office, at $2.50 a week. Not only was this affluence; he could now be outdoors. He might even learn a useful and romantic trade. As he wrote home to his favorite uncle, George Lauder:

"If I had been in Dunfermline working at the loom it is very likely I would have been a poor weaver all my days, but here I can surely do something better than that, if I don't it will be my own fault." The American yeast was already at work.

What would any young hero do in such a situation? Why, he would arrive early to sweep out the office, learn Morse code when everyone thought he was idling, and then at a critical moment save his boss' reputation by taking a message for him while he was out and promptly delivering it.

All this Carnegie did. At a time when telegraphers read their messages from a printed tape, Carnegie read directly from the click of the receiver—the third man in the country to master the trick. So at sixteen he was getting twenty-five dollars a month as an operator. Thanks chiefly to Andrew, the little family was comfortably established, owning its own home within five years of arrival.

Then at seventeen, seeing greater possibilities, Andrew jumped at an offer from Thomas A. Scott to manage the telegraph office of the Pennsylvania Railroad, at thirty-five dollars a month. But of course he did not long remain a telegrapher.

One day, when Scott was nowhere to be found, the whole railroad line was tied up as the result of a serious accident. Instead of waiting for the superintendent, young Andrew worked out the entire strategy for getting the trains moving again, sent wires in Scott's name, and soon had the whole railroad back to normal.

Said Scott later on to a friend:

"Do you know what that little white-haired Scotch devil of mine did today?"

"No."

"I'm damned if he didn't run every train on the division in my name without the slightest authority."

"And did he do it all right?"

"Oh, yes, all right."

So Andrew moved quickly up the ladder until he was superintendent of the Western Division. In a day of inadequate equipment and unscientific operation, wrecks were frequent. Carnegie always rushed to the scene to clear things up.

Before he was twenty he had made his first investment—in Adams Express.

When, shortly thereafter, a man named Theodore Woodruff

showed him the model of a sleeping car he had invented, Andrew was enthusiastic. He persuaded the Pennsylvania Railroad to build two of them. When the grateful inventor offered Andrew a one-eighth interest in the new company, Carnegie accepted without knowing where he would get the money to pay the first installment. But he found it, the public was delighted with the sleeping car, and the Carnegie fortune was founded. By the time Andrew was twenty-five, he was drawing five thousand a year in dividends from this investment alone. With this, he could build further—and did.

Now he could provide some comforts for his mother as he had longed to do. But Scotch thrift was a habit hard to upset, and it was difficult to get her to accept domestic help. His father had died at the early age of fifty, just as Andrew's fortunes had begun to rise. Thomas, his brother, was already clinging to the ladder a rung or two behind Andrew as telegrapher and then as assistant on the railroad job. He continued an able partner until his early death at forty-two.

What Carnegie regarded as "one of the few justifiable wars in history" was about to break out. When Fort Sumter was fired upon, Scott was called to Washington to organize railroads and telegraphs for the government, and Andrew went with him as his assistant.

But before he could get there, Andrew had to organize a crew to restore the rail service to Washington which had been cut off by saboteurs. With soldier help, he repaired the twenty miles of ruined track between Annapolis and Annapolis Junction. Carnegie rode the engineer's cab on the first train to enter Washington from the North. After a perilous period, the capital had been reunited to the loyal states. Carnegie's energy, knowledge and leadership had accomplished it.

During the Battle of Bull Run, he worked from a nearby telegraph office, despatching troops to and from the battle. In November, 1861, he returned to Pittsburgh, now an important rail center for troop movements. In 1862, still suffering from the results of a sunstroke experienced while he was in Virginia, he got three months' leave from the railroad and went off to Scotland.

The next year, when he carefully totted up his income in order to pay the wartime tax, he had earned nearly fifty thousand dollars! In today's money it would be nearer four times that much. And he was twenty-seven. His salary, $2,400, was a small part of the total; the biggest item that of a venture into Pennsylvania oil which had turned out very well.

In the year when he was to turn thirty, Carnegie resigned from the Pennsylvania Railroad. He no longer needed an employer. Within a month he had organized the Keystone Bridge Company just in time to supply iron bridges to a big country that was expanding everywhere after the Civil War. Iron now became the center of Carnegie's activity. He was soon organizing companies to make rails, locomotives, beams. He then put business aside and spent five months wandering around Europe with a company of congenial friends.

In 1867 he moved his home from Pittsburgh to New York, where he found that he could easily add large commissions to his income by placing American securities with English firms. At the end of 1868 he wrote himself a memo which began:

"Thirty-three and an income of $50,000 per annum! By this time two years I can arrange all my business as to secure at least $50,000 per annum. Beyond this never earn—make no effort to increase fortune, but spend the surplus each year for benevolent purposes." The "Gospel of Wealth" was already in his mind— that a wealthy man is merely the custodian of the riches that come to him and that it is his duty to invest them wisely for the welfare of mankind.

But Carnegie was not to leave business as quickly as he thought.

First there was the Pullman Company. When it threatened the Woodruff Company, Carnegie suggested a merger, was smart enough to flatter Pullman by naming the company after him, and won his point. The merged companies monopolized the sleeping car business.

The other item that prevented Carnegie from retiring was steel. Once convinced that this wonder metal could really be produced as Bessemer said it could, Carnegie switched his attention to it from iron. While other mills stood cold and idle during the panic year of 1873 and after, Carnegie was busily building a modern steel mill. He knew that the depression was temporary and that the best time to build was when others were idle and prices low. But competitors lacked either his faith or his finances, or both. He drove his men hard, rewarded them well, made them partners once they had shown promise, and was never satisfied with last week's record of production.

When one of his managers proudly wired Carnegie that Number Eight Furnace had broken all records that day, Carnegie shot back:

"What were the other ten furnaces doing?"

When he dropped around to say good-by to his chief steelmaker, Bill Jones, before taking off for Europe, he said:

"When I once get on a steamer and feel myself rounding Sandy Hook, with this long vacation ahead, you don't know what a relief it is to me."

"You don't know what a relief it is to all of us!" said Jones.

By the seventies, Carnegie was spending most of his summers in Scotland, and they were long ones. His mother, as she grew older, preferred to stay at their summer home at Cresson in the Allegheny Mountains, where Andrew would linger with her a month or so before crossing the Atlantic. Other Pittsburgh friends also came here, and since most of them dined at the nearby Mountain House, it was a congenial, clublike atmosphere.

In 1881 he got the notion of touring England in a coach with four horses with a privately invited party of twelve. In seven weeks, the party traveled eight hundred miles, seeing England and Scotland from the seats on top. And Carnegie was the life of the group, rousing them in the morning, planning excursions to points of interest, keeping up a lively flow of good talk.

But when his mother died in 1886 within days of his brother, Carnegie found himself suddenly alone. The following year, at the age of fifty-two, he married Louise Whitfield, an attractive young woman of thirty whom he had known since her girlhood. It was a good marriage, a happy marriage, despite the difference in ages. But what kind of adoration is it that keeps a man tied to his mother as long as she lives?

Always eager to tidy up his business affairs, to get all his eggs into one basket and then watch the basket, as he put it, Carnegie had finally gathered together all his iron and steel firms into one company, Carnegie Brothers & Company, in 1881. He then began to reach out toward an empire which would embrace every aspect of the industry including raw materials and transportation. Inevitably he became acquainted with a young man named Henry Clay Frick who had taken advantage of the depressing seventies to make himself master of the coking coal and coking ovens of the Pittsburgh area.

Carnegie began investing in Frick's company, which was in need of capital, and ended by bringing Frick into his own management group after his usual custom of setting aside shares for him and using the dividends to pay for them.

Carnegie's way of doing business is well illustrated in the case of the Homestead mill which he acquired in 1883 when the owners found that they were losing money on it. He offered to reimburse the owners for every penny they had invested in it, either in cash or in Carnegie stock, and to take them onto his staff as well. The owners, expecting to be beaten down, gratefully took cash and got out. All but one. He accepted both the stock and the job and within fifteen years saw his fifty thousand rise to eight million.

Of all his working partners—and Carnegie had a genius for picking good ones—the outstanding one was Charles Schwab. Tired of clerking in a store, he had asked the steelmaster Bill Jones to give him a job at the factory. He proved so adept that within six months he was assistant manager at the Braddock mill. And he had a genius for keeping records. One day Jones sent him to Carnegie with the usual report. When the boss began questioning him about operations at the mill, Schwab's answers were so well-informed that Carnegie was delighted.

"Have we ever met before?" he asked.

"Yes, Mr. Carnegie," said Charles. "I used to hold your horses at Cresson."

Schwab soon became superintendent of the Homestead mill and Carnegie's right-hand man.

Dark days were ahead for Homestead, where one of the bloodiest strikes in our history occurred in 1892, after a less serious one in 1889. Carnegie's way of handling a strike was to shut down until a settlement could be reached. But he was in Europe. Frick, who was handling the negotiations as chairman of the Carnegie Steel Company, managed matters badly when there was every sign that an agreement could have been reached with the union. He prepared the property as if for war and brought in Pinkerton detectives. A bloody battle followed, and in the aftermath an assassin tried to kill Frick in his office. Carnegie was for rushing home, but Frick begged him not to—naturally enough, since this would have put an end to his career as head of Carnegie Steel.

Hating violence of any kind, Carnegie was bitterly disappointed in Frick's handling of Homestead. Before long Frick and Carnegie parted company. But in Britain, where Carnegie had bought some newspapers and was carrying on a campaign to democratize the old country, the Tory press was happy to compare the Homestead tragedy and the martial law which followed with Carnegie's statements about the superior opportunities of the American workingman.

Meanwhile the Carnegie empire went on growing. To break the grip of the Pennsylvania Railroad and its discriminatory rates, Carnegie began a parallel line of his own which would connect with steamers on Lake Erie and thus bring the rich ores of Minnesota within his reach. Although John D. Rockefeller had beaten him in the race for mining properties, they had signed an agreement which gave Carnegie guaranteed access to the ore and which bound him to buy of Rockefeller. The railroad —and his own lake ships—brought him ore at a fraction of previous charges.

And now, his empire complete, the time was aproaching when Carnegie would separate himself completely from the fabulous business he had built up. Morgan offered to buy out Carnegie and establish United States Steel. Carnegie asked $400,000,000 and got it immediately, with another $92,000,000 worth of common stock thrown in. But this he considered merely "water" and would not touch a drop of it. The transaction took place in 1901.

A year or two later Morgan and Carnegie happened to sail for Europe on the same ship.

"I made one mistake when I sold out to you," Carnegie said.

"What was that?"

"I should have asked for one hundred million dollars more than I did."

"Well," said Morgan, "you would have got it if you had."

With his gift for making friends, Carnegie knew all the great men in England and America. Though business had been his career, it had not kept him from loving literature, travel, music and sports. Even in his later years he golfed, fished and swam— sometimes all three the same day. Each home he built had a pipe organ in it, and at his Scottish castle he kept a bagpiper.

As he freed himself from business, he took an increasingly active part in public affairs, and this participation concerned itself more and more with peace. Even as a young man he had written that he hoped instruments of war would some day be seen "only in the Museum as relics of a barbarous age." When Britain and Germany blockaded Venezuela, he appealed to his friends in the British government to modify their action. The blockade had been set up in an effort to collect debts owed in Europe. Actually, as he pointed out, Americans were far worse out of pocket, but our government did not propose to use battleships as bill collectors. When the British went on to seize Venezuelan warships and bombard Puerto Cabello, the United States objected. The British promised not to occupy Venezuelan soil, but the Germans refused to make any promises. Teddy Roosevelt thereupon issued an ultimatum, promising to send Dewey and the whole American fleet in unless the Germans would submit their claims to arbitration.

The letters Carnegie received from Balfour, Morley and others suggest that his influence was helpful in averting a more serious situation. Peace was to occupy more and more of his thought. "The abolition of war grew in importance with me until it finally overshadowed all other issues," he confessed later. But first, there were other benefactions.

His libraries, for instance. Carnegie, Scot that he was, simply knew that everyone thirsts for an education. The betterment of mankind had to begin there. From his own experience and the memory of a kind man, James Anderson, who had opened his library to boys, Andrew felt that he could do the most good most efficiently by offering to build libraries. He would pay for the building if the community would stock and maintain it.

By the turn of the century he was getting about a thousand requests a year from the English-speaking world, to which he had restricted himself, and was actually giving away libraries at the rate of two or three a day.

Much of his beneficence, in libraries as in other things, went to Scotland. In 1902 the students of the University of St. Andrews chose him to be their rector. Nothing could have pleased this unschooled but highly educated Scotch-American more. When he reached St. Andrews station and stepped into his waiting carriage, students freed the horses and placed themselves in the shafts, drawing him and his wife to the home of the principal. The city was gaily decked; a torchlight procession delighted fun-loving Andrew. Part of the tradition was that the students interrupt and make a mockery of the formalities. Andrew took it all in stride and was happy when the students chose him for a second term.

In his installation speech he dealt with Europe's fear of growing American strength and proposed what has begun to emerge only in our time—a united Europe, politically and economically federated like the United States.

Encouraged by the Hague Conference which the Russian czar had called in 1898 (it met in 1899), and the Permanent Court for the settlement of international disputes which had come out of it, Carnegie was willing to tell his St. Andrews audience that there was now no excuse for war. He especially based his hopes upon the bright outlook for arbitration, which, he said, had been used to settle 571 disputes since the Jay Treaty of 1794 had established the modern use of arbitration. Supposing that even one out of ten of these differences had led to war, said Carnegie, arbitration had prevented at least fifty-seven armed conflicts.

From the comfortable mansion Carnegie had built at 2 East Ninety-first Street in New York, he continued giving away money at a rate never known before. Anyone who came begging for five thousand was likely to get a brusque negative. He could never hope to live long enough to give money away at that rate. No, his figures were more likely to be for ten million, or more.

His method was to fix upon an objective, such as the hero awards, then properly endow a foundation to carry on the work in perpetuity. In this way he established the Carnegie Foundation for the Advancement of Teaching, the Carnegie Institution of Washington for scientific research, the Carnegie Institute and the Institute of Technology at Pittsburgh, and the Carnegie Endowment for International Peace. Finally, finding that he still had $150,000,000 on his hands, he established the Carnegie Corporation with $125,000,000 of it, so that for all time the kind of work he believed in could go on in ways that would be appropriate to new needs and challenges. When he tried to take $10,000,000 of this for a similar purpose in Britain, the lawyers told him he had already given up the right of disposing of the money, so he cheerfully parted with another ten, leaving the remaining $15,000,000 to his family but providing also for a long, long list of private pensioners whom he had been supporting for years.

From the house at Ninety-first and Fifth Avenue he loved to cross to Central Park and take a brisk walk around the reservoir, or stop to chat with people who had no idea who he was but were fascinated by his open friendliness, his chatter about his own family (a daughter had been born in 1897 when Carnegie was in his sixty-second year), his interest in their own families and ways of earning a living. He was equally at home among presidents, prime ministers, and kings. Or with literary men like Mark Twain or Richard Watson Gilder or Matthew Arnold. Once a year a splendid literary banquet took place at the Carnegie home. Those attending for the first time would sign their names on the tablecloth, and the following year it would appear, embroidered to mark their places.

Gilder, who knew Carnegie best and who made a trip to Canada with him in 1906, wrote back to his wife:

"A. C. is really a tremendous personality—dramatic, wilful, generous, whimsical, at times almost cruel in pressing his own convictions upon others, and then again tender, affectionate, emotional, always imaginative, unusual and wide visioned in his views."

More and more Carnegie's concern focused upon peace.

Wrote Herbert Spencer to him in 1900:

"I wish very much that you would spend some thousands out of your millions in employing a few capable men in the United States and Great Britain to war against war." Several years went by, however, before he found a project which looked promising.

Meanwhile he continued to be used as an informal channel of communication between statesmen.

In 1906 he wrote to Roosevelt to urge that he propose the submission of all international disputes to arbitration at The Hague or some other tribunal, and that governments agree not to use force until or unless an offer to arbitrate had been rejected. And he concluded:

"The man who passes into history as the chief agent in banishing or even lessening war, the great evil of his day, is to stand for all time among the foremost benefactors."

Roosevelt promised to consider with Elihu Root whether to make such a proposal. He also had one of his own for restricting the size of battleships, but Britain turned it down.

In 1906 Carnegie also became president of the New York Peace Society. The next year he was chiefly responsible for convening the National Arbitration and Peace Congress, as well as three later congresses. Peace was in the air in those days. Peace societies flourished, newspapers were full of proposals for putting an end to war, and arbitration was popular.

Even before his principal benefactions for peace began, Carnegie had given away a great deal of money to the cause. He gave generous support to peace societies and arbitration associations in various parts of the world. He supported speakers, helped pay for peace literature, subsidized books that would otherwise not have come out, helped pay the costs of conventions and international gatherings, and made it possible for those giving their lives to the cause to be fed and clothed. In these ways he gave away a large sum of money, of which no record was kept.

The first major challenge to his purse in the interest of peace came in the form of a letter in the summer of 1900 from one of his many statesmen-friends, Andrew D. White. White, as the American delegate to the First Hague Conference, had succeeded in getting the Kaiser to accept the Arbitration Court, even though reluctantly. Now White's letter simply passed on the plea of a Russian delegate, de Martens, that Carnegie build a home for the new international court. But in subsequent letters he urged the idea.

Carnegie was not much taken with the proposal. The governments involved, he argued, ought to foot the bill. But in the end he said that, although he would certainly not make the offer, he would if called upon provide one and a half million dollars.

The call was not long coming. It came from the Netherlands government, which set up a corporation to handle the funds, invited plans from a dozen outstanding architects, and then chose one that shocked Carnegie. He had thought of a "temple of peace"—simple, grand, dignified. The trustees chose a showy, overdecorated palace. But as with all his giving, Carnegie left the responsibility of execution to others. Still, in this case he protested.

"The building proposed is no Temple of Peace, but shouts all over of the pomp, pride and vain circumstances of inglorious war." It was twice too big for its intended purpose.

Although cut down in size, the pretentious design remained, and Carnegie never cared for it.

"Of course I must bow my head and say 'all right,' " he wrote Gilder. "That is the part of the giver always."

Although disappointed in the building (which was not completed until 1913), Carnegie was deeply interested in the meetings of the Second Hague Conference of 1907 which, it was hoped, would take real steps toward disarmament and universal arbitration.

For some time the German Kaiser had indicated an interest in having Carnegie visit him. Most men would have regarded such an intimation as a command, but not Carnegie. He would visit the Kaiser if and when he got round to it. But it now began to appear to him that the Kaiser was the one who would determine whether Europe was to have peace. He also felt that the essential instrument should be a league of peace, or a league of nations. So he sat down and wrote a sort of soliloquy, imagining what he would do if he were in the ruler's place. What could he do for peace?

"I am the only man who can bring Peace among men," wrote Carnegie. "Can it be that God has destined me so to work his glory, and so to benefit the world? . . . I have it! Eureka! An International Police! A League of Peace! Propose to the Hague Conference that this be formed."

He closed with a stirring appeal to the Kaiser to make himself remembered for all time as the man who had the power to bring about a peaceful world, and who did it. If after reading this the Kaiser still wanted to meet him, he was ready to make the trip. The Kaiser did, and Carnegie made it, in 1907.

"I have read your books," said the Kaiser. "You do not like kings."

"No, Your Majesty," said the ever-ready Carnegie, "I do not like kings, but I do like a man behind a king when I find him."

Carnegie afterwards reported that he had three interviews with the Kaiser and dined with him twice.

"A wonderful man, so bright, humorous, and with a sweet smile. I think he can be trusted and declares himself for peace." It was one of the very few times Carnegie had so mistaken a man. Far from proposing a league of peace, the Kaiser's government rejected both disarmament and compulsory arbitration, so the achievements of the Second Hague Conference were marginal.

After Roosevelt left the White House and went off on his African safari, Carnegie began urging him to call on the Kaiser on his way home to see what he could do to persuade him toward peace. Elihu Root also wrote out a series of proposals and suggestions. Plans were made for a follow-up conference with British leaders. But then word was passed to Roosevelt that no suggestion for disarmament or arbitration should be made by him when he met the Kaiser. All Carnegie's planning, therefore, went down the drain.

Still he would not give up. Scot that he was, he believed in the mighty power of education to change minds, and he believed in the essential rationality of man. Why would man, endowed with a mind, not use it? How could he abrogate the rule of reason?

And reason made it all so obvious—the utter futility of wars, the senseless wastage of human and material resources, the damage to trade and to society. Arbitration, limitation, federation —these were the rational, self-evident answers.

From about the time of his visit to the Kaiser in 1907 Andrew Carnegie made peace his prime concern. He was not alone. Men had suddenly wakened to the terrible burden of armaments the nations of Europe were building up, and the danger they threatened.

"The most prolific mother of war in our day is preparation," warned Carnegie in his pamphlet, "Peace versus War."

In 1908 Dr. Nicholas Murray Butler of Columbia University drew up a proposal which he labeled "Carnegie International Institute." It called for a major endowment to do educative work in peace and arbitration. But Carnegie was not impressed. He was, as always, looking for something practical. And he thought he had found it in the idea of a league for peace, with an international court to arbitrate disputes and an international force which would make possible the reduction of national arms and armies.

The disappointment he felt over the Kaiser's refusal to discuss disarmament or arbitration was modified when President Taft, speaking to the New York Peace and Arbitration Society in 1910, said he could see no point in excluding questions involving "national honor" from arbitration. In all the arbitration discussions of the past this restriction had been preserved. No one seemed to know how it had crept in or what it meant. It had come to be taken for granted. Taft's comment drew a tremendous response. The United States and Great Britain promptly negotiated a treaty requiring that they submit all differences to the Hague Court. Everyone praised it; the Senate rejected it.

But Taft's speech had one decisive result. Carnegie now saw the way open for a major undertaking in the field of peace.

"President Taft, foremost among rulers of men, has really bridged the chasm between peace and war."

That was the way the Taft speech had affected him.

"The crime of war is inherent," he wrote. "It awards victory not to the nation which is right but to that which is strong." It is, he felt, "no longer actual war itself which the world in our day has most to dread. This is not our greatest curse. It is the everpresent danger of war which hangs over the world like a pall."

Once his mind was made up, he moved swiftly. At a meeting called at the Carnegie Institution in Washington on December 14, 1910, Carnegie turned over $10,000,000 in U.S. Steel bonds to a distinguished board of twenty-six trustees, thus establishing the Carnegie Endowment for International Peace. This gave the organization $500,000 a year income. Nothing like this had ever happened to the peace movement before.

"Altho we no longer eat our fellowmen nor torture prisoners," he wrote in his letter to the trustees (he had taken up simplified spelling), "nor sack cities killing their inhabitants, we still kill each other in war like barbarians."

He ended with a paragraph so noble in concept and so reveal-
ing of the greatness in him, that it needs to be read in full:

> *When civilized nations enter into such treaties as named, and
> war is discarded as disgraceful to civilized men, as personal war
> (duelling) and man selling and buying (slavery) hav been dis-
> carded within the wide boundaries of our English-speaking race,
> the Trustees will pleas then consider what is the next most degrad-
> ing remaining evil or evils whose banishment—or what new ele-
> vating element or elements if introduced or fosterd, or both com-
> bined—would most advance the progress, elevation and happiness
> of man, and so on from century to century without end, my Trus-
> tees of each age shall determin how they can best aid man in his
> upward march to higher and higher stages of development un-
> ceasingly; for now we know that man was created, not with an
> instinct for his own degradation, but imbued with the desire and
> the power for improvement to which, perchance, there may be no
> limit short of perfection even here in this life upon erth.*

Wrote Carnegie's distinguished British friend, John Morley:
"This last noble stroke of wisdom and beneficence is the
crowning achievement, and is universally recognized for what
it is—a real ascent in the double spheres of ideal and practical.
. . . Today, my dear Carnegie, you have truly made us who are
your friends, proud of you."

The Endowment went immediately to work to carry out Carnegie's intent. Three major divisions were established—Intercourse and Education under Nicholas Murray Butler, Economics
and History under John Bates Clark, and International Law
under James Brown Scott.

The first was to foster those personal contacts among men and
institutions interested in peace which would stimulate further
acts for peace. It was to set up an office in Europe, greatly stimulate exchange of persons among nations, and give support to the
American Peace Society. It also undertook a campaign to get
popular understanding and support for then-pending treaties of
arbitration which the Senate was beginning to balk at.

The second division took as its main work a thorough exploration of the causes of war. With the aid of many scholars in Europe and America, it began publication of a long series of studies which still continues.

The Division of International Law had three major objectives: to assist the development of international law and its acceptance, to foster a better understanding of international rights and duties, and to encourage peaceful methods of settling international disputes. An early task was to be the cataloguing of all treaties, judicial decisions and national laws bearing upon world law.

In the fifty years of its existence the Endowment has published hundreds of monographs and studies of war; the studies of World War I alone comprise a library. It has sponsored hundreds of conferences, promoted the exchange of scholars, financed other organizations working in its field. It has raised its endowment to $25,000,000, its yearly income to more than $1,300,000. Its building on the United Nations Plaza provides a common roof and center for many of the organizations working for world peace and understanding.

Nowadays it throws the weight of its interest into programs which will help tighten the rather precarious grip the United Nations has got upon world problems. To develop existing institutions into ever more successful ones, able to cope with a world moving towards internationalism in spite of itself—this seems to be the emphasis.

So the Endowment looks into problems of international organization, such as financing the United Nations. It studies the work of the UN Secretariat and the concept of an international civil service. It tries to assay the impact of science upon world affairs, and ways in which science could be applied more helpfully. It is concerned with the old problem of arms control and the newer methods of indirect aggression—subversion, terrorism, guerrilla war.

It is in the midst of a world-wide action program to train young diplomats for newly independent nations.

Meanwhile it continues its work in international law and sponsors a series of lectures each summer at The Hague. It has been active in such fields as the recruitment and training of technical assistance people, the analysis of economic cooperation in Asia, and the meeting of the United States' needs for specialists in foreign affairs. It continues to maintain a European office in Switzerland which arranges round-table discussions for officials who come to Geneva. Its publication, *International Conciliation* (begun in 1924), includes a book-length issue each year on the major questions facing the UN General Assembly.

It no longer supports peace societies as it once did, nor does it have a program aimed at the general public through mass media or voluntary organizations. Its work reflects the tendency of our time—toward specialization in technical fields requiring a good deal of training, toward the sophisticated development of the techniques and instruments which might make peace possible.

In Carnegie's day it was enough to work for broad objectives such as the use of arbitration. In our time it is essential to make the best use possible of the instrument we have at hand—the United Nations and its associated agencies. A balky great power can upset the smooth functioning of the UN or hamstring its efforts. But its chance of doing so is lessened if the UN staff are fully capable of doing a professional job within the limitations that fence them round.

Yet—is the Endowment fulfilling the real need? Has the time not come for a massive assault upon all the errors and superstitions about war, peace and world affairs that still clutter men's minds? Might it not put some of its vast funds into such a program? Or even into motivational studies that would tell us how you influence men and nations to follow reason instead of blind emotion!

We do not seem to have had much success with this, since

Ikhnaton. Yet without success here, all the studies and advances will suddenly be thrust into one towering fire again, as they have been before.

Early in 1914 Carnegie came to the conclusion that peace was closely related to moral conviction and that men might best be led to peace through their religions. He therefore called religious leaders to meet with him in his home and ended by endowing the Church Peace Union with two million dollars.

Even in late July of 1914 Carnegie had no glimmer of the war ahead. Nor did his friend John Morley, member of the Asquith cabinet, who saw in Ireland and Mexico the only current threats to peace.

Realist that he was in most things, Carnegie was too much the optimist to believe that Europe would run headlong into war. His whole business experience had taught him that men sought their own interests, but that though they were certainly greedy, they were not inclined to destroy themselves.

He still believed in the Kaiser as a man of peace. Only the year before he had headed the American delegation which carried best wishes to Wilhelm II on the twenty-fifth anniversary of his reign.

"Remember, Carnegie!" Wilhelm had said. "Twenty-five years! —and twenty-five years of peace! If I am Emperor for another twenty-five years not a shot will be fired in Europe!"

When Germany plunged into Belgium, Carnegie was stricken.

"All my air castles have fallen about me like a house of cards," he said.

Yet he kept up his correspondence with world leaders, especially in Britain and the United States. In February of 1917 he wrote Wilson:

"There is only one straight way to settlement. You should proclaim war against [Germany] however reluctantly, and then settlement would soon come. Germany sought peace recently because she knew her weakness. Britain and France cooperating with us would ensure peace promptly beyond question, and at next meeting at The Hague we would abolish war forever."

He still felt that a league of peace would do the trick, and that it should be embodied in the peace treaty—as of course it was. Carnegie lived to see the end of the war and the signing of the peace treaty at Versailles. In that same eventful year of 1919 his daughter married Roswell Miller, the son of an old railroad associate.

Carnegie was an old man now, in his eighty-third year, and he had had several illnesses. In August he apparently caught cold while fishing in the lake which bordered his beautiful estate, Shadowbrook, at Lenox in the Berkshires. He died within a few days, on August 11, and so was spared the bitter knowledge that the United States Senate would reject the treaty and the League.

Perhaps it was a stroke of prescience that led him to make his gift to the Endowment in perpetuity. For this seems to match the tempo of man's motion towards peace.

12. Norman Angell
(b. 1874)

The Illogicality of War

 Mystery confronts us whenever we try to say why this particular man out of millions should make a unique contribution to peace. When he has made it, it seems obvious, as with all great contributions. Why had it never been made before? Why did it have to wait for this particular man? And what led him to his discovery?

Norman Angell was born to a comfortable but average middle-class merchant family of Lincolnshire, England. He never had a college education. He had no training in diplomacy or statecraft or politics. He had no advantages of birth to make him familiar from boyhood with the ways of governors and rulers.

His early career in fact sounds like that of many a teen-age rebel who finds home stuffy and who wanders off in search of a freedom more fancied than real, more romantic than realizable. Norman Angell's early life could quite handily be used as an example and a warning to other would-be rebels.

At seventeen, as he himself tells us with a touch of irony, he admired Mill's "Essay on Liberty" and was in revolt against his comfortable family and what he took to be their callous indifference to life's injustices.

"One more quotation from John Stuart Mill," his brother Tom warned him, "and in the interest of family peace I'm going to give you a first-class hiding."

What does a sensitive, misunderstood youth do under such circumstances? Why, he leaves home. He goes off to America, to the Wild West, where a man is taken at his true worth. At least, he still did in 1891. Norman Angell's father contributed fifty pounds to the venture and off he went, on a ship carrying sails in her lockers in case the engine failed.

He went without passport, visa or immigration quota. None were needed in those days. When he leaned over to open his bag for a casual inspection in New York, the customs officer said:

"What's that in your hip pocket?"

"A six-shooter." Any European youth knew you had to have a six-shooter to live out West. So the future Nobel Peace Prize winner had bought a cheap Belgian-made weapon before leaving home.

"Keep it there," said the inspector. When Angell lost it several months later, he did not bother to replace it. By then he knew that the problems he had to face were not solved by a six-shooter.

On the train going west he met a man who immediately identified him.

"Limey?" he said. "From the old country? England?"

"Yes."

"What are you going to do?"

When Norman told him his plans, he offered him a job clearing a quarter section of land. Wages would be a dollar a day, plus food, if he proved out. "You got blankets?" he asked. Mystified, Norman admitted he had not. He hadn't had time to learn that blankets made up the equipment of a migrant worker.

After clearing desert for several months, Norman was promoted to cattle herding. Except for roping, he learned to be a pretty good cowboy. After two years as a cowboy, he was bringing a herd north from Mexico when at Tejon Pass, impressed by the look of the land, he decided to try homesteading.

He had miserable luck. Then he took on an already irrigated piece of land seventy miles away for a brother who wanted to come to California. When it came time for Norman to "prove up" his own claim, the whole countryside turned out to testify that he had not lived on his property as required.

"Why pick on this claimant?" his friend Covert argued. "He is a genuine settler, has put a lot of work on the place, dug a deep well, and has even been mail carrier for the district."

"Because he's a damn Britisher and wears those funny breeches."

That settled it. Norman Angell lost his land. Five years of drudgery—digging a deep well by hand, building a hut to live in, readying the land—had come to nothing. So he went on to San Francisco, was "taken" by a plausible gentleman who turned out to be a confidence man, and then got into newspaper work—first in San Francisco, then in St. Louis and Chicago.

On a sudden impulse he decided to return to England. Within a few weeks of his return he answered an advertisement which landed him a job as editor of a small and struggling English newspaper in Paris. He was soon earning a gold ten-franc piece a day. Compared with ranching, this looked like opulence. To this he added work as correspondent for a French paper and for several American papers. In 1904 he founded the *Paris Daily Mail* for Lord Northcliffe, czar of the popular press in England.

It was the Dreyfus affair which aroused his interest in the "passions and irrationalisms" of political combat. Former friends became bitter enemies over the case. Angell remembered the passionate Anglophobia and ignorant prejudice he had found in America. Each side in the Dreyfus affair constructed its own mythology, its own set of symbols and sacred cows to which un-questioned allegiance must be given. Listening to the speakers in the Chamber of Deputies or the remarks of respected leaders, he discovered the same defiance of evident fact, the same blind, emotional prejudice. For ten years the Dreyfus case dominated French politics. Partisanship grew so strong that a man might be denied his appointment as surgeon in a hospital because he was Dreyfusard. Emotions became so polarized that one had to be passionately for or against; there was no middle ground.

Norman Angell thought he could see the same pattern of behavior in the emotional agitation which had brought on the Spanish-American and the Boer Wars.

"Men," he concluded, "are not guided by facts but by their opinions about the facts, opinions which may or may not be correct; and usually are not, precisely because of these distorting forces." Such forces, arising within the self, are subjective, irrational, and often unconscious.

How did it happen, he asked himself, that the United States never worried at all about its 3,000-mile border with Canada, but when Britain got into a dispute with Venezuela over a bit of jungle frontier thousands of miles away, Theodore Roosevelt and the jingoist press whipped up a frenzy over this dire threat to the safety of every American?

In 1903 Angell published his first book, *Patriotism Under Three Flags*, as a study of this strange phenomenon and as "A Plea for Rationalism in Politics" as his subtitle put it. In the case of Venezuela, the Spanish-Amerian War, the Dreyfus affair and the Boer War, "passions were excited most in defence of a policy which affected welfare or interest little or not at all; or affected it adversely." Emotions blind us, not only to proper interpretation of facts but even to self-evident facts themselves.

The more he became acquainted with political leaders, journalists, and "practical" businessmen, the more he was amazed at their tendency to accept as truths what to him seemed clear fallacies or at least half truths:

1. That man can do nothing to prevent war since it is a part of his nature

2. That you can't expect men to act according to reason

3. That the "unavoidable" coming war with Germany was a struggle for bread

As to the first, men had successfully overcome anarchy and violence within municipal and national jurisdictions, while groups or races once thought implacable enemies had learned to live peaceably together, as in Switzerland or Belgium. War between states such as, say, Great Britain and the United States, had become unthinkable (I am extending his argument here), while even such bitter historical enemies as Great Britain and France had given up fighting each other.

As to the second point, all of human history was a testimony to the gradual abandonment of brutishness. Bad as man's record was, he no longer considered warfare a way of life or glorified mass murder.

As for Germany, it was at that very moment buying wheat and other foods in the British dominions on the same terms as Britain.

But the fallacies persisted in spite of his book—a fate which frequently overtakes writers. So, with that optimism which must be in the blood of every man who takes up a cause, he tried again. His new manuscript went the rounds of the publishers. A book on peace? Nobody was interested. Some publishers were even belligerent.

"This war is coming," they told him, "and we must face it and be prepared, and the only effect—if any—of books like the one you propose is to weaken our will to be prepared and to face facts." And so on.

Finally in 1908 Norman Angell boiled his book down to a pamphlet of a hundred pages, called it "Europe's Optical Illusion," and sent out a hundred review copies.

Nothing happened. No reviews, no sales. At last, having the whole edition on his hands, he sent between two and three hundred copies to public leaders in Britain, France and Germany. Within three months people began talking about it—important people. At Angell's request, the *Nation* gave it a two-page review. Now other reviews began to pour in from the Continent and the United States. A full edition was published under the title, *The Great Illusion*. Translations into more than twenty languages spread its message from Norway to Japan, from Finland to India.

"Even King Edward VII read it," D. C. Somervell noted in *The History of the Reign of King George the Fifth*, "and he seldom read anything that was neither official nor amusing."

People began misquoting and misunderstanding it. They affirmed that it said war had become impossible, when the main point was that a war was on the way which would solve none of the problems the nations were preparing to fight over.

What *did* the book say?

War arises not because bad men take a course they know to be wrong but because good men on both sides follow a course they think right. But their thinking is based on demonstrable fallacies.

A nation's wealth does not depend on its military power, since some of the world's most prosperous nations—Switzerland and Sweden, for example—have no significant military strength.

It is also a fallacious argument that a nation must own or control all the raw materials its economy requires. Such control is necessary only for war, not for peace. Nations are always eager to part with raw materials in the world market, since their value turns to wealth only when they are sold. So eager are the nations to sell their products that the chief complaint is not over a scarcity of any sort but rather that nations are "flooding the market" by their low prices.

Although in any normal situation we would welcome low-priced goods as a bargain, yet internationally every nation tries to keep foreign goods out and get rid of its own, so no peaceful nation has to worry about being able to buy what it wants.

War, by upsetting the applecart, can only depress the world economy; no one can gain by it. A conqueror cannot enrich himself from the nations he conquers, for if he confiscates resources, he dries up the ability of that nation to produce and thus he chokes off the very profits which tempted him, while if he leaves things alone, why did he go to war in the first place?

A war which upsets business in Britain will inevitably affect Germany. Assets are often international. So is shipping, credit, securities, insurance, markets. If Germany should succeed in crippling Britain, it would severely cripple its own industries. The German ironmaster makes locomotives needed in Argentina to get wool down to the ports for shipment to England. England turns the wool into cloth which it sells to the United States, which pays for it with the grain it ships to England. Trade is not a battle between two competitors, but a flowing river which fertilizes as it flows.

War in the modern world is not economically advantageous. Military force cannot transfer wealth, trade or property from the vanquished to the victor. Nor can the defeated be made to pay the costs of the war. The proof of that point had to wait for the 1920's. The Allies ended by getting from the defeated something less than they had lent him in order to pay them!

Far from being inevitable, Angell continued, war results from a failure of human wisdom. But we need not assume that we must always fail. People don't want war, he argued. They don't want cholera either, but where cholera continues it is because they fail to see the connection between bad sanitary conditions and the disease. Our international anarchy makes war as certain as accidents would be if we had no traffic rules.

Recognizing the dangers of nationalism and patriotism, and the failure of national coercive power to bring peace, he argued that only an international police power can prevent aggression.

"Armies are instruments used by rival litigants; police, the power behind the judge." Somehow police power must replace armies. The dispassionate and impartial judgment of a judge and jury must be applied to world affairs. In 1909 (and even in a revised edition of 1933) Norman Angell saw as the solution a concert of Europe which would deter the aggression of those who wanted to impose their will upon others.

It was an epochal book, forcing Europe to face some truths it had ignored. It should have prevented World War I.

Instead, it was immediately attacked. "The cause of war is Germans," said Lord Cromer. The Socialists said the cause of war was capitalism. Pacifists thought armaments themselves cause war. The debate went on until war came.

Meanwhile Viscount Esher, an influential adviser to the king, told Norman Angell that a wealthy industrialist, Sir Richard Garton, was eager to form a foundation to promote the ideas of *The Great Illusion.* So Angell, while still carrying on his editorship of the Paris paper, directed the foundation with the help of a paid secretary and assistant. The object: to change public opinion so as to prevent the coming war.

These were the points it was to hammer home:

1. Political control of sources of raw materials is not necessary to a nation's existence or well-being.

2. No war can be economically advantageous.

3. The victor will not be able to make the vanquished pay the costs of war.

4. War is not inevitable; it is not made by nature but by men.

5. Human behavior is susceptible to change: we no longer boil people in oil, burn them alive, or fight duels.

6. Nonresistance is no remedy, but rather the proper use of power to deter aggressors.

7. Defense against aggression rather than peace itself is the first objective.

8. Differences with Germany should be aired. The nations

should work toward a concert of Europe rather than continue to maintain an always unstable balance of power.

Agreeing with George Meredith that "When men's brains are insufficient to meet the exigencies of affairs, they fight," Norman Angell began in 1912 through the Garton Foundation to hammer home the truths he hoped might permeate the public mind and prevent war.

His ideas were being talked about everywhere. Groups organized as War and Peace Societies or Norman Angell Leagues. Men and women of the highest repute contributed their prestige. A monthly paper began publication. Debates, conferences, Hyde Park orators added their bit. Norman Angell went on a tour of German universities. In Berlin the argument grew so hot that the audience began to hammer home their convictions with chairs and benches. Five years' work among German students, Norman Angell thought, might dilute Prussianism enough to prevent war. But it was now 1912.

On July 27, 1914, he returned to London from a conference at Jordans (burial place of William Penn), where a group of American, German, English and French students had frankly discussed the differences dividing their countries. He had been deeply impressed and encouraged by the depth of the talks, the perceptiveness of the young people.

The next day, Austria declared war on Serbia.

Convinced that Britain's only chance of averting a major war was to declare its neutrality so that it could put pressure on both sides, Norman Angell quickly formed the Neutrality League. He had the support of many eminent men. Half a million copies of its manifesto were distributed by two hundred volunteers. Mass meetings gathered in Trafalgar Square. Three hundred sandwich men carried the message through London's main streets.

On August 1, Germany declared war against Russia, and on August 3 against France. When Germany marched into Belgium and then refused to guarantee Belgian neutrality, Great Britain declared war against her.

Yet even while public attention was focused on the war, Norman Angell began to look for ways to end it which would not repeat all the old errors. He came to the United States to write and lecture, mostly on the theme of what America's role should be and how we could help build a lasting peace through sponsoring a league of nations.

After the war he became more and more closely affiliated with the British Labor Party, until in 1929 he sat for a term in Parliament but found its frustrations unsuited to his interests and temperament.

Finally, two years after he was knighted in 1931, the Nobel Peace Prize came to him.

"No one in this country, or perhaps in the world, has done more for peace than you have," Robert Cecil wrote him. And Philip Noel-Baker, who was to win the prize in 1959: "If peace comes it will be more your doing than that of any other man alive."

From 1940, when war had already broken out again in Europe, until 1951 Sir Norman lived in the United States, where he continued to write and lecture on the world situation and once again urged men not to make the same old mistakes that would lead to still another war.

"The insistent belief," he wrote in the introduction to *For What Do We Fight?* "that the simple destruction of Hitlerism will of itself free us from the evils for which it stands is an insidious and dangerous fallacy."

His arguments did not prevent Roosevelt from siding with Stalin against Churchill, with the result that Russia occupied most of the Balkans and Eastern Europe, including East Germany, so that the United States ever since has had to keep troops in Europe and sit on a powder keg in Berlin.

Progressive opinion in the United States, he found, was more friendly to Russia than to Britain. The mistrust of British imperialism, a natural outcome of our history, still controlled American attitudes. It was this which forced Churchill to concede as much as he did to Russia. To combat this American tendency to regard Russia as the instrument of progress and Britain as the apostle of reaction, Sir Norman wrote *Let the People Know,* a best-seller.

In that book, Sir Norman was willing to leave the nature of international cooperation to the future—whether league, federation or Locarnolike treaty. Unless day-to-day policy and action in the early postwar period showed far greater wisdom than in 1918, he doubted that any international order would develop. He ended his book with the hope that we would not again destroy our Wilsons, blame our failures on each other or on some convenient scapegoat, and turn to isolationism.

After All, Norman Angell's autobiography, portrays a man whose entire life except for a bit of vacationing was his public one. There is hardly any mention of women except mother, sister, and young nieces. For most of his mature life, and even as a boy, he was immersed in work which left little time for anything else. His own account suggests a man whose life derives its meaning from a cause. The cause, a kind of enlarged self, actually embraced the whole world—which is not a bad thing to be devoted to. If we could all learn the secret of such self-enlargement, we would have solved the problem of world order.

His books—forty-three by his own count—are those of a pamphleteer and journalist. But no one has better exposed the folly of war than Norman Angell in *The Great Illusion.*

When it comes to solutions, he seems to favor something like an alliance of the "good" powers against the bad. That might have sufficed in dealing with a maniac and a racist like Hitler. But how can it handle a political faith like communism which, despite the iron rigidities of its doctrine and its bleak suppression of liberties, does speak to the underprivileged?

Alliances beget counteralliances. Our problem is how to break out of the historic circle of conflict as allies realign themselves for the next war.

We have now reached the stage of two superalliances presided over by two superpowers holding the power of life and death in their hands. If they should fight, half of mankind might be wiped out. What becomes of foreign policy, diplomacy and international negotiation when one power can start a war that may poison or annihilate populations not even involved in the quarrel?

The great merit of Norman Angell's contribution to world peace is that he saw, as early as 1903, the major fallacies on which international relations were based. The tragedy is that it no longer seems to matter to us that war settles nothing. Nuclear war can annihilate us all. Not only does war not pay; it can wipe us out as quickly as a dog can break the neck of a rabbit. The interlocked world of trade and commerce Norman Angell described is being transformed into competing worlds, each determined to prove its own politico-economic system the best, and willing to destroy the other's economy to prove the point.

So for the folly Sir Norman exposed we have substituted another folly, another conflict, and—perhaps—another war. This time the result will not be mere catastrophe but annihilation. So much for progress in the last sixty years!

13. Wilson
(1856-1924)

War to End War

 It is a tribute to the universality of Woodrow Wilson that we rarely think of him as the Southerner he was. Born in Staunton, Virginia, in the year (1856) when civil war broke out in Kansas, he was three years old when John Brown raided Harper's Ferry, little more than a hundred miles north of Staunton, and four when the war began. By the time it was over, he was in his ninth year. The boy came to know half a dozen communities as his father, a Presbyterian minister, moved from one church to another.

Growing up in wartime and Reconstruction Georgia and South Carolina, Tommy, as he was called in those days, knew at first hand the horrible effects of war, and the echo of those days and memories can be heard in his eloquent effort to keep us out of the war that blazed up in Europe in 1914.

Wilson's road to the White House was unique—almost miraculous. How could a college president—and one about to lose his job, at that—suddenly without any previous experience in politics become governor of a state? Before he became a candidate for the governorship of New Jersey, Woodrow Wilson had never run for office. Indeed, he was so little known even in the small

[239]

town where as president of the university he was the leading citizen that when he tried to charge a small item in a local shop, the clerk asked, "What name, please?"

Yet Tommy's preparation for politics was far wider and deeper than his career indicated. As a youngster he had insisted on organizing his baseball team along parliamentary lines. He had practiced eloquence from early days, having come by it naturally through a long line of Presbyterian preachers. And he was fond of telling his Princeton classmates that he would meet them in the Senate. He even wrote out a few cards declaring himself a senator. He went in for debating.

Politics may still have been in his mind when he went to the University of Virginia to study law and then to Atlanta to practice it. He never did argue a case. After a year, during which he got interested in writing about government and politics, he went back to study—this time to Johns Hopkins and political science.

Did his brief view of the law and the rough and tumble of litigation make him draw back to the other and more gentlemanly side of politics as seen and analyzed from a professorial chair?

From boyhood, Tommy Wilson had been more given to the power of the word, as demonstrated by his revered father, grandfather and uncles, than to the power of the body. The world of the Presbyterian parsonage had moved him more toward eloquence, idealism and a sense of destiny than toward combat, realism and the hard learning that you have to fight for what you get. Words—"the deep eloquence which awakens purpose," he called it—were stronger in his experience than muscles. A father who could move a whole congregation and be revered by them proved it. Many years later a newspaper headline reported: PEN IS MIGHTIER THAN SWORD SAYS WILSON. He believed this. (Unfortunately the compositor left out the space between the first two words.)

Moreover, Wilson was always an aristocrat. The contact of

minds stimulated and excited him rather than bodily contact. So instead of plunging into the hurly-burly of politics with its inevitable compromises and its hard contacts with other wills and purposes, Woodrow—as he began to call himself when he began to have a public—turned to books and audiences.

Even in Atlanta he had begun to find a satisfactory outlet in writing. At Hopkins he finished *Congressional Government* and thereafter several more books on American government which had a good sale.

"I have a sense of power in dealing with men collectively which I do not feel always in dealing with them singly," he confessed. Obviously, then, his was the mentality and the equipment of a teacher, a preacher, a lecturer. And that was the course he took, except for the amazing last ten years of his active life.

In 1885 (nearly twenty-nine now) he went with his lovely bride and childhood sweetheart Ellen Axson to teach at Bryn Mawr College just outside Philadelphia. Ellen, "a luminous personality" as William Allen White called her, was a beautiful young lady, combining an exquisite sweetness and delicacy with a stern religious spirit that was quite the equal of Woodrow's. He was delightfully happy. In her presence all his best qualities came out—his humor, his playfulness, his warmth. It was an ideal marriage and remained so until Ellen's too early death in the White House nearly thirty years later.

The quality of their relationship comes into focus with one very small anecdote. Woodrow expressed himself rather forcefully in a direction that Ellen did not approve.

"You don't really think that," she told him.

"Madam," he said, surely with the beginning of a grin, "I was venturing to think that I thought that until I was corrected."

When three daughters came into the family, Woodrow was surrounded with four feminine admirers, all of whom no doubt felt free to correct him, but all regarding him as their oracle, their bard—he loved to read poetry to them—and their defender. They modified a little his rocklike Presbyterianism, perhaps, yet more important they tended over the years and in spite of the anecdote to build in him the conviction that he was oracle, prophet, defender of the right. A noisy, slightly rebellious boy in the family might—who knows?—have modified Wilson's character, made him see that logic and fine ideals do not settle all problems, forced him down off his high horse, and perhaps even have changed world history.

It is dangerous for a man to be totally surrounded by admirers, and this was Wilson's happy and tragic fate. First in a girl's college—where a young bridegroom of a teacher gets adulation as Freudian as it is flattering—then at Wesleyan and finally at Princeton, Wilson was a tremendously popular professor. He joked with his students but also inspired them. Listening to his lectures was an experience in eloquence, an inspiration which men remembered for the rest of their lives. Four times the Princeton boys voted him the most popular professor.

When the students proposed that chapel attendance be optional he told them:

"Why, gentlemen, it is optional. If you wish to go to chapel you may."

The feeble joke was sufficient to dispose of the matter.

Meanwhile his influence was spreading beyond the campus. His books on government were popular; they were not greatly original but because they filled a need they brought him money and fame. Then he began to get a reputation as a public lecturer. His eloquence, which he had worked at since his teens, and his gift of speaking in apparent spontaneity without notes, also paid dividends. He was lucid and precise, yet passionately sincere— the greatest orator of his time.

If, with his high cheekbones and jaw thrust forward, he was not a handsome man, he was an impressive one. Listeners felt that he believed what he said and knew what he thought. Never a great scholar, rather poorly read even in his own field and ignorant in most other fields except for romantic poetry, he had the gift of absorbing ideas rapidly. He could cut through verbiage as a scythe cuts hay and quickly come to the essence. The gift made him impatient with wordy people and thus unpopular with them. It also led him into the error of thinking he had a first-class mind, and thus to being impatient with those who in his opinion hadn't. Political fealty is not built this way.

Politics is compromise. Except in a totalitarian state it cannot be anything else. Yet Wilson felt intuitively certain that his judgments once he had made them were incontrovertibly right.

"I am sorry for those who disagree with me," he once confided to a friend. Why? "Because I know that they are wrong."

Although he recognized the necessity of compromise in politics, at the moment when his career and human history hung upon his willingness to accept it, he could not drink of that cup.

"There can be no compromise in individual morality," he told a Princeton class. "But there has to be a compromise, an average, in social morality. There is indeed an element of morality in the very fact of compromise on social undertakings." Wise, even profound words. If only he could have remembered them in 1919!

The difficulty lay in his very strength. He knew that God had ordered the universe from the beginning and that it was His will to use men for His own purposes. Because he felt himself an instrument of the divine purpose, Woodrow Wilson tended to think his motives purer, as he tended to think his mind better, than others. And since he lived most of his life within campus or parsonage walls, these assumptions were not challenged.

They never made a prude of him. As friend, father, husband he was a delightful companion—"one of the most kindly, courteous, considerate, genial and companionable of men," said S. G. Blythe.

Yet the world came to think of him as aloof, stiff, uncompromising.

Could it be that unconsciously he had absorbed in childhood the difference between the father in the pulpit and the father in the home, and that when he stepped into that high pulpit of the presidency he knew he had to lay aside the familiar manner and speak the words God gave to him?

Another strong influence, and one that helped shape his own character, was Edmund Burke. Wilson admired him above all other statesmen.

"A man of sensitive imagination and elevated moral sense, of a wide knowledge and capacity for affairs, he stood in the midst of the English nation speaking its moral judgments upon affairs, its character in political action, its purposes of freedom, equity, wide and equal progress."

Writing this in the 1890s in his essay, "The Interpreter of English Liberty," Wilson was not only describing Burke but also the man he hoped he might himself become. From Burke he took that tendency to view a nation as the embodiment of spiritual and moral qualities which was to lead him to his greatest triumph and then to his greatest failure.

"I am so tired of a merely talking profession," said Woodrow to his brother-in-law, Stockton Axson. "I want to do something."

When he became president of Princeton in 1902 he had taken one step at least out of the talking profession. He immediately began to do something. He proposed the preceptorial system as a means of raising the standards of instruction by providing a more intimate working relationship between students and teachers. He made headlines by proposing to abolish the eating clubs and establish an academic community that was truly democratic. And then he got into the argument over the graduate school that ended in his resignation and his entry into politics.

As anyone knows, there is politics aplenty on a college campus, and Wilson's fight with the trustees and the alumni over the eating clubs and the graduate school gave him first-hand experience with factions, influence, hidden deals and the necessity of compromise. To gain support against the affluent trustees, he visited the alumni in the West, as he was to visit the West twenty years later to gain support for the League of Nations. Neither trip succeeded. Wilson always thought that American politics, like British, should be so devised that a man could go to his constituency to prove himself right and those obstructing his program wrong. But American politics does not operate that way—a lesson he never learned.

He did see, however, that the United States would have to give up its isolationism. In *A History of the American People* he concluded that as we conquered international markets we would be forced to make sure that our ideals and principles had a chance to exist in those parts of the world where our interests lay. As early as 1887 he favored the idea of "governments joined with governments for the pursuit of common purposes in honorary equality and honorable subordination." The United States, because of its success with federalism, would he thought be a leader in this sort of international cooperation.

So when a combination of chances led him to the governorship of New Jersey in 1910 he had spent most of his life thinking about government and the last few years learning some practical lessons in politics. When the political bosses came to his Princeton home to sound him out, Jim Smith walked out into the beautiful garden Ellen Axson had made and, with a wistful look along its fine vista, said:

"What in hell a man wants to leave this for to get into politics is more than I can see."

Would-be reformers were certain that Wilson would do the bidding of the bosses who had pushed him through the convention.

He astonished both sides, first by refusing Jim Smith the senatorial appointment he coveted, then in a brilliant five-month campaign by pushing through a thoroughly liberal lot of laws which established direct primaries, controlled corrupt practices and utility rates, reformed city administrations and provided for employers' liability. He then toured the country expounding his program and, thanks to the split in the Republican Party brought on by Theodore Roosevelt, was elected president of the United States in 1912 just two years after his election as governor.

What progress! Had anyone ever walked into the White House so easily? No wonder then if he thought he could do wonders, and if he expected men to follow where he led.

He had promised the country the same sort of program he had given New Jersey. The New Freedom, he called it. Starting off, he showed that he had learned something from the Irish politicians of New Jersey. He even brought one of them along as his secretary—Joe Tumulty. Joe's job was to handle the press and the machine politicians. Wilson also took pains to keep in touch with the various factions of his party. As a result of convention maneuverings, he appointed William Jennings Bryan Secretary of State. Strategically, Bryan was Wilson's contact with the agrarian left and the West. Albert Burleson, Postmaster General, took care of operations on the Hill, especially among the Southern Democrats. William Gibbs McAdoo (Secretary of the Treasury) handled the liberal Democrats, while William B. Wilson (Secretary of Labor), a union man, kept in touch with labor.

By giving or withholding favors, these men could force a consensus upon the party and thus assure the success of Wilson's program. For Wilson had decided to depend upon his own party rather than a progressive coalition to carry his reforms through. His success in this may have laid the groundwork for a greater failure later on, for his reliance upon Democrats to carry the League proved disastrous.

During his first term, however, the strategy worked well. He got his reforms, and they were impressive—lowered tariffs, currency reform, the Federal Reserve Act, regulation of trusts, the Federal Trade Commission. He had entered the White House after years of thinking about the role of the president—"the vital place of action," as he called it, in the American system. He also believed in a strong cabinet, and though he did not appoint an eminent one, still he consulted its members regularly, running its sessions like a Quaker Meeting, taking opinions but not putting things to a vote. The president, he told Congress, is not merely a department of government, but "a human being trying to co-operate with other human beings in a common science." The chief fault in Wilson's idea of the presidency is that he failed to distinguish between the president as leader of his party and as chief of state. This was to lead him to one of his most tragic blunders.

There was no sign of this in the early months. But even then Democrats on the Hill felt far removed from him, and that sense of distance was also to be a factor at the climax of his career.

"What do you fellows make of Wilson?" a congressman asked a couple of leading Democratic legislators. "How do you get on with him?"

"Not a bit," said Claude Kitchin. "We never get near him."

"No more than you do," added Oscar Underwood.

Yet Wilson's first four years proved the fastest in our economic and social history up to that time. Even in foreign policy, despite the vexations and errors in his dealings with Mexico, he showed that he could put world order ahead of America's material interests. He was eager, as was Bryan, to make the United States the leader toward world peace; he had joined the American Peace Society in 1908 when he was president of Princeton. So he began immediately to negotiate treaties providing for investigation of disputes and a pledge to avoid war until an international commission had turned in its report. He supported arbitration of international disputes, sponsored a third Hague Conference, and toward the end of 1913 discussed with his personal emissary, Colonel E. M. House, a plan to get the nations of Europe to reduce their armaments.

As war flared, Wilson lost his beloved wife Ellen, on August 6, 1914. It was a bitter blow.

Pulling himself together, he sent Colonel House to see if the belligerents would agree to negotiate a peace. There was plenty of support around him. Theodore Roosevelt in 1915 came out for a league which would unite the nations against any aggressor. Charles W. Eliot of Harvard and Hamilton Holt were among the founders of the League to Enforce Peace, which was to have many eminent supporters. And in 1915 House was able to get from the British an agreement to Wilson's ideas for a permanent peace settlement which would include a holiday on naval and arms manufacture and a general guarantee of territorial integrity.

The British, however, naturally wanted to be sure that the United States would come into any such agreement. Wilson assured them that he regarded the league idea as essential to world peace. He saw that the United States must involve itself in the world community and must lead the way to world organization. On February 1, 1916, at Des Moines he called for an international tribunal and a joint guarantee of peace. On May 27 he stated that the war might have been avoided if it had been clear that the United States would have come to the aid of any nation that was attacked. Moral force, he felt, could and must be brought to bear against militarism and aggression, and this force could prevent war.

In the midst of his struggle to end the war he married Edith Bolling Galt on December 18, 1915, sixteen months after Ellen's death. The White House and the presidency were lonely places; he needed the support of a loving companion.

Wilson's effort to keep the United States out of the war was based not only on his conviction that circumstances could justify a nation in being "too proud to fight" but that by maintaining our neutrality we would be in a position to serve as peacemakers in a "peace without victory."

"Only a peace between equals can last," he said. A true prophecy. But such a peace was not to be.

Still he kept trying. He sent House to Europe again in 1916, to see whether a conference of belligerents could be arranged under American auspices, and was deeply disappointed when nothing came of it. At a meeting of the League to Enforce Peace in May of 1916 both he and Senator Henry Cabot Lodge spoke in favor of such a league. Wilson declared that the United States was "willing to become a partner in any reasonable association of nations formed in order to realize these objects [self-government, peace, freedom from aggression] and to make them secure against violation."

But were we really willing? Although the platforms of both parties in 1916 approved some form of world association to guarantee peace, the Senate debates early in 1917 gave warning that it would be a tough job to take the country into any such league.

On January 22, 1917, Wilson produced one of his great papers when he gave the Congress his vision of the foundations of world peace—"peace without victory." No nation should seek to rule another, and every people should be free to determine its own policy, "the little along with the great and powerful."

In a world that had gone mad with battle, Wilson nobly tried to preserve sanity. He has been criticized for assuming that foreign relations consisted of intercourse among civilized gentlemen controlled by enlightened public opinion, that decency and good will must prevail, and that a tone of moral admonition would bring the Germans around. It is further alleged that the moral tone he took soon became self-righteous and therefore led to chauvinism and to that hatred of "the Hun" which persisted for years among us and is not entirely dead yet. Yet none of his critics has supplied an alternative that would have had any hope of success.

For three years he tried to mediate, to stop the war, to halt attacks on unarmed ships. As Will Rogers put it, twirling his lariat, the President seemed to be losing the contest with Germany; he was five notes behind.

He got a good deal of encouragement and assistance from the peace movement, and even from Congress. In August, 1916, Congress had authorized him to invite the major powers to a conference once the war was over in order to establish an international peace-keeping organization, which was what the League to Enforce Peace had been urging. Wilson had already—if somewhat vaguely—supported its principles in his speech of the previous May. Indeed, it was instrumental in putting the League of Nations seed in Wilson's mind. Most of the Fourteen Points he enunciated had been brought to his attention by peace-minded men or organizations: freedom of the seas, the removal of trade barriers, fair treatment for backward regions and all the rest. The Emergency Peace Federation had presented just such a program to Congress and the President in February, 1915.

The Women's Peace Party, launched early in 1915, sent delegates (including Jane Addams) to an International Congress of Women which met at The Hague in April, then sent representatives to the prime ministers of the belligerent countries. They got little more than a polite brush-off, and even Wilson, in spite of a flood of supporting telegrams, refused to take up their suggestion of offering to mediate. Yet he was influenced by their ideas. When Wilson saw Jane Addams, he asked her for another copy of the peace terms the women had devised, he had so crumpled and soiled the one he had.

While Wilson held back, Rosika Schwimmer, one of the more active women, persuaded Henry Ford to charter the peace ship which undertook to get the boys out of the trenches before Christmas, 1915. It was her idea—and a good one—that if public opinion could be dramatically appealed to, responsible leaders would speak up and the senseless slaughter end. But the American press laughed it all to death and Ford deserted the ship at Christiania. Still, the Neutral Conference for Continuous Mediation which was set up at Stockholm did help to organize and popularize the demand for a reasonable peace. It also brought about informal talks between people who had the confidence of the belligerents.

As late as February, 1917, peace groups were urging the President not to declare war. But by this time the man who had kept us out of war and who had been too proud to fight had so far changed his mind that he showed contempt for ideas that had once been his own. On April 2 he asked Congress to declare war.

Before the overwhelming vote came on April 6, the stalwarts had their say. La Follette, in a brave and brilliant four-hour speech, exposed the fallacies of Wilson's arguments, showing that both sides were at fault and that we were, too, in failing to remain truly neutral.

Perhaps the saddest note of all was the about-face of the American Peace Society. Its official journal now argued that "We must help in the bayoneting of a normally decent German soldier in order to free him from a tyranny which he at present accepts as his chosen form of government. We must aid in the starvation and emaciation of a German baby in order that he, or at least his more sturdy little playmate, may grow up to inherit a different sort of government from that for which his father died." Most of the other peace groups followed suit.

Wilson felt that he had done his best to avoid war, knowing that America too would now get caught up in the war hatred and that the peace would be vindictive. Yet all his pronouncements were aimed at preventing just such an outcome. He saw the war as one for the freedom of all peoples, Germans included. Ironically, the nationalist aspirations nurtured by his statements were to grow faster than the international ideals he also sponsored, and were to overtake him at Paris.

"It is a fearful thing," he said, "to lead this great peaceful people into war. . . . But the right is more precious than peace, and we shall fight for the things which we have always carried nearest our hearts—for democracy, . . . for the rights and liberties of small nations" and "to make the world itself at last free."

Still attempting to preserve for America a moral superiority which would enable it to win a just peace, he said: "We desire no conquest, no dominion. We seek no indemnities for ourselves, no material compensation for the sacrifices we shall freely make."

We were in the war less than twenty months. Yet during that time Wilson, as William Allen White said, "created a world as it must be when his major dream is realized." His voice was heard around the earth—"the words of a righteous man spoken in the passion of a great exhortation." Ironically, Wilson was finding that only a war could put all his talents to full use—his moral earnestness, his gift of words, his knowledge of our history, his skill as a teacher, his growing ability as an administrator.

The mobilization of men, transportation, industry and food resources was astonishingly quick and efficient, and amazingly free of corruption. Americans truly felt in that day that they were working together to make the world safe for democracy. It was perhaps our last age of innocence, but it was elevating while it lasted and one looks back upon it today with a deep and piercing nostalgia.

Throughout those exciting, buoyant, sacrificial twenty months Wilson kept goading the world toward glimmering goals of peace with justice for all. Never before had it been given to a man to speak the dreams of all mankind and everywhere to find a response. So eloquent and so deeply felt were his words that men believed for once that the baseless fabric of this vision would not dissolve or prove an insubstantial pageant. Wilson convinced them that it could be.

It is true that Wilson kept his statements in a somewhat starry realm. He seems to have felt (wrote Samuel Flagg Bemis) that the United States would be so strong at the end of the war as to be able to dictate the terms of peace. But to have discussed specifics while the war was going on would merely have set the allies to quarreling amongst themselves.

So his great speeches—and quite rightly—were planned to keep the wagon of wartime effort hitched to the star of postwar peace with justice.

In January, 1918, he announced his Fourteen Points. They sounded like a charter for a new world: open covenants openly arrived at, freedom of the seas, equality in international trade, disarmament, equal rights for colonial populations, self-determination of peoples and a general association of nations to assure the continuing operation of international justice.

"We believe," he told a joint session of Congress a month later, "that our own desire for a new international order under which reason and justice and the common interests of mankind shall prevail is the desire of enlightened men everywhere."

Then came the four points in his Mount Vernon speech: the destruction of every arbitrary power that can disturb the peace of the world; the settlement of every question by free acceptance of the people immediately concerned; the consent of nations to be governed in their conduct as individuals are governed in theirs; an organization to preserve peace by checking every invasion of right.

In the Fourth Liberty Loan speech in September he again asserted that the "indispensable instrumentality" was the league of nations which must be a part, "the most essential part, of the peace settlement itself."

Wilson was getting strong encouragement from the radical wing of the Liberal Party in England. They favored a fair and just peace; they kept supplying him with documents and pamphlets, often through Colonel House. They believed he could lead the world to the kind of peace he and they wanted, but in England they had to buck a strong current headed by Lloyd George, a former antiwar man who had become a very vindictive wartime prime minister.

This liberal group, which included Ramsay MacDonald and Norman Angell, had set up the Union of Democratic Control shortly after war broke out. The four principal points they stood for were clearly echoed in Wilson's more eloquent restatements of them: no transfer of territory without consent, no treaties to be made without the sanction of Parliament, a foreign policy devised not to maintain a balance of power but aimed toward concerted action to build international agreements and abiding peace, reduction and nationalization of armaments.

The League of Nations Society began its work in England as early as 1915, and throughout the world it attracted a valiant band of distinguished men and women who knew that a just peace had to be worked for. These leaders looked to Wilson as the one man who might materialize their dreams. They welcomed his leadership. Wilson, in turn, made good use of the material they sent him. The idea that the United States could no longer avoid entanglement in the world's wars and therefore must help to preserve peace came from the editorials of Norman Angell appearing in *The New Republic*. The Liberty Loan speech was a response to Ray Stannard Baker's report from London that British labor and liberal groups needed Wilson's support.

"National purposes have fallen more and more into the background, and the common purpose of enlightened mankind has taken their place," said Wilson.

It was Wilson's skill with words and ideas, says Herbert Hoover, that turned the German request for an armistice into a complete surrender—one of the most monumental feats of international action in history.

"Single-handed he had maneuvered the Germans from their island of safety where they might have negotiated with their armies still standing, into almost complete surrender." He also brought the allies around to a peace which was to be based upon the Fourteen Points, the chief exception being Britain's insistence that freedom of the seas must be further discussed.

When the armistice came and the war was won, no man had ever stood higher among men than Woodrow Wilson. Yet in this mighty growth the worm was already gnawing.

Wilson had made the mistake of asking the voters to return a Democratic Congress in the 1918 election, as an essential support to carrying out his plans for a just peace. This was a logical enough sequel to his earlier decision to rely upon Democrats rather than upon a liberal coalition to put through his domestic reforms. But it was strategically wrong-headed. People had been thinking of Wilson as their leader; now he forced them to think of him as the Democrats'. Republicans took it as a rebuff and a challenge. The people gave Wilson a Republican Congress.

Even then Wilson might have appealed to liberal Republicans to help him forge a just peace. The tangible way of doing this would have been to appoint a couple of leading Republicans to the Peace Commission—such men as Taft, Root, or Hughes, all of them favoring a league to enforce peace. Instead, Wilson went himself—thus inevitably involving himself in all the postwar quarrels of Europe, and taking with him men who had no weight either in America or abroad. Only one of them, Henry White, was a nominal Republican, but he had no political influence.

Despite all his fine words, Wilson never succeeded in explaining to Americans why he must go to Europe. It was easy for the opposition to say that he went in order to be applauded, and the tremendous ovations he received there seemed to bear them out.

It was, of course, unprecedented for an American president to leave the country, and Americans generally do not approve unprecedented behavior in a president. Wilson seems to have felt that only he had all the facts in mind and could deal with all the issues at hand; there may have been a touch of megalomania in it. Perhaps every good president must be so touched.

Wilson had failed to draw up a plan of action. He wanted to sense the situation at first hand, meet the leaders, convert them to his principles as he believed he had converted the world and—this was his dominant idea—to see to it that the League of Nations should be embedded in the treaty of peace.

The leaders of Europe who sat down with Wilson at the conference table came with shopping lists in hand. Wilson, says Herbert Hoover, was "a menacing intruder in the concepts of British, French and Italian statesmen, and a threat to their secret treaties dividing all Europe." The people of the world might agree with Wilson—up to the point where their own interests came in. But then they expected their leaders to bring back annexations and reparations if they wanted to stay in power.

This ambivalance—the desire for a just peace and the demand for special rewards and privileges—spelled defeat for Wilson's high aims before he ever reached Europe. France went back to her ancient policy of trying to dominate the Continent, and Britain to her ancient policy of keeping any one nation from dominance. And while Wilson struggled against these old reflexes in his effort to bring a new world to birth, his own country was returning to its ancient policy of keeping out of Europe's quarrels.

The European allies had bound themselves by secret treaties to support each other's claims. They now held the territories they wanted. Wilson wanted nothing comparable, and this very lack of demands left him little to bargain with. To be sure, Europe depended heavily upon the United States for food to keep alive and money to get the wheels turning again, and Wilson might have used his position as grocer and as money-lender to whip them into line. At the very moment when he sat with them in conference, Herbert Hoover was operating a continent-wide system of transportation, communication and supply to feed Europe and to stamp out disease. Without this American aid the whole of Europe would have collapsed in hunger, disease, and economic breakdown. Perhaps a tougher or less idealistic bargainer than Wilson would have made capital of this.

But he still believed in his ideals and in their power to move men.

"It is moral force as much as physical force that has defeated the effort to subdue the world," he said at Carlisle, his mother's birthplace. "Words have cut as deep as swords."

And still he might have moved them, had he insisted upon his own principle of open discussion at Paris. A great drama was playing itself out there, but behind closed doors. If the press had been given complete access to what was going on, public opinion might still have been aroused. The French press was under strict

[256]

government control, but American newsmen, hungry for material and generally—in the beginning, at least—favoring Wilson, would have made an exposé of every selfish demand, every vindictive article. Yet they were kept in the dark until they too began to suspect Wilson along with the rest.

William Allen White wrote that Wilson was as honest as daylight but could not bear daylight. Drama irked him, so he avoided it. The result was that he traded the substance of Europe's demands for the shadow of America's ideals.

Harold Nicolson, a bitter critic of Wilson, said that few diplomatic conferences have operated in such secrecy as the Peace Conference, and that under this cover one after another of Wilson's Fourteen Points was violated.

"The collapse of President Wilson at the Paris Peace Conference is one of the major tragedies of modern history," he concluded.

Other critics, including his Secretary of State Robert Lansing, criticize him for having worked too much alone, separated from his advisers and spending day after day in the Council of Four where he was no match for Lloyd George, Clemenceau and Orlando. Since Wilson had no complete plan, they worked usually from a French or British draft, which meant that Wilson had to operate as an objector and obstructor.

Quickly seeing that Wilson was afraid of losing the League, they forced him to give up point after point in exchange for supporting his League, and pacified him by giving lip service to the Fourteen Points in the very act of scuttling them. Thus they created the preposterous "free city" of Danzig which was really Polish, prevented the logical *Anschluss* of Austria with Germany, and continued colonialism under the name of mandates. Such verbal hocus-pocus duped Wilson into abandoning his principles at the very moment when he thought he was fulfilling them.

Only the United States could save Europe from starvation and bankruptcy. Yet Wilson was too much a gentleman to take advantage of this. So he surrendered in the matter of reparations and let Germany be saddled with two hundred times the load which it had imposed on France in their previous war. He surrendered again on the Rhineland, Shantung, the Saar.

The real villains were quite willing in addition to throw the blame upon Wilson. So Lloyd George, Clemenceau and Wilson each agreed to issue a statement on why Fiume had to be denied to the Italians. Wilson did so; the others did not. When Wilson inquired why they had broken their word, they blandly replied that his own statement had covered the matter so well as to make others superfluous. So Wilson alone had to shoulder the hatred of Italy.

His position was difficult because he was always trying to refuse something to somebody, and thus he appeared like a willful obstructionist. He put up a good fight against greedy, vindictive and war-weary men. It is a strange irony that he has been blamed for the errors of Versailles rather than they.

He knew that the three premiers were creating the conditions for the next war and tried to tell them so. At the end of one eloquent argument, Clemenceau with tears in his eyes, said:

"Mr. President, I want to say that you are not only a great man but you are a good one, and I am with you."

Then they went back to their bargaining again. Soon Clemenceau was saying to the President:

"You have a heart of steel."

"But," said Wilson, "I have not the heart to steal."

This bit of dialogue epitomizes many dreary hours of negotiation.

Yet when it was all over, Lloyd George could say in all sincerity:

"You have brought the two countries closer together than any other individual in history."

Wilson was damned by his perfectionist supporters, who expected him to achieve all his aims, and by the cynical opposition who had no faith in his ideals. While young William Bullitt was resigning from the American delegation because he thought

[258]

Wilson had sacrificed his principles, House was urging him to give in so as to save the League. Secretary of State Lansing opposed having the League in the treaty at all, which led Wilson to exclude him from any real part in the negotiations.

Lansing, a somewhat precise and colorless man with a legalistic mind, complained that Wilson rarely consulted him, never accepted his advice, and ignored whatever memoranda he forwarded. Wilson, he said, gave his delegates no plan of work and no opportunity to prepare and advise him. By his secret diplomacy he lost point after point instead of insisting upon open sessions that would have rallied public opinion behind him.

Lansing, who favored judicial means of composing disputes, argued that Wilson so devised the League as to give the power of decision to political bodies. This, said Lansing, would have led to political compromises instead of justice. It apparently did not occur to him that in international disputes no one wants justice—he wants what he wants. This is the paradox of international settlements—that juridical decisions will be ignored, while political decisions based on power are bound to be unfair to someone. Wilson, however, saw that power could not be ignored and hoped that by providing a public forum for international affairs he could rally public opinion so as to force just decisions.

Lansing also opposed the idea of mutual aid against aggressors (Article X). He preferred a negative guarantee not to encroach on the territory of others. He disliked the dominance of the great powers in the League, as well as the system of mandates. Wilson's own Secretary of State was thus against him in the most important items of his design for world peace. He had that to contend with, too.

When Wilson insisted on producing the text for the League of Nations Covenant during the ten days that remained before he had to return to America, Lansing was aghast. He thought that the treaty was "unwise and unworkable, that it was conceived in intrigue and fashioned in cupidity, and that it would produce rather than prevent wars." And he said British statesmen agreed with him.

But Wilson's greatest failure was in the sphere of economics, where, despite his legislation against the trusts at home, he had the least knowledge and interest. The League was not designed to grapple with the commercial rivalries which motivated world politics. It was to take another war before such cooperation as the Common Market and the General Agreement on Tariffs and Trade could come to birth.

Yet Wilson was less faulty in his economics than Lord Keynes, who denounced the Versailles Treaty for imposing impossible conditions upon Germany, conditions which would ruin the economy of Europe. Despite Keynes' predictions, the output of iron, steel and coal increased. Instead of falling, production rose beyond demand. In each of the six years preceding 1939 Germany spent on rearmament alone seven times as much as Keynes said she could possibly pay in reparations.

Wilson's critics usually overlook the fact that, in addition to negotiating the peace, he had to give his attention at the same time to many other problems. Europe's railways, communications and mines were disrupted, her crops short, pestilence threatening. The French killed every effort to raise the blockade on food to Germany and neutral Europe. Five revolutions occurred in Hungary while Herbert Hoover was trying to feed its people. Italy refused to let food pass to Jugoslavia in retaliation against Jugoslav outrages against Italians. It was in such an atmosphere that Wilson, the idealist, had to work for results.

Latter-day critics have had a field day with Wilson's idealism, finding in it the seed of every failure at Versailles. Yet as Paul Birdsall points out, "idealism and justice are the very rudiments of common sense. They amount to a practical realization of what the traffic will reasonably bear. They require the sacrifice of immediate vengeance for the sake of long-term enlightened self-interest." It was reactionary nationalism in Europe and America which defeated Wilson.

Even as he saw his cherished ideal of a just peace being undermined by the erosive hatreds of Europe, he persuaded himself that all could be recovered if the League were incorporated into the treaty. For hatreds would die down, and in the process of working together, and before the bar of public opinion, governments would through the League learn to behave like gentlemen. The Covenant of the League was so interwoven with the peace settlement that they could not be separated. Therefore, Wilson persuaded himself, all the nations would have to accept it. And in time, as they lived under it, they would be molded by its high principles.

So he told himself. And who can say that, if America had trusted him, he might not have been right?

Lansing and House, with the benefit of hindsight, said he should have included in the treaty only the broad principles of a League, that this would have passed the Senate, and that a League governed by a commission which the treaty could have set up would then have been able to function even without Senate approval.

In Wilson's mind the League was idealism made practical: principles embodied in a sacred covenant which public opinion would force the wily rulers of old Europe to honor. By coming into such an arrangement, the United States could see to it that European quarrels never again came to the point of general war.

It was a bitter irony that the concessions he had to make in order to have his League were the very ones that ultimately killed it.

Despite the endless provocations, he had remained patient, calm and conciliatory in conference, well-informed on most issues, humane, and administratively competent. To him alone goes the credit of having established for the first time in history a systematic and powerful organization of nations to keep the peace. His too is the credit for incorporating the Permanent Court of International Justice, the International Labor Organization, the right of all peoples to political independence. Despite its faults, the peace treaty brought Europe closer to ethnic independence than it had ever been before or has ever been since.

So, while American aid was saving Europe from famine and pestilence by providing ninety-five per cent of the materials and money, Wilson was trying to save Europe for the future too. "His forceful and clear mind, his administrative strength and his courage," according to Herbert Hoover, were always in evidence.

Wilson left for the United States on February 14, 1919, in order to carry out his duties at home. He returned exactly a month later.

Lansing complains that since Wilson left no instructions with his commission, the whole month was wasted.

"The whole world wants peace," wrote Lansing. "The President wants his League. I think that the world will have to wait."

On June 28, 1919, the treaty of peace was signed in Paris to the booming of cannon. But on Capitol Hill in Washington a *New York Times* correspondent was unable to find a single Republican senator who thought it could be accepted without revision.

At last, on June 29, having done the best he could, Wilson sailed for home. He had tried to save Europe from itself. Now—though he was not yet fully aware of it—he was going to have to save the United States from itself.

Wilson had gone to Paris in the first place against his physician's advice. In the spring of 1919 he had had a bad attack of influenza followed by asthma which badly interrupted his sleep. Never robust, he had needed sleep to keep him healthy. And under the pressure of his many commitments, he had abandoned the health regime which had kept him going. At the very moment when he was to need all his strength, his health was balanced on a precarious fulcrum.

On July 4, Wilson was in mid-Atlantic on his way home. To

the soldiers and sailors sailing with him on the *U.S.S. George Washington* (he had insisted on taking them aboard to help get the boys home from Europe) he said, speaking from the after hatch:

"This is the most tremendous Fourth of July that men ever imagined, for we have opened its franchises to all the world."

A few days later New York gave him the most enthusiastic reception the city had ever seen. He was nearly overwhelmed by the rush of people who wanted to shake his hand or even touch his coat.

The next day at noon he went before the Senate. When he entered the chamber, he looked entirely well again. He walked with elastic step, good color had replaced the grayness his face had taken on at Paris along with a sag and twitching of the features, his figure was erect and confident, and his eyes had the brightness of an alert and dedicated man.

"My services and all the information I possess will be at your disposal and at the disposal of your Committee on Foreign Relations at any time, either informally or in session, as you may prefer," he told them. He went on to explain that, throughout the long sessions of peacemaking, the framers had realized again and again that the only way they could make peace was to set up a world body to maintain justice among nations.

"What had seemed a counsel of perfection had come to seem a plain counsel of necessity," he told them. And so "The League of Nations was not merely an instrument to adjust and remedy old wrongs under a new treaty of peace; it was the only hope of mankind." From now on the United States could not escape its position of world leadership.

"The stage is set, the destiny disclosed. It has come about by no plan of our conceiving but by the hand of God who led us into this way. We cannot turn back."

It was a noble peroration, but only a handful of men on the Republican side applauded and some did not even bother to rise as the President left the hall. The treaty was too bound up with

Wilson—the man who had asked the nation to defeat them in the recent election—for them to swallow it. Many of them were still angry that a Democrat had run the country during its greatest war effort and, worse, had done a good job of it; they had not even been able to dig up any real scandals or graft. Republicans, moreover, did not put it past Wilson to run for a third term. They therefore had to thwart and humiliate him.

They had an able leader in the "lean and acid" Senator Henry Cabot Lodge who, since the campaign of 1916, had been a bitter enemy of Wilson and who was now—thanks to a majority of one in the Senate—Chairman of the Committee on Foreign Relations. Fate had stacked the cards against Wilson and, as time would prove, against world peace.

Lodge was small, aristocratic, cold, precise. Proud of his learning, he had resented it when Wilson's election to the presidency had made him Washington's leading scholar. Lodge cherished the fact that Wilson had once made a faulty classical allusion and also that he did not quote widely from the classics in his speeches, as any true scholar would naturally do, at least by Lodge's standards.

Henry Adams, a fellow Bostonian, had summed him up this way: "Cabot's lofty principles compel him to help no member of his family but himself."

It was this regard for self—a self which he believed Wilson had undermined and violated—which was to be a prime factor in a vital American decision.

We have seen how, in 1916, shortly after Wilson's inauguration, Lodge had come out strongly for a world league when speaking to a convention of the League to Enforce Peace. Wilson—whose position until then was unknown—had eloquently backed him up. Since the League was largely Republican, it had looked as if partisanship on this issue could be avoided.

The trouble began during the campaign of 1916 when Lodge, who naturally resented Wilson's use of his office as wartime President to appeal for the election of Democrats, took the trail against him. Relying merely on hearsay, Lodge charged that Wilson after sending a strong protest against the sinking of the *Lusitania* had followed it with a secret note telling the Germans not to take it seriously—he was merely trying to satisfy outraged opinion at home.

Wilson bluntly answered, "Let me say that the statement made by Senator Lodge is untrue."

Lodge took this as a personal insult. The ridicule which followed in the press was more than this carefully groomed and bearded aristocrat could take.

Thereafter he made it his business to destroy Wilson while at the same time convincing himself that he was a loyal patriot defending his country against a man who, in his own words, was always "thinking of the country only in terms of Wilson, never of the country's interests alone."

"The key to all he did was that he thought of everything in terms of Wilson. In other words, Mr. Wilson in dealing with every great question thought first of himself."

Psychologists have told us enough of the mechanism of projection so that we can easily see through Cabot Lodge, who in turn saw in Wilson the very fault he could not acknowledge in himself. And time had made plain the relative calibers of the two men. The tragedy was that they had to shoot it out against each other, and that the world had to pay for the damage done.

When Wilson proposed a League for Peace to Congress early in 1917, Lodge replied with a lengthy and carefully prepared rebuttal, setting forth the usual isolationist, nationalist position.

The next year Lodge met with two other men whom Wilson had offended—George Harvey, an old supporter, and Theodore Roosevelt, to whom Wilson had denied a command in France. They met at the home of former Senator Beveridge of Massachusetts, who also opposed the League idea. Roosevelt and Beveridge promised 20,000 subscribers to Harvey's *War Weekly* which would spearhead the attack on Wilson and his League.

Wilson only added fuel to their already well prepared combustibles when he went to Europe without any real Republican on the peace commission—the obvious reason being, of course, that he would have had to take Lodge, the Chairman of the Senate Committee on Foreign Relations. And Lodge would have spiked the League. Indeed, he handed to Henry White as he was leaving for Paris a secret memorandum for Lloyd George and Clemenceau, stating that no treaty of peace would pass the Senate if it had the League in it. White never showed the memorandum, but Lodge's position had been made clear.

When the war ended and Wilson had been wildly welcomed in Paris, an ailing Roosevelt called Lodge to his hospital bed to plot the rejection of the League. They agreed that the country was for it and that it would therefore have to be killed slowly, by alteration and discussion and confusion and reservations. A few days later Lodge lectured the Senate on its right to revise and reject treaties.*

When Lodge asked Senator Watson from Indiana to keep the Republican senators in line during the fight against the League (which did not yet exist), Watson said:

"Senator, I don't see how we are ever going to defeat this proposition. It appears to me that eighty per cent of the people are for it."

"Ah, my dear James," said Lodge, "I do not propose to try to beat it by direct frontal attack, but by the indirect method of reservations." He then explained his strategy.

On February 14, 1919, Wilson presented the Covenant of the League of Nations to the Peace Conference, and the next day it was widely praised in the American press. A few days later, former President Taft, firm supporter of the League, was worrying about the opposition already apparent in the Senate—"the vicious narrowness of Reed, the explosive ignorance of Poindexter, the ponderous Websterian language and lack of stamina of Borah, the vanity of Lodge. . . . It is their American selfishness, their American littleness, blinding them to the real interests of the

* See Alan Cranston, *The Killing of the Peace*, pp. 41–45.

world, that arouses me," he concluded. He had good cause to be worried.

The next blow at Wilson was a senatorial round robin, signed by more than one third of the senators and engineered, of course, by Lodge, which stated that the League of Nations "as it was understood was to be proposed" could not pass. Lodge then skillfully introduced it on the floor at a time when it was clearly out of order, so that objection would be made and it could not be put to a vote. For if it had been voted on, it would have been voted down. It all went as he had planned. The world had been put on notice that Wilson could not expect the necessary two-thirds support.

Wilson, back in Paris in March, reluctantly pushed through the four amendments which Taft and others assured him would take care of Senate objections. Yet Wilson had no sooner got the amendment relating to the Monroe Doctrine than Lodge began denouncing it. As Senator Williams of Mississippi sourly pointed out:

"His objection to the exclusion of mention of the Monroe Doctrine increased to virulence when he was faced with the inclusion of it."

Meanwhile support of the League swept across the country in the form of resolutions by all sorts of associations—farm, labor, merchant, professional, church, and women's groups, even including the D.A.R. A popular vote would have adopted it over-whelmingly. The League to Enforce Peace, with solid Republican leadership, had 10,000 officers, 50,000 volunteers and 300,-000 hand-picked members throughout the country who busily promoted resolutions, held state conventions, and brought pressure to bear on senators.

The opposition was in deep gloom until Harvey got $150,000 from Mellon and another large but unspecified amount from Henry Clay Frick to fight the League.

When the peace treaty came to the Senate, Lodge, who by clever parliamentary moves had gained control of a majority of the Foreign Relations Committee, blandly announced that he would read the entire treaty to the committee before asking them to consider it. That would use up two weeks of valuable time.

When Senator Watson, Lodge's collaborator, got to worrying about the possibility that the Lodge strategy might defeat itself if Wilson were to accept the reservations, the Senator from Massachusetts said:

"But, my dear James, you do not take into consideration that hatred that Woodrow Wilson has for me personally. Never under any set of circumstances in this world could he be induced to accept a treaty with Lodge reservations appended to it."

This was no doubt an accurate guess, and one that came from the bottom of Lodge's own heart. But Watson was not satisfied.

"But that seems to be rather a slender thread on which to hang so great a cause," he said.

"A slender thread!" said the strategist. "Why it is as strong as any cable with its strands wired and twisted together."

Lodge's tactic of delay soon began to pay dividends. Taft, in coming out for reservations, had caused a rift in the League to Enforce Peace. Its collapse put an end to effective organized support for the League. Some good speeches were made in favor of the League on the Senate floor, but the Democrats had no one to match Lodge in parliamentary strategies.

On August 19 (1919) the members of the Foreign Relations Committee went to the White House, where they subjected Wilson to a barrage of questions which seemed designed to wring out of him a confession that the treaty had been written by the British, that he had blundered badly in allowing the Japanese to take over German rights in Shantung, and that he had made secret agreements in Paris. Some of the questions seemed no better than polite heckling, or calculated to catch the President in lapses of memory or to get him in a corner on extraneous questions and then to use the result against the League.

There was irony in the exchange between him and his successor-to-be, Warren Harding, when Wilson had to instruct the man who was to be made famous by Teapot Dome as to the nature of moral obligations. But the committee had a point in their worry about what would happen if an American member of the League Council should vote to move against an aggressor, thus binding Congress either to confirm his judgment—possibly against its wish—or to veto it and show the United States to the world as having two minds.

The lengthy conference changed nobody's mind.

Meanwhile the committee was hearing witnesses—preferably those opposed to the treaty. In a confidential letter to a friend, Lansing said of his treatment by the committee:

> To tell you the truth the whole proceeding disgusted me with the principal actors and their manifest object. The personal animosity to the President and the endeavor to discredit him before the American people are only too evident. Appreciating this my position was embarrassing because I did not propose to give the slightest aid to such an unworthy purpose. The character of the questions asked, the public hearings, the unjustifiable and what seemed to me undignified comments of some of the Senators are so contrary to the usual sedate and temperate conduct of senatorial business that I really felt ashamed to think that I was before a committee of the Senate of the United States.*

Lansing had found plenty to criticize in Wilson, had felt continuously frustrated under him in Paris, and did not favor the League. Even so, his sense of fair play rebelled at what the committee was doing to Wilson and the treaty.

A few days later (August 23) the committee began amending the treaty. Before finishing, it had more than fifty amendments, and the *New York Times* was disgusted, along with a good many other papers. "This small body of Senators repudiates the work and signatures of the plenipotentiaries, it maims and transforms

* From a personal letter to Edward N. Smith of Watertown, New York, dated August 18, 1919, in the possession of his son, Chard Powers Smith.

the whole meaning of the Treaty by amendments—some fifty of them in a day, we might say in a bunch. If such things can be, what respect and consideration will be shown to plenipotentiaries of the United States in future serious negotiations?"

But Hearst's papers and the *Chicago Tribune* were reaching a much wider audience with their own particular brand of vilification.

Six disgusted Democrats on the committee turned in a minority report which said:

"We deplore the long and unnecessary delay to which the treaty has been subjected while locked up in the committee, whose majority decisions and recommendations were from the start a foregone conclusion. They could have been made in July as in September and would have been the same."

The delay, of course, was what Lodge wanted. It gave Hearst time to do his work. It allowed time for confusion and boredom and disgust to set in.

On September 16 the Secretary of the Senate began the two-week task of reading the Versailles Treaty to an empty chamber. Two more weeks of delay and confusion and behind-the-scenes maneuvering.

But Wilson, convinced at last that he must go out to the people, had left Washington to cross the continent in order to save the League.

He had no doubt made mistakes all along the way—first in failing to take a Republican delegation to Paris, then perhaps in returning to Paris instead of remaining in the United States where he might have stiffened in what he would agree to, then in the air of aloofness which had created the impression that he was arrogant and unwilling to compromise. A few small compromises in July might have saved more drastic ones later on, but Wilson could not bear the thought of compromise; there had been enough of that in Paris, and remembering those painfully long hours he feared that any tampering with the treaty as it stood would bring the whole structure down.

He had not believed that the Senate would really reject the treaty, for how could they send him back to beg Germany for new terms?

But now his fighting blood was up. For three weeks he barnstormed the continent, talking to huge and usually enthusiastic audiences. He spoke in a friendly folk idiom without talking down to them.

"As I came through that line of youngsters in khaki a few minutes ago," he said in Columbus, "I felt that I could salute them because I had done the job in the way I promised them I would do it, and when this treaty is accepted, men in khaki will not have to cross the seas again. That is the reason I believe in it."

Moving westward, he explained that the treaty was made to protect the weak from the strong, that the alleged loss of sovereignty was an illusion, that under the treaty no secret agreements could ever again be valid.

He tried to remove the issue from partisan politics, pointing out that both party platforms had advocated a league of nations. He argued that the document he had brought from Paris was "penetrated throughout with the principles to which America has devoted her life," and that the idea of a league had been advanced twenty years ago by Republicans like Senator Burton of Ohio. He reminded them that both houses of Congress had several times authorized the president to invite the world's governments to a conference to set up a system of international arbitration. "Now that they have got it, they do not like it," he said at Billings.

"If there is a better scheme," he said at Kansas City, "I for one will subscribe to it, but I want to say now, as I said the other night, it is a case of 'put up or shut up.'

"My ancestors were troublesome Scotchmen," he went on, "and among them were some of that famous group that were known as Covenanters. Very well, then, here is the Covenant of the League of Nations. I am a Covenanter!"

Wilson grew whiter, his face thinner and more fatigued as the trip wore on. He suffered from bad headaches. But he would not give up. He told correspondents that his constitution might be exhausted, but he would live on his by-laws for a while. The speeches went on, admirable in the way they made difficult issues plain.

On Shantung he said, "Are you going to institute war against Japan and France and England to get Shantung back for China?" And he pointed out that while Great Britain and France were retaining their interests in China, Japan had promised to give up the sovereign rights Germany had, retaining only the economic interest.

Arguing that the League was China's only chance, he said, "It affords the only hope that China can get of the restoration to herself not only of the sovereignty of Shantung, but of the sovereignty other nations as well have taken from her."

Pointing out that he had taken back to Paris and pushed through the alterations suggested by the Senate Foreign Relations Committee, he said, "To hear some men talk about the League of Nations you would suppose that it was a trap set for America."

Opponents kept drawing attention to little details in a way which destroyed the perspective of the great plan.

"Clear the deck of these criticisms, that really have nothing in them, and look at the thing in its large aspect, in its majesty," he begged.

At Portland he read a brief statement:

> *Nations must unite as men unite in order to preserve peace and order. The great nations must be so united as to be able to say to any single country, "You must not go to war," and they can say that effectively when the country desiring war knows that the force which the united nations place behind peace is irresistible.*

That statement had been made by Senator Lodge at Union College in 1915, Wilson revealed. "I entirely concur in Senator

Lodge's conclusion," said Wilson, "and hope I shall have his co-operation in bringing about the desired result."

To the argument that the League would drag us into war he replied, "My calm judgment is that it is ninety-nine per cent insurance against war. . . .

"If the fight is big enough to draw the United States in, I predict they will be drawn in anyhow, and if it is not big enough to bring them in inevitably, they can go in or stay out according to their own decision."

As for the old bromide about entangling alliances, it was the League and only the League which would put an end to them. "The day we have left behind us was a day of alliances."

But the basic question, he kept saying, was very simple. "Shall the great sacrifice that we made in this war be in vain, or shall it not?"

At Pueblo, Colorado, on September 25 he made one of his most eloquent speeches.

"The one effective move for obtaining peace," he said, "is by an agreement among all the great powers in which each should pledge itself not only to abide by the decisions of a common tribunal but to back its decisions by force."

He concluded: "There is one thing that the American people always rise to and extend their hand to, and that is the truth of justice and of liberty and of peace. We have accepted that truth and we are going to be led by it, and it is going to lead us, and through us the world, out into pastures of quietness and peace such as the world never dreamed of before."

At four the next morning Wilson's physician, Admiral Grayson woke Joe Tumulty, Wilson's secretary, to say that the President was very ill. Together they went to his drawing room on the train. The President's face was white, one side sagged perceptibly, and tears were running down his cheeks. When he tried to move, his left arm and leg refused to respond. Still he did not want to give up, fearing that Lodge would call him a quitter and that the treaty would be lost.

But it was obvious he could make no more speeches. With a pilot engine ahead, the President's train raced back to Washington.

For seven vital months Wilson was too ill to take charge of the situation. For the first weeks he was desperately sick. "For days life hung in the balance," according to his wife. As he got better, she stood between him and anything that might irritate him or cause a relapse. Only the most essential matters were brought before him and she, without any training to guide her, decided what those things should be. Then she condensed them to a brief summary of her own which tended to shield him from anything exciting or troubling.

The battle droned on in the Senate. Lodge had his hands full as he tried to hold in line the men who wanted no League at all, those who wanted a League but with considerable modification, and those who would accept mild reservations. The mild ones threatened to join with the Democrats, while the irreconcilables with the colorful and orotund William E. Borah as their leader kept coming close to upsetting Lodge's precariously balanced applecart.

The mood of the country still seemed to be pro-League. Polls kept showing it. Petitions for the League kept issuing from such important organizations as the American Federation of Labor, The American Bankers Association and the American Bar Association. Even the Massachusetts Republican State Convention defied Lodge in his own bailiwick by approving the Covenant.

But Lodge was not discouraged. He still intended to send Wilson a treaty so altered that he would be bound to veto it. On November 8 the Senate began voting on Lodge's fourteen reservations. By November 17 it had passed them. The Democrats failed entirely to substitute milder reservations. As it now stood the treaty allowed the United States to decide for itself when and under what conditions it would withdraw from the League; it renounced American responsibility for the territorial integrity of any other country or for the use of its armed forces except by joint resolution of Congress; it left the United States free to refuse mandates, to decide for itself what was or was not the League's business and what was a Monroe Doctrine issue, to repudiate the Shantung settlement and any disarmament plans the League might make, and several other matters.

Supporters of the League were thrown into confusion. Should they support the amended treaty or reject it? The League to Enforce Peace was itself riven apart. But Wilson was clear. In a letter to Senator Hitchcock intended for all Democratic senators, he said: "I sincerely hope that the friends and supporters of the treaty will vote against the Lodge resolution of ratification." And so they did.

Thus by a bitter irony it was at the command of the man who had conceived and fought for the treaty that it was killed in the Senate. The men who voted against it were the Democrats who had fought for it and the Republican irreconcilables who had fought against it. Lodge and his coalition were for it!

The country was bitterly disappointed and sick at heart, but no one seemed able to offer a solution. Lodge managed to defeat Senator Underwood's resolution for a conciliation committee. The League to Enforce Peace came out for the Lodge resolutions as the only way out. House, himself now a sick man, wrote two letters advising Wilson that having rejected their amendments he should now let the Senate work out the problem in whatever way it could. It would then be up to the Allies to decide whether to accept the reservations. But it appears that Mrs. Wilson never let her husband see the letters.

In January (1920) Wilson wrote a Jackson Day message proposing that the election that year be used as a solemn referendum on the issue.

By another of those ironies which surrounded Wilson, at the very moment when the treaty had been consigned to limbo by the Senate, he called on the Council of the League of Nations to meet in Paris, as it had been agreed he would do when enough countries had ratified the treaty to make it operative.

After a good deal more conferring and skirmishing in the search for a compromise, the Foreign Relations Committee reported the treaty back again—with the same reservations. And the debate dragged on.

On March 19, the treaty with the reservations was defeated once again.

In June the Republicans got into a bitter fight at their National Convention over the League issue. When it was finally suggested that the Convention support membership based on the Lodge reservations, Lodge violently disagreed! Now that they had successfully killed the League, he was done with them.

In his own book, *The Senate and the League of Nations*, Lodge tried to put the whole blame on Wilson. Written after Wilson's death, it gives the impression of a man stabbing repeatedly at a corpse and therefore does nothing to help Lodge's stature.

He argued that a real idealist would have accepted the reservations.

"No one could have destroyed such a vast opportunity except the man to whom it was given, and in this work of destruction, unaided and alone, Mr. Wilson was entirely successful."

This charge comes with a sickening thud from the man who had devoted himself day and night to defeating the League and to fixing the blame upon Wilson.

To justify himself he wrapped himself in the flag, certain that he would find plenty of support in this cheap gesture:

"I have loved but one flag and I cannot share that devotion and give affection to the mongrel banner invented for a league."

So he let the secret out in spite of himself. He would not have accepted any league at all, but he wanted to fix the blame upon Wilson for all time and wrote a book to be sure of it. It is a book which even now leaves a very bad taste in the mouth.

Not that Lodge was the only one to blame for the fiasco in the

Senate. Wilson, because of his stiffness, his somewhat holier-than-thou attitude, his assumption that what he wanted was inevitably right, bears some of the blame too.

What had happened to the political skill and parliamentary finesse which had been his when he had accomplished so many domestic reforms, or even during the terrible ordeal at Paris? As he became the messiah of a cause, did he also acquire the inescapable fate of messiahship—to be rejected of men and martyred? Do we still have to murder the god, the embodiment of the ideal, so that his death will somehow redeem us? Is there—as there appears to be in the world today—a darkness in man which will not turn to the light even when the means are at hand? Is there within us something which must always murder and befoul the good and the just?

Does this in any way explain the motives of men like Borah who, sure that they were right, would have nothing to do with international cooperation?

Ignorance, prejudice, political maneuvering, a traditional suspiciousness of Europe, a half-baked application of Washington's phrase against entangling alliances, and a habit of being persuaded by their own oratory—all these were present in the Senate and elsewhere. But that is not all.

Every possible emotion and division was worked upon to whip up opposition. The Irish were agitated with the claim that Great Britain would dominate the League and might use American troops to quell an Irish rebellion. The Germans in America thought the treaty a devastating blow to the fatherland. These relatively small minorities made so much noise that it began to appear as if the country were truly going against the League. Wilson's name was booed and hissed in their meetings. Republicans in Washington talked of Wilson as if he were the chief enemy of the country. The process of crucifixion was under way and seemed to grow more virulent after Wilson's collapse. One recalls that the scapegoat driven out into the desert to die for the sins of the tribe is usually crippled or has his legs broken.

Unemployment, inflation, strikes, Red scares—all coming along in the wake of war—had agitated the people and made them eager to find a scapegoat. The Hearst papers made the most of this.

Yet today we still ask whether there was no way Wilson might have saved the League.

Walter Lippmann says he failed to make Americans see what was in it for them—that we needed the League to prevent Germany from rising again. Wilson's arguments tended to be too idealistic.

Ironically, he might have saved it by dying. If he had died, we probably would have entered the League and Wilson, as one of his bitterest ememies remarked, would have eclipsed Lincoln as a martyr.

It is clear now that the European powers would have accepted our reservations. Indeed Lord Grey and Jusserand both tried to make this plain to Wilson. When Jusserand went to the White House and told Wilson that if he would accept the reservations the treaty would be ratified, the President told him:

"Mr. Ambassador, I shall consent to nothing. The Senate must take its medicine."

Wilson thought the reservations killed the treaty; the opposition thought they were necessary to save the United States from disaster.

Finally Mrs. Wilson herself pleaded with him:

"For my sake, won't you accept these reservations and get this awful thing settled?"

"Little girl," he said, "don't you let me down." And he explained—what he apparently believed—that he had no moral right to accept changes.

"Better a thousand times to go down fighting," he said, "than to dip your colors to dishonorable compromise."

And on that position he stood pat. When public opinion forced the Senate to its second consideration of the treaty, he could then have let his senators vote for the treaty with reservations while making it clear that he did not approve. But this he would not do.

So the final irony was that he himself defeated the League. A word from him, and 47 Democrats uniting with the 34 Republicans would have put it through. He was like a father who preferred to kill his own child rather than see it live in what he regarded as a maimed and helpless condition.

When Harding came in, Wilson retired, his health shattered, to a modest house on S Street in Washington, still confident that the League was mankind's best hope. He lived three years after leaving the White House, going out but little, seeing a few friends, his faith in the League unshaken.

"The world is run by its ideals," he said near the end of his life to a friend. "Only the fool thinks otherwise." And to another, with tears running down his cheeks: "You can't fight God."

In 1923 he made his last public address, an Armistice Day speech on the radio. "When the victory was won," he said, "we . . . withdrew into a sullen and selfish isolation, which is deeply ignoble because manifestly cowardly and dishonorable." And he concluded: "The only way in which we can worthily give proof of our appreciation of the high significance of Armistice Day is by resolving to put self-interest away and once more formulate and act upon the highest ideals and purposes of international policy."

A crowd gathered before his house that Armistice Day to give him an ovation, and he appeared briefly. Lansing, whose resignation as Secretary of State he had ultimately asked for, saw it this way:

> The ovation to Mr. Wilson yesterday was depressing in that it exhibited the ravages of disease upon a once powerful and commanding personality. It was to me pitiful to have the shattered body and weakened mind paraded before the public, however sympathetic that public might be. . . . It is a misfortune for any man to be canonized as a martyr during his lifetime, particularly

*one who conceives himself to be the inspired mouthpiece of Provi-
dence, since it nourishes his egotism and keeps alive, in spite of
defeat, a vanity which is a weakness rather than a strength of
character.**

When early the next February Wilson was near death, quiet
crowds came and stood in the snow before the house, some
kneeling—a last tribute to a man and a dream. He died on February 3, 1924.

"Great reformers do not, indeed, observe times and circumstances," Wilson wrote early in his career. "Theirs is not a service of opportunity. They have no thought for occasion, no capacity for compromise. They are early vehicles of the Spirit of the
Age. They are born of the very times that oppose them."

It sounds like a clairvoyant prophecy of his own eminence and
martyrdom.

It is easy for us now to see where his errors lay, but by comparison with his antagonists whose errors were fundamental and
moral his were only tactical and human.

The result of our refusal to follow the course Wilson marked
out was a Europe so unsettled economically and politically that
it was soon preparing for another war. Liberal opinion everywhere was thrown back and we became isolationists again, raising our tariff walls so that debtors could not pay us, and thus
bringing on a world depression, and further announcing our
irresponsibility by legislated withdrawal from world affairs. If
we had entered the League, the League Wilson wanted, World
War II might not—probably would not—have come. Failing to
enter it let loose those twin scourges of communism and fascism
which have bedeviled us ever since.

The fight for the League exposed an antiquated mechanism
of dealing with our international relations which has still not
been corrected. A few senators could still block a policy the
country wanted to adopt, just as they now block civil rights,
medical care, or indeed any sort of reform legislation.

* Private letter to Edward N. Smith of Watertown, New York, dated
November 12, 1923, in the possession of Chard Powers Smith.

Even so, most of Wilson's principles and policies have become so integrated into our thought about world affairs that we take them for granted. And Wilson as much as anybody was father to the United Nations—our sponsorship of which was a belated testimony to his essential rightness.

Wilson was against the European policy of the balance of power, and for the American system of strength through federation. In that system, state and federal governments do not as a rule conflict; each has its stated duties and powers. So, in a civilized world, another step would be added to the federal pattern to make it possible for nations to cooperate without disturbing their functioning as nations. The idea of the mutuality and equal dignity of all nations was Wilson's. It has been embodied in the United Nations. This in turn is based on an essentially religious faith in the equality and brotherhood of all men. Religion was admittedly at the very center of Wilson's life and thought.

Even in his errors Wilson contributed to our foreign policy. Franklin Roosevelt (Wilson's Assistant Secretary of the Navy) carefully studied the record and carefully insisted on unconditional surrender (a questionable improvement over Wilson's "peace without victory"), informing and involving the rival political party in postwar plans and keeping the United Nations separate from the peace treaties.

We see Wilson today as one of the great prophets of world freedom and justice. We understand that his politics was a religion because he deeply believed that only those who knew freedom could know God. We know him for one of the great enunciators of our history, able to make our ideals so clear and living to us that they seem within our grasp. And in our hearts we know that he was right, though we betrayed him.

Wilson made collective security an American policy. He assumed that nations could be brought to act in their affairs like men of honor in personal relations. He assumed that they could be brought to combine against an aggressor. He expected that diplomacy would be based on law and justice. He did not have to deal with the phenomena of fascism and communism as world powers. So his world was simpler than ours—one in which he could expect men to act with reason under a kind Providence.

Today his concept seems unworkable because it was rooted in nineteenth century liberalism and progressivism. It assumed that democracy would spread throughout the world. It had no way of grappling with totalitarian power states. So we need to develop principles and methods, as Dag Hammarskjöld did, which will meet the new conditions.

Still Wilson will remain as one of the great ones of all times. His faith in self-government, independence, and international justice and order inspired the whole world.

"His lofty moral idealism," said General Smuts, "seemed for a moment to dominate the brutal passions which had torn the old world asunder."

Josephus Daniels, his Secretary of the Navy, remembering Wilson near the end of his own life, said:

"What Wilson left us was not merely a plan for peace, but the imperishable pattern of the courage with the faith, the sacrifice with the vision. He took his faith from the heart's desire of an unhappy world. But he added flame to that faith. The troubles which we face now would not have dismayed him. They will not dismay other living men who not only guard his faith, but keep his spirit now."

He was a failure, but a magnificent one, as are all great men who reach as high as he did.

"Ideas live; men die." He said this once, and he could have said it of no one more truly than of himself. His was a great life, a great program, a great mission. So the failure was great too. But it made our present failure less of a catastrophe than it would otherwise have been. A hundred years from now, if we have the wisdom and the luck to avoid nuclear annihilation, we shall see Wilson's ideals finally triumphing in a world peace and a world government, for that is the inescapable direction in which men are walking, even in this time of troubles.

14. Gandhi
(1869-1948)

Nonviolence as Philosophy and Technique

 The greatest man of our century, as any competent jury would decide, was a person who never held an elective office yet could command the vote of millions, who possessed no wealth yet could put his hand into the pockets of rich and poor alike, who wore nothing but a loincloth when he conferred with the leading statesmen and rulers of the world, and who found himself at home in all religions.

Although he was the son of the prime minister of one of the small princely states of India, Mohandas Gandhi as a youth and young man had seemed to lack all the qualities of greatness.

In the fascinating autobiography which, characteristically, he calls *The Story of My Experiments with Truth*, he tells us about his child marriage at thirteen to an illiterate girl, and about the temptations to eat meat—to which he succumbed—and to visit a prostitute—which he escaped. And he tells us how, married at thirteen and a father at fifteen (that baby died), he left India at seventeen to study in England so that he might advance rapidly in the law when he returned home.

In London young Gandhi outfitted himself like a dandy—

striped trousers, frock coat, high collar. Spending lavishly, he began lessons in elocution, French, dancing and violin.

But he had vowed to his mother that he would not eat meat. Difficult as it was in an English boardinghouse to keep the vow, he kept it. Desperate from the insipid food, he discovered a vegetarian restaurant, then moved out of his expensive suite to a plain room where he cooked his own simple breakfast and supper. Giving up all his fancy lessons, he buckled down to study and to a regime which allowed him to live on a shilling and threepence a day.

Gandhi—the real Gandhi—was beginning to emerge.

He returned to India after three years, trained to the law. His mother had died in his absence, but the news had been kept from him. (His father had died long before.) But there was his wife, and a four-year-old son whom he hardly knew. Before he could get acquainted with them, however, he decided to move to Bombay where he would have a chance to put his English law training to use.

He began with a very small case in the Small Causes Court. But when he arose to cross-examine the plaintiff's witnesses, his head reeled with fright and he could think of no questions to ask. He returned the fee, fled the court, and soon left Bombay for home.

Then, through his brother, came the opportunity to go to South Africa, where a large Indian trading firm felt that it could use his services. All they offered him was £105 and all expenses for a year's work. But he was still smarting from his failure at Bombay and eager to try something new. So leaving his family behind again—there were two children now—he set out in 1893, not knowing that the turning point of his life lay just ahead.

His employer, Abdulla Sheth, met him at Durban. Abdulla, though he had no formal education, was one of the wealthiest businessmen in Natal. Although other lawyers were already working on his lawsuit, which involved £40,000, Gandhi soon saw that his client had the stronger case but would be ruined by the endless litigation. He persuaded Abdulla to accept an arbitrator, who ultimately made the award to Abdulla.

"My joy was boundless," Gandhi recalled. "I had learnt the true practice of law. I realized that the true function of a lawyer was to unite parties riven asunder."

He was to carry this lesson far beyond the sphere of a commercial law case.

Gandhi's stay in Africa stretched well beyond the year he had intended.

He was about to leave, and a farewell party had been prepared for him, when he chanced to see a newspaper article about a legislative proposal to deprive Indians of their voting rights in Natal.

"This bill," he told Abdulla and his friends, "if it passes into law, will make our lot extremely difficult. It is the first nail in our coffin."

So the farewell party turned into an organizing meeting to fight the bill, and Gandhi agreed to stay on another month, without salary.

He stayed, as it turned out, for three years before going home to his family, and then only to bring them back with him. Altogether he spent some twenty-one years (1893–1914) in South Africa. He was forty-five years old before his career in India really began. All the instruments he was to use in his battle for Indian freedom had already been perfected in Africa.

Gandhi had had his first view of what it meant to be an Indian in Africa when, on his arrival, he had tried to travel first class from Durban to Pretoria. A white passenger started to enter the compartment, saw Gandhi, and left. He soon returned with three railway officials, who told Gandhi to get out.

"But I have a first class ticket," he said.

"That doesn't matter. I tell you, you must go to the van compartment."

"I tell you, I was permitted to travel in this compartment at Durban, and I insist on going on in it."

When he refused to move, a constable was sent for to push him out. Gandhi sat through the cold night in the waiting room, wondering whether to go back at once to India. He concluded that he would stay on and see what he could do to combat the prejudice against Indians.

So when he plunged into the fight against the disfranchising legislation, it was with the feeling that this was a work to which he was called. Meanwhile he had suffered a good many other indignities at the hands of whites and was to experience more. To overcome color prejudice became his crusade.

Indians had come to Africa as indentured laborers. After five years, they might stay another five as free laborers. Some chose to remain permanently in Africa. But in 1894 all this was changed when the laborer, if he stayed, must agree to be a serf forever or pay an annual tax of three pounds—not only for himself but for each dependent. Three pounds was all an indentured worker earned in half a year. Indians were subjected to many other disabilities, some of them insulting. Gandhi himself had once been kicked off a sidewalk.

Now a prosperous lawyer and widely respected among the seventy thousand Indians of South Africa, Gandhi threw himself into addressing conferences, drafting memorials to government, sending letters to the newspapers and preparing petitions for signing. In everything, his method was to appeal to the good will and good reason of the adversary rather than to stir up hatred.

The cause gave him courage. No longer was he the shy, bashful young man struggling with his English or too abashed to speak up. Small and lithe (as a contemporary reports), he had refined and earnest features. His skin and eyes were dark, but the smile which lighted his face and the direct fearless glance "took

[286]

one's heart by storm." After a few years in Africa he spoke English perfectly.

Gandhi felt that he must first establish the principle that Indians as citizens of the British empire were entitled to equal treatment wherever they might live in that empire. Ultimately the Natal legislature did vote for equal rights for all British subjects, and Gandhi won his point.

But the undercurrent of hostility never died, and as usual the prejudiced sought other ways to make their prejudice felt. In 1906 an ordinance was proposed in the Transvaal which would force Indians, alone, to register with government, be fingerprinted, and carry a certificate at all times.

Gandhi assembled a mass meeting at Johannesburg. Under his influence, everyone present swore not to obey the law if it should pass. Gandhi went to London to lobby against the legislation, was assured the king would not allow it, and returned happy— only to learn that London had quietly informed the Transvaal government it could do as it liked when it ceased being a crown colony on January 1, 1907. So it promptly passed the Asiatic Registration Act or "Black Act," as its opponents called it.

Most Indians refused to register, Gandhi among them. He was haled before one of the courts in which he had practiced and on January 11, 1908, sentenced to two months in jail. General Jan Christian Smuts, having Gandhi brought to him from jail, promised that if Indians would register voluntarily he would get the law repealed. Gandhi assented.

He was bitterly criticized for giving in to Smuts. When he started for the office to register, a group of big, husky Pathans from northwest India assaulted him in the street, knocking him down with a heavy blow and kicking him where he lay. But he completed his registration.

Then Smuts betrayed him by not rescinding the law.

Indians by the thousands burned their certificates in defiance,

among them Gandhi. He was soon back in jail. The fight
went on.

Now greatly sought after as a lawyer, Gandhi was earning the
equivalent of thirty thousand dollars a year—a fantastic income
in that time and place. (In today's equivalent, it would more
nearly equal a hundred thousand.) He kept a fine house and
dressed his family lavishly.

But gradually he came to feel that no man should enjoy such
wealth for himself. Reading Ruskin, Tolstoy and Thoreau had
led him to ideas about man and society which were to form the
basis of his later campaigns for freedom.

He now completely revised his way of life from one of luxury
to one of self-denial. As early as 1904 he had moved to a farm
in order to simplify his style of living. Six years later he founded
Tolstoy Farm on a thousand-acre plot twenty miles from Johannesburg. About eighty people were soon living there. Gandhi, as
general manager, made the bread from wheat they ground themselves, supervised the making of marmalade from more than a
thousand fruit trees, took charge of the primitive sanitation
system, and soon persuaded everyone to do without tobacco,
alcohol and meat. Always a dietary experimenter, he insisted on
light meals—mostly fruit and nuts. Yet he often walked the
twenty-one miles to town and back—all in the same day. This
he managed by starting out at 2 A.M.! He also, at the age of
thirty-seven, gave up sexual intercourse. This ancient Indian
custom of brahmacharya apparently gave Gandhi a feeling of
spirituality, self-denial, and complete dedication to the public
service he had assigned himself. No doubt it helped channel all
his energies in that direction.

He had also been working toward a philosophy which would
embrace his deepest feelings about human relations and which
would provide a stable platform for the struggle to achieve
equality and dignity for Indians in Africa. Gradually, from his

[288]

reading of the Bhagavad–Gita, the New Testament, Ruskin's *Unto This Last,* Tolstoy's works and Thoreau's essay, "Civil Disobedience," he began to know where he stood.

Wealth should be held only in trusteeship for the good of all. Physical labor was not debasing, as Indians thought, but ennobling, and all men should engage in it. Life should be reduced to its simplest terms, whether in dress, food, or possessions. At Tolstoy Farm they did without chairs and beds. Not possession but self-possession was the thing to be aimed at.

Out of all this Gandhi developed his philosophy of Satyagraha —Truth-force or Love-force (since love and truth were the same) —the way of winning over opponents not by conflict or hatred but by force of the truth, by love, by gentleness which lacked nothing of firmness, by seeking out the best in the adversary and trying to win him through what was good in himself.

It was one of the great discoveries—or rediscoveries—in human relations.

But to be a Satyagrahi required courage. It was Gandhi's conviction that one had to meet violence and hatred fearlessly, ready even to suffer death if need be. As he wrote on the occasion of being attacked by the Pathans:

> *Nothing better can happen to a Satyagrahi than meeting death all unsought in the very act of Satyagraha, i.e., pursuing Truth. All these propositions are true only of a struggle like the Satyagraha movement, where there is no room for hatred, where self-reliance is the order of the day, . . . where there are no leaders and no followers, or where all are leaders and all are followers, so that the death of a fighter, however eminent, makes not for slackness but on the other hand intensifies the struggle.*

Satyagraha was a sacrificial act of love, the outcome of a deeply religious point of view. To Gandhi, Truth *is* God.

"My uniform experience has convinced me that there is no other God than Truth," wrote Gandhi in his autobiography.

[289]

The only means for the realization of Truth is Ahimsa [nonviolence]. . . . To see the universal and all-pervading Spirit of Truth face to face one must be able to love the meanest of creation as oneself. . . . Identification with everything that lives is impossible without self-purification. . . . God can never be realized by one who is not pure of heart. . . . So long as a man does not of his own free will put himself last among his fellow creatures, there is no salvation for him.

Gandhi also discovered that the law which governs all life is God, that every human being partakes of the nature of God as every drop shares the glory but is not the ocean. "God never appears to you in person but in action."

He believed that all religions contained Truth, and that each man should blend into his own faith every acceptable feature of other faiths.

"If I could popularize the use of soul-force, which is but another name for love-force, in place of brute-force, I know that I could present you with an India that could defy the whole world to do its worst."

To Gandhi religion was not separated from life but was at the very center of it, the necessary motivation for all one did and achieved.

Without this religious base, Gandhi could hardly have succeeded in his quixotic notion of turning the British out of India. Precisely because he rediscovered in himself the deep religious roots of Hindu culture and because he spiritually reawakened the hopeless, somnolent people of India was he able to inspire a whole nation to achieve freedom.

"Gandhi has in him the marvelous spiritual power to turn ordinary men around him into heroes and martyrs," said Gopal Gokhale, president of the Servants of India Society. Gandhi had that power because, through sacrifice and self-denial, he had made himself a Mahatma, a Great Spirit. No other kind of leader could have recalled India to the glory of her great tradition

of saints and holy men and seekers. But Gandhi was a man of
action too. For him these were not separate but complementary.
Right action could proceed only from right thought, right preparation. Gandhi embodied his principles in a set of vows which he
expected all Satyagrahis to be bound by:

> *The vow of truth, which implies a steadfast witness despite con-*
> *sequences*
> *Ahimsa—nonviolence*
> *Brahmacharya—chastity*
> *Control of the palate*
> *Nonthieving, by which he meant not storing up anything be-*
> *yond day-to-day needs, until the hungry millions could be fed*
> *Swadeshi, meaning local self-sufficiency in production and trade*
> *Fearlessness*
> *Abolition of untouchability*
> *Learning through Indian languages rather than English-based*
> *education*
> *Khaddar, or manual labor for all*
> *The religious use of politics—that is, recognizing that the good*
> *of the individual is contained in the good of all, and good and*
> *effective political action can only develop out of the realization that*
> *God is Truth and Love. One must reach the God that is in every*
> *man. Sound religion is the best politics.*

Poverty, chastity and humility had always been the basis of
religion in India. Gandhi was only returning to his own roots
when, through the writings of Ruskin, the New Testament,
Tolstoy and Thoreau he found his way back to the Gita and the
Upanishads. No, he was doing more than that—he was achieving
a way of life in which religion, politics, society and the family
merged, and which one day would catch the imagination and
feed the hope of the disadvantaged and deprived everywhere.

In spite of twenty years' labor on behalf of the Indians in Africa,
Gandhi found himself in 1913 facing as great a challenge as at
any time in the past. Further immigration had been prohibited.

The three-pound annual tax on every Indian who wished to remain in South Africa was still enforced. Only Christian marriages were recognized as legal—which meant that most Indians
were treated as if they were living in adultery with their own
wives!

Gandhi's solution was to make a mass protest which would
persuade the government to rescind these unjust laws.

So a group of women crossed from the Transvaal into Natal,
thus breaking the law against immigration. They walked to New-
castle where they persuaded indentured Indian laborers in the
coal fields to strike. When they were jailed, the strike spread.
Meanwhile some women volunteers had also walked from Natal
into the Transvaal and had also been jailed.

Suddenly, Gandhi found that he had five thousand strikers on
his hands in Natal, with no preparation to feed them and more
coming in every day. He advised them to walk into the Transvaal,
thus courting arrest and leaving it to the government to feed
them. But first he told them what jail would be like and tried to
persuade them to go home. Instead, more came in.

On October 13 Gandhi and more than two thousand strikers
began to march. Gandhi let the government know what he was
up to, offering to call off the march if the three-pound tax was
cancelled. The government made no reply.

Gandhi now planned to lead the marchers to Tolstoy Farm,
160 miles away, in eight days. But then he and his lieutenants
were arrested en route, tried and jailed, while the strikers were
loaded into trains and taken back to detention camps near the
mines, which they steadfastly refused to work. Resistance now
spread throughout South Africa, until fifty thousand indentured
workers were on strike. India, electrified by Gandhi's campaign
for justice, sent funds. English sympathizers in India and
England backed Gandhi.

Suddenly, on December 18, Gandhi was set free. A commission was set up to examine Indian grievances, but Gandhi

[292]

charged that it was prejudiced and threatened another march. At last Smuts recognized the strength of Gandhi's method.

"You can't put twenty thousand Indians into jail," he said, and began to negotiate. After weeks of bargaining, they reached an agreement on June 30, 1914. The next month it was passed into law. Marriages under Indian faiths were recognized. The three-pound tax was abolished. No indentured laborers would be brought in from India after 1920. Although Indians born in South Africa could enter the Cape Colony, free movement from one province to another was still forbidden.

Years later, Smuts himself said of Gandhi:

"He never forgot the human background of the situation, never lost his temper or succumbed to hate, and preserved his gentle humor even in the most trying situations." Not a bad description of a Satyagrahi!

Gandhi returned to India in 1915 a famous man. Indians expected to see an impressive personage, large of stature, of commanding presence, and—what all Indians love—a great orator. Instead they saw a little man in a big turban, with a voice so weak that he could not be heard in a crowd and with none of the orator's tricks.

Almost his first act was to establish a Satyagraha ashram at Sabarmati near Ahmedabad similar to his Tolstoy Farm. The standard of living was that of the poor Indian peasant. Everyone worked—at farming, spinning, cooking, cleaning. Soon the young men and women who would carry out India's struggle to be free began to gather around Gandhi. He urged them to give up their English clothes for the costume of the peasant, to get out to the villages and speak the languages of India. For India must be reformed from within, he told them, before it would have the strength or the right to gain its freedom.

He himself, by this return to the ancient, timeless India, restored India's pride in its ancient traditions and gave it the hope that it might rule itself.

But India, he taught, must first clean its own house. And the first task must be to root out untouchability, "the inhuman boycott of human beings."

When he admitted an untouchable family to his ashram, his wife refused to have the woman in the kitchen and wealthy Hindus withdrew their support. But he quickly won over Kasturbai and adopted the daughter as his own. New supporters of his program appeared unbidden.

One day a peasant from the Champaran district, far to the north near Nepal, came to see Gandhi and told him of the hardships his fellows suffered from, being forced by the British to raise indigo. Then, when the British learned that the Germans had begun to produce artificial dyes, they had demanded compensation for releasing the peasants from the agreement. Gandhi went to Champaran, was ordered to leave, refused to go, was tried but ultimately released without sentence.

A commission of inquiry found against the landlords, but Gandhi settled for restitution of only a quarter of the money taken from the peasants. He gave nearly a year of his life to this case, but it was worth it, for he proved that civil disobedience could work as well in India as in Africa. A turning point had been reached in India's long history.

The end of the First World War found Indians discouraged and disaffected. More than half a million of them had fought for Great Britain. London had indicated that Indians would have increasingly responsible roles in government. At war's end, the censorship and the jailing of prominent leaders by secret tribunals was expected to end. Instead, the Rowlatt Act, passed in March, 1919, imposed bitter restrictions on civil liberties.

The next day Gandhi told a colleague:

"Last night the idea came to me in a dream that we should call on the country to observe a general hartal." A hartal was Gandhi's version of a general strike, but much more paralyzing than anything known in the west, since employers too would cooperate. Factories and shops would shut, transportation would be at a standstill.

On April 6, the chosen day, all India ground to a halt. At last, after more than two hundred years, Indians had found a way to assert themselves against the foreign ruler. In Gandhi's view, it was a way of basing politics upon moral force.

But then matters got out of hand. Violence flared in Delhi, Bombay, Ahmedabad. A frightful massacre occurred at Amritsar when General Reginald Dyer ordered his troops to fire into an unresisting crowd. Gandhi announced that he would fast for three days. He asked the people to fast with him for a full day. On April 18 he announced an end to the civil disobedience movement. The people had not yet understood Satyagraha, or they could not have grown violent. Now he realized that he must train a band of devoted leaders.

He had not abandoned his principles; he had only to perfect his method.

"Noncooperation with evil is as much a duty as is cooperation with good."

In 1922 he was sentenced to six years in jail for writing a series of articles which condemned the government and urged his readers not to serve or cooperate with it. He was released after an operation for appendicitis early in 1924.

Thereafter he traveled throughout the country, urging the use of homespun upon city and country people alike. It was his way of trying to bridge the gap between peasant and townsman, ancient India and modern. Gandhi had a genius for picking out some simple, tangible thing which caught the imagination of the humble and the privileged alike, appealing to their common heritage and providing a spur to action.

This was the case with khadi. The well-born leaders of the India National Congress smiled at Gandhi's use of this rough, home-made country product and at his insistence upon spinning the thread from which it was woven. But they soon discovered that Bapu ("Uncle," as all his colleagues now called him) had hit upon something of importance. The arts of spinning and weaving had almost been forgotten as English mill cloth had replaced homespun. But now, by setting the example himself through daily weaving, Gandhi had shown the country people a way to provide clothing for themselves at no cost and at the same time to advance their independence, demonstrating their economic strength by nonpurchase of English cloth.

Soon all the Congress leaders, once resplendent in Bond Street clothes, went into khadi. Even today in India most politicians find it advisable to wear these rough but attractive materials, while spinning remains an almost religious ritual among Gandhians. I have attended memorial services to Gandhi where a whole stage full of his followers kept up their spinning throughout a long program of songs, prayers and speeches. True, most Indians today prefer the harder, more even mill cloth and the government-subsidized khadi industry has a hard time disposing of its output. But khadi both as a symbol and as a means of economic relief played an important role in lifting India toward independence.

As the people learned what Gandhi really meant, and that his method was completely nonviolent and respectful toward the antagonist, they became more expert in applying it. In 1928, eighty-seven thousand peasants in Bardoli peaceably revolted against a twenty-two per cent rise in taxes imposed by the British. Officers took away their buffaloes, their cooking pots, their carts.

Gandhi persuaded the mayor of Ahmedabad, Vallabhbhai Patel, to help them.

"Pull your carts to pieces," he told them. "Keep the body in one place and the wheels in another." The government announced that it would sell off all the lands. Gandhi, calling for a nationwide hartal, went to Bardoli himself. And the government capitulated. Satyagraha had proved itself again.

In 1930, bowing to the Congress Party's decision to press for independence, Gandhi again looked for an issue on which to base a civil disobedience campaign. He knew instinctively that the only way he could appeal to India's illiterate millions was through some symbol, some simple thing which touched them all. This time he hit upon the salt tax, by which the government collected revenue from every ounce of salt sold in the country.

Characteristically, he wrote to the Viceroy, Lord Irwin, to say in advance what he intended to do and why.

British rule, he said, had reduced India to a land of serfs crushed by unfair taxes and had imposed the most expensive administration in the world.

"Take your own salary," he wrote. "You are getting over 700 rupees a day against India's average income of less than an eighth of a rupee [two cents] per day. Thus you are getting much over five thousand times India's average income. The British Prime Minister is getting only ninety times Britain's average income. . . .

"Nothing but organized nonviolence can check the organized violence of the British government. . . . My ambition is no less than to convert the British people through nonviolence, and thus make them see the wrong they have done to India. I do not seek to harm your people. I want to serve them even as I want to serve my own."

Irwin refused to see Gandhi. So on March 12, after prayers, he and seventy-eight members of the ashram left Sabarmati for the seacoast two hundred miles away.

"I go to the ocean of God, and I make salt with my hands, and the foreign government will arrest me for it, but this is my truth and I will die for it," he said.

If all India was not concentrated on that march at the beginning, it was when Gandhi reached the ocean after twenty-four days. Thousands knelt by the road as he passed. Often he stopped to talk to them. He told them to make khadi, to keep clean, to give up child marriage and, when the moment came, to break the salt laws. By the time he reached the sea on April 5, his group had grown to several thousand.

After a night of prayer, Gandhi walked into the sea, then turned back to the beach and picked up a pinch of salt left by the waves. He thus became a criminal under British law; he possessed salt not purchased from the monopoly.

At once, all along India's seacoast, villagers popped up with pans and began to make salt. The police arrested them in crowds, beating and even biting them. Volunteers openly sold salt in the cities, courting arrest. In Bombay where Congress Party members were making salt on the roof of their headquarters, a crowd of sixty thousand gathered. The police herded hundreds off to jail. Indian village officials resigned when government pressed them to enforce the salt law.

Gandhi had planned to lead a raid on the government salt works at Dharasana, but when he was again thrown into jail his colleagues carried on. Weaponless, they advanced toward the salt works. Police with heavy sticks smashed their heads and shoulders, but as they fell others took their places without wavering, only to be knocked down and kicked in the stomach or testicles. Webb Miller, a hardened correspondent, was so sickened by it that he had to turn aside.

"I cannot understand how any government that calls itself civilized could deal as savagely and brutally with nonviolent, unresisting men as the British have this morning," he wrote.

The brutality went on for several days. But the moral superiority of nonviolent resistance over brutal suppression had been made clear to the whole world.

Finally on March 5, 1931, Gandhi and Irwin reached an agreement. Gandhi did not get the promise of eventual complete independence which was his goal, but by calling off the campaign of civil disobedience he got the release of those jailed in the salt controversy and permission for Indians to make salt on the coast.

In August, elected sole delegate of the Congress to the second Round Table Conference, Gandhi sailed for London. But the Conference, which seemed to have been designed to illustrate all the various ethnic, religious and political conflicts of India, was a disaster from the point of view of a free India.

Yet in a way it was a triumph for Gandhi because the English people—even those whom his khadi movement had put out of work—came to know and love him.

"I want you to suffer," he told the conference and through it all of Great Britain, "because I want to touch your hearts; and when your hearts have been touched then will come the psychological moment for negotiation."

The British plan of separate electorates seemed to Gandhi and his associates an obvious device to divide and rule. When the government's position became clear in 1932, Gandhi wrote from jail to Ramsay MacDonald:

"I have to resist your decision with my life."

He announced a fast unto death, beginning September 20. The nub of the difficulty was the plan of separate electorates for Hindus and untouchables. Under the impact of the fast, the untouchable leader Dr. Ambedkar and the Congress leaders finally worked out a compromise Gandhi could accept and the British government would agree to. After six days Gandhi, who had seemed close to death, broke his fast with a glass of orange juice.

The so-called Yeravda Pact clearly stated that no one should henceforth be regarded as untouchable because of his birth. The main achievement of Gandhi's fast was thus to make clear to all of India the injustice of untouchability. Attitudes and customs rooted three thousand years in Indian society could not be wiped out overnight. But now all of India had been made to look at untouchability and to know that it was wrong. Thus, in the very midst of his struggle with the British, Gandhi had achieved the

[299]

triumph of leading his people to reform themselves from within
—the only means by which they could gain the strength with
which to overcome the external bar to their freedom and independence.

This was the genius of Gandhi—that he could convince men
of the necessity of purity and integrity as the only basis for
freedom. A people who practiced a form of slavery or discrimination against their own kind could hardly expect to win freedom
from foreign rule. And the fast was a symbol of self-purification
all India could understand. Gandhi happily risked his life to
encourage his people to purify themselves of superstition and
prejudice.

As for the people, they knew a saint when they saw one. India
always has. And they were happy to follow him.

So he went on, in jail or in his ashram (moved to Wardha in
1936 and named Sevagram in 1940), or on long journeys into
the heart of village India, living the life of a Satyagrahi, rising as
early as four in the morning for prayers, removing his own night
soil, eating a few dates and nuts and drinking goat's milk, going
for a walk with some of his admiring staff (well sprinkled with
pretty young women), joking in his gentle way as they went
along. Every day brought a hundred letters to be answered, and
many visitors. He saw them all—people with personal problems;
workers in the various voluntary organizations he had initiated in
order to carry out his ideas in education, relief to untouchables,
or the production of khadi.

From 1933 to 1939 he was nominally out of politics, but he
still remained the biggest landmark in the Indian political scene,
and Congress leaders kept coming to him for advice.

His program for India he had condensed to three words—
khadi, swadeshi, swaraj: homespun, self-sufficiency, self-government. By making their own cloth, Indians would take the first
step toward self-sufficiency and break the back of Britain's economic dominance. So successful had this campaign been that the

weavers of Lancashire and Yorkshire had been thrown out of work by the hundreds. Gandhi had made a point of visiting them when he was in England. Instead of holding it against him, they had given him a warm welcome, such was the power of the man in his unaffected humility and in the warm human contact he made with all sorts and conditions of men.

Self-sufficiency must extend into every aspect of life, and it must begin in the village. So he took a lively interest in every kind of village industry, encouraging the production of things that would first meet every basic need, then of items that could be sold. India must use its own language or languages instead of relying on English as the only nationwide tongue. It must have schools to tackle the almost universal illiteracy which prevented progress. And they must be schools appropriate to India—not copies of the British system. So Gandhi worked out his system of basic education, with emphasis on practical learning. Instead of starting with academic subjects, he started with the needs and problems of the village and went on from there.

Gandhi was suspicious of industrialization, which seemed to encourage or at least magnify the wars that were sweeping the world. He had faith in the village, in the small human group, in the dignity of poverty and self-denial and in a way of life reduced to the bare essentials. Perhaps because he could see no way and no need to make the villages wealthy, he emphasized the virtues of doing with little so long as that little was the work of one's own hands and so long as it liberated a people from foreign control. This was what Gandhi sought through self-sufficiency, which would provide the base and the continuing support for the great goal of self-government.

Men could not govern themselves, he knew, until they had achieved freedom within.

In 1942, with the war on India's doorstep, Gandhi was jailed again along with most of the Congress leaders. The Congress had stated that if India were made free it would cooperate to the fullest in the war; otherwise it would be obliged to begin a campaign of civil disobedience.

Well, the jailings started off an unpremeditated wave of violence throughout the country. An underground developed. It burned police stations, tore up rails, and pulled down wires. In many areas it set up independent local rule. Gandhi, accused by the viceroy of having started all this, began a fast on February 10. It went on until the second of March, and left him prostrated. Then his wife died, and soon after that his health took another downward turn. On May 6 the British released him from jail. Altogether, he spent over six years of his life in prison.

The subsequent freeing of India and its tragic separation into two nations with all the accompanying mass butchery is well known. Gandhi did his best to stop it, traveling on foot from village to village in the most dangerous areas, trying to prevent the partition which the Muslin leader Mahomed Ali Jinnah demanded and which Congress and the British accepted at last out of desperation.

The British left, the rioting grew worse, and once more Gandhi attempted to convert the hearts of men by a fast unto death. When he began his fast on September 1, 1947, Indians were murdering each other in many parts of the country. Immediately some of the worst hooligans came to see him—big, tough men who wept and promised to give up killing.

Community leaders of all factions came to promise that there would be no more trouble in Calcutta if he would break his fast. He asked to see it in writing. Calcutta and Bengal remained true to that promise. He gave up his fast on the fourth.

Gandhi hurried on to Delhi where in the city and in nearby Punjab unspeakable murders even of little children were taking place. Even the police, inflamed by communal hatred, pitched in to compound the murder and destruction. And there again he fasted. He would not break his fast until Delhi became truly peaceful.

He forced India to turn over $180,000,000 to Pakistan as its due share of their joint assets. Again leaders signed pledges and the fast ended. Said Zafrullah Khan, Pakistan's foreign minister:

"A new and tremendous wave of feeling and desire for friendship between the two Dominions is sweeping the subcontinent in response to the fast."

But Gandhi had only a few days to live. On January 25, 1948, a fanatical Hindu shot and killed him as he walked out of the house where he was staying in Delhi to attend daily public prayers in its grounds—a martyr, as perhaps every peacemaker is in the end, to his own idea and ideals.

Gandhi was the towering peacemaker of our time. He developed a unique technique soundly based upon an unshakable philosophy which offered men that substitute for war which William James had sought. Philosophy and technique were indivisible: that was their strength. More, the philosophy was itself based upon a conviction of universality—of the oneness of man and the whole creation.

If this is true, then conflict is only a brief interruption in nature. To dispel it, one must seek more earnestly to discover the truth of human unity that undergirds all living. If that truth could be earnestly pursued by both parties in a dispute, the conflict would disappear and the essential oneness become manifest. For Gandhi, Truth and God were indistinguishable. To pursue one was to discover the other. If one approached an antagonist in the proper spirit, his truth and yours would merge and a solution satisfactory to both would be found. Indeed, there was but one truth which, once discovered, would make brothers of opponents. Compromise, conciliation, consideration were therefore essential in any difference of opinion.

Gandhi always told the British in advance of every move he planned. He was invariably kind to his judges and jailers. When well-to-do Indians sent blankets to rain-soaked demonstrators in Bombay, they in turn offered the blankets to the police who opposed them. That was the Gandhian way. When Gandhi, bargaining with the landlords of Champaran, suggested a settlement of fifty per cent and they offered twenty-five, he immediately agreed. They would have been glad to pay the fifty, but Gandhi preferred to be magnanimous—to wipe out bitterness, to establish a spirit of love.

By what miracle did this bashful, diffident failure become the greatest man of our century?

Called to Africa merely to act as an assistant in a commercial law case, he ended by transforming himself, the Indians of South Africa, and in some degree even the government there.

The influence of Ruskin, Thoreau, Tolstoy, the Bhagavad-Gita, The New Testament and the Christian friends he came to know in Africa all had their effect. No one can say by what subtle chemistry all these things—as well as the memory of his religious-minded mother and the whole impact of Indian religion, so interfused throughout the culture—led him to his unique discoveries.

The embarrassment and shame he suffered at the hands of the British, in India, England and Africa, surely prodded him to rediscover the virtues embedded in Indian culture, and to that extent led him to recapture the spirit of the Bhagavad-Gita, with its emphasis on action, and the spirit of Vedanta in its emphasis on the unity of truth.

Respect for the many Englishmen who befriended him in England and Africa also gave Gandhi a warm regard for that fundamental sense of justice and fair play which ultimately brought most of them onto his side. Shrewdly, he knew how to appeal to what was best in them. Indeed this was the heart of his whole method—to appeal to the best in a man, holding his own ideals before him as a mirror so that he must face them, and then acting as if he were bound to follow them.

As an Indian, Gandhi instinctively knew the value of suffering. No one can stay very long in India without feeling moved both by the involuntary suffering of the poor and the voluntary suffering of those holy men who hope to purify themselves by

[304]

undergoing physical hardship and deprivation. Gandhi must have known from the beginning that suffering or deprivation voluntarily undertaken on behalf of others is a powerful weapon. His fasts came to have world-wide consequences because they were testimonies to the truth he wanted to make known to all. When this one man fasted, the whole world knew it. The moral force of his simple act ultimately (along with the current of world events, to be sure) removed the British from India.

From deep Indian roots Gandhi also imbibed the knowledge that religion and politics are not to be separated from the rest of life, or from each other. As he insisted, politics—the art of governing men—cannot succeed apart from religion—the faith that human life has meaning, unity and divinity. This, as much as anything, embodied Gandhi's secret and his truth. Politics is not the art of the possible, but the art of the ideal. You ask men, on their own behalf since the good of the individual is contained in the good of all, to sacrifice their comfort, wealth, convenience, even life itself on behalf of the total welfare—the welfare of British raj as well as of Indian peasant. You raise a nation out of torpor and stagnation by demanding the impossible of its members.

But first of all you set an example yourself, by renouncing the world and receiving it back again as the gift of God. This Gandhi did in the most literal way, by reducing his food intake to a minimum and eating only those things which require no cooking, by dressing himself in a loincloth and occasionally a shawl, by owning nothing but a dollar watch, a pair of spectacles, and a pen.

Yet when Gandhi needed money for his activities or charities, rupees by the thousand poured into his lap. When he insisted on traveling third class, the government put a car, or at times even a special train, at his disposal. As his followers used to joke among themselves—and still do—"It cost a lot of money to keep Bapu in poverty."

[305]

Only a man with an absolutely unswervable standard of personal morality could have succeeded in such a course. Lesser men would have been tempted by the wealth that could so easily have been turned to the uses of their own family. Gandhi leaned over backwards, even to the point of denying his sons the sort of education he had himself received.

Only because he had given up everything to the cause—even conjugal love, profession, large personal income—could he make his outrageous total demands upon others. Those who knew him have told me that he was absolutely fearless, ready at any time to face death. This was what made it possible for his followers to walk straight into the crowds of waiting policemen, knowing they would be struck down, their skulls crushed, their shoulders broken.

The goals Gandhi set for India and Indians expressed the dreams of a whole people—freedom from foreign rule, self-sufficiency, education, a restoration of past greatness and a realization of India's glory as a civilization.

But whether Gandhi, with all these virtues and skills, could have captured the heart of India and of the world without his absolutely uncanny sense of drama and timing must remain an unanswered question. From what source did they come to him? The South African experience revealed them to him and to us, but who knows what originated them? Indian culture is full of the dramatic gesture as a revelation of a message: the naked sadhus wandering the streets in absolute poverty, the widespread renunciation of the world at the age of fifty-five or sixty and retirement to an ashram for a life of asceticism, the temple sacrifices, the colorful religious festivals. As a boy, growing up in the household of a father who was prime minister to one of the smaller maharajahs, Gandhi must have imbibed all this unconsciously.

He not only imbibed it but added to it his own dash of genius. Hence the mass marches and imprisonments in South Africa, the salt march, the renaming of untouchables as Harijans—children of God.

Based on unswerving nonviolence, Gandhi's methods nonetheless embraced all the appeals of war—the noble declaration of principles; rallying to their banner; sacrifice; danger; movement of large bodies of people with the resulting sense of group strength and excitement; a life of hardship and excitement rolled together; the thrill of knowing what one was about, of marching under an inspiring leader, of direct action to which one could give himself without the need of introspection or reflection; and the clear hope of ultimate victory.

The triumph of great men like Gandhi is sheathed in an inescapable irony: their success turns out to be in the end a failure. Gandhi, the great peacemaker, was himself violently murdered. He brought freedom to India, only to see the subcontinent plunge itself into one of the worst blood baths of history as Muslim and Hindu slit each other's throats, burned each other's houses, even ripped innocent children in half. Perhaps a million people died thus, and fifteen million were made refugees. Yet his method of peacefully bringing about major changes remains the great spiritual achievement of our century and works at this moment in our South, in South Africa, in India itself.

Any discussion of Gandhian techniques is bound to meet the challenge:

"But he was working on the British, and they're essentially decent people. He couldn't have worked it on Hitler."

He couldn't have worked it on Hitler. Nor, though it has often been suggested, could the Jews. Only the German people could have worked it, because it was their business. Massive nonviolent resistance to Hitler on the part of Germans at the stage when he was trying to win converts could without question have changed world history. And if you protest that this would mean a change in the hearts of the German people, Gandhi would answer:

"Yes, of course. That is always the case. Did I not have to change the hearts of the Indian people—yes, and of the British?"

A change of heart through unswerving devotion to truth through love—this is what Gandhi always sought and what, to an amazing degree, he brought about. It is the inescapable challenge of all peacemaking.

In foreign affairs, this means a set of goals that are truly human rather than nationalist, an openness to truth as the antagonist sees it, an honest search for common ground. It means less reliance on governments and more upon the voluntary associations in which Gandhi placed great faith, and which are an organic and vital part of American democracy. Indeed it would mean that there are no "foreign" but only international or human affairs. For no man would be alien in Gandhi's view.

So to India and to the world he became the Mahatma—the great soul. Gurdial Mallik, who knew both Gandhi and Tagore intimately, having taught for nearly a quarter of a century at Tagore's Santiniketan and worked on many a project at Gandhi's call, once told me that "With Tagore it was the truth of love, with Gandhi the love of truth."

"Gandhiji sang the song of service to the accompaniment of the spinning wheel," Gurdial writes in his little book, *Gandhi and Tagore.** "Gurudeva [Tagore] spent himself in the service of song.

"One was a devotee of Duty, the other an adorer of Beauty. But both worshipped, though at two different corners, at the selfsame shrine of Truth."

We have still not understood Gandhi's truth, though it is simple. We still have not understood the truth of Buddha or of Jesus. Rather, we do our best to make it into something else. Therefore much of Buddhism has become abstruse and ornamental, whereas the truth Buddha taught was simple. Christianity has become a structure incorporating all sorts of rituals, myths and beliefs from many sources such as would surely shock Jesus if he returned to view it. And so with Gandhi, the work of corruption is going on in India today, as Gandhi societies build

* Ahmedabad, Navajivan Publishing House, 1961.

museums and centers to enshrine Gandhi but only succeed in losing him.

Gandhi's message is simple, direct and inescapable. Give what you have to the service of man—wealth, talents, energy, love—and receive it back at God's hands. Discover that truth is one, and that it is in the heart of the antagonist as well as in your own. Then meet on common ground. Never compromise on principles, but do not mistake a desire for personal or national advantage as a principle. Go out to meet your antagonist in love, humility and openness, and you will change him. Let your faith be in the truth wherever it leads, your armor nonviolence. Then you will find that the antagonist is a friend. And your truth and his will merge, and you will be at peace with one another.

15. Dag Hammarskjöld
(1905-1961)

Peace by Juridical Sanction

Although he held an important post in the Swedish cabinet, few people outside of Sweden and European diplomatic circles had ever heard of Dag Hammarskjöld until the Soviet delegation to the United Nations Security Council cast its fifty-eighth veto to prevent Lester Pearson from following Trygve Lie as Secretary General. That was on March 13, 1953. The French then proposed Dag Hammarskjöld, who won approval March 31 and was confirmed by the General Assembly a week later.

"A clerk," said Trygve Lie.

Early in April Dag Hammarskjöld stepped from a plane at Idlewild airport into a crowd of reporters and cameramen. He looked young—he was forty-eight—trim, rather scholarly, and perhaps a little scared.

"I was hoping that I could get out of it alive," he later told a friend.

When he stepped out of the plane, Dag Hammarskjöld was stepping into what Trygve Lie had called "the most impossible job in the world." Yet he kept it until his death eight and a half years later. During that time he walked calmly up to half a dozen crises which threatened to turn into major conflicts. By quiet diplomacy, by skillfully fitting means to situations, by combining firmness with conciliation, he made his office and the UN effective instruments of peace.

Son of a prime minister who had also served as president of the Nobel Foundation and on the International Court of Justice, Dag Hammarskjöld was a born aristocrat. The first Hammarskjöld was a cavalry captain knighted for bravery in 1610. Dag grew up with his three brothers in the palace at Uppsala where his father was Governor of Uppland. He was devoted to his parents—to his stern father and to his mother with her warmly emotional nature and her "child-like openness toward life" as he himself put it.

Perhaps the personality that became Dag Hammarskjöld is best understood as a compromise between the patriarchal, conservative, authoritative father and the loving, emotional mother. Dag gave the impression of being cool and reserved. Yet his patience and integrity, his quickness to grasp points of view and to find areas of agreement, showed a sensitivity we more often think of as feminine.

His university friends found him a good companion as well as a brilliant student. He loved hiking, mountain climbing, bicycling, skiing. His inborn sense of direction made him a welcome guide. At the end of a hard day, he was ready for an evening of talk on anything from Swedish nature poetry to abstruse economic theory. A music lover, he cared especially for Bach and Vivaldi.

When his father moved to Stockholm in 1930 Dag, now twenty-five, went along. Well grounded in law, philosophy and economics, he was almost immediately drawn into government work but managed to complete his doctorate in 1933.

Even at this early stage of his career he had developed the involuted way of speech for which he was to become world famous. He not only defended his thesis in this remarkable language, but

[311]

carried on at dinner afterwards, leading Gunnar Myrdal to inquire in wonder:

"Do you speak at home, too, in these long, eloquent, carefully
constructed cycles?"

Also in these early years he had already committed himself to
that regime of hard work and long hours which was to impress
people at the UN. Often he stayed in his office halfway through
the night. And this, no doubt, was one reason why he never
married. He had already seen the effect of such a career on his
gentle, loving mother. "How could a man ask a woman to share
this sort of life?" he once said to a friend.

His reverence for his mother, and his sense of the alienation
she felt from the preoccupations of his father, had touched him
deeply. He too preserved something of the paternal stiffness and
was never able to unbend and be fully at ease, except perhaps in
a small group of intimate friends. But inside, he had his mother's
quick perceptions.

When friends introduced him to a charming and brilliant girl,
they thought they might be able to topple him. But his only
response was: "She didn't appreciate T. S. Eliot."

He was hardly thirty when he became under secretary in the
Ministry of Finance under Ernst Wigforss. Hammarskjöld,
Wigforss later wrote in his memoirs, "had a talent for winning
people personally, straightening out differences and filling a
leading role in a big organization." He also had a canny sense of
what was politically possible. During the years when Sweden's
response to the world-wide depression was a revitalizing of its
economy by building up a "middle way" of cooperatives and
social legislation, this was important.

A foretaste of his UN assignment as a conciliator came just
before World War II when Sweden sent him over to calm
American feelings regarding Sweden's neutrality.

In 1941 Dag Hammarskjöld became head of the state bank
(Riksbank). After the war he and Wigforss decided on a low-

interest policy which, though it involved sacrifices for Sweden, would help her war-stricken neighbors. Financial interests bitterly opposed it. In this crisis Dag tried to convince them that they were oversimplifying the problem. To his refined and subtle mind, perhaps, nothing was simple—which fitted him ideally to deal in a world where in fact nothing is. In this case he baffled even the professional economists arrayed against him.

"He has a tremendous power of expressing himself orally in a way that people can't quite follow," mused a puzzled opponent.

Returning from negotiations about dollar arrangements in the United States, said the same man, Hammarskjöld "presented the results to businessmen so beautifully and complicatedly that no discussion was possible; it was all so interrelated in so complex a fashion that no grip was possible on any part of it."

In 1947 Hammarskjöld was Sweden's top representative in discussions that prepared the way for the Marshall Plan, still speaking in the same complicated way that had entranced Gunnar Myrdal. Only now he was doing it not only in Swedish but in French, German and English!

Quite logically, his work with the Organization for European Economic Cooperation led to his becoming an adviser to the Swedish Ministry of Foreign Affairs. In 1951 he became vice minister, with cabinet rank, and headed the Swedish delegation to the UN.

When Dag Hammarskjöld entered the UN Secretariat Building as Secretary General, he was taken to an elevator which he was told would be reserved for his use. His first official order was to release the elevator for general use.

Once he had settled into his office on the thirty-eighth floor, his executive assistant, Andrew Cordier, suggested that he might like to meet all the staff members. It would take about two months, Cordier estimated, to shake hands with the several thousand employees. Dag, going from floor to floor, saw them all in two weeks. Soon after, one of the typists standing in the cafeteria line happened to glance behind her. The Secretary General was standing there. He refused, with thanks, her invitation to step ahead.

Colleagues found him shy, even withdrawn. "Beneath the icecap is a genuinely nice man," one of them concluded, "though he tries his best to disguise it."

His capacity for work soon became evident, his tidiness as an administrator. Memoranda left with him one evening were usually answered the next morning. But reporters went away baffled by his press conferences. They understood all the words, yet when they tried to make a news story out of them, the meaning seemed to vanish. It was not only that he was incapable of oratory or dramatics. His vagueness, which was to become a trademark, simply could not be cast in headlines.

The vagueness was not manufactured to fit the UN situation, though it often came in handy there as a way of avoiding partisanship when tensions were acute. It came from being steeped in the law and from the firm reliance upon law which had been the foundation of Sweden's national life since the fourteenth century. Sweden's delicate position between Eastern and Western Europe made it alert to maintain its independence through encouraging the whole international community to function by law rather than by raw power.

Dag Hammarskjöld's words often seem to wash away the supporting facts until only the pure legal principle remains. Such a method removes to the background the very items which irritate and anger. When discussion is focused on the purely legal factors, tempers tend to grow calm.

Not that he ignored the political realities; in fact, he was extremely sensitive to them. But he had to think out the principles first, and take his stand on them.

As administrator, he soon reorganized the Secretariat in such a way as to hold all the reins in his hands, though he was ably assisted by a few aides who worked nearly as hard as he did. It was a very personal method, depending upon a core of deeply committed people. But it had worked in Sweden, and it would work at the UN, as events were to show.

Chief of these aides was Andrew Cordier, a former professor of history and political science who had worked in the Department of State as an expert on international security and had been involved in the UN ever since its formative days at San Francisco. His intimate and thorough knowledge of the UN and his wonderful good humor and common sense made him invaluable. Ahmed Bokhari of Pakistan, Ralph Bunche, Philippe de Seynes of France, the German Heinz Wieschhoff and C. V. Narasimhan of India were among his close collaborators, along with his Swedish aide, Per Lind. A few other top officials somehow did not find places on the team and eventually left.

Although the public image of Hamarskjöld was that of a shy, reserved man who managed to conceal more than he revealed when he opened his mouth, his co-workers learned that his blue eyes had steel in them, that he was capable of anger though usually able to control it, and that stupidity irked him.

Another side was the deep vein of mysticism—not surprising in a man who loved poetry, music and high mountains—which led him to the UN Meditation Room whenever he faced a tough problem. When the room was dedicated, he said:

"When we come to our deepest feelings and urgings, we have to be alone, we have to feel the sky and the earth, and hear the voice that speaks within us." Mysticism, an all-embracing love of humanity, and peacemaking often go together. They did so conspicuously in Dag Hammarskjöld.

After his appointment to the UN, he used to go for long walks in the woods around his hideaway at Brewster, New York, or in the winter along the sands at Jones Beach. He loved to have a few friends along, but treated them without fuss—bacon and beans and coffee for breakfast and, after six hours of vigorous hiking, beans again.

Mountain climbing had taught him the value of moving forward cautiously, being sure of each foothold. "One who is really serious in his determination to reach the top," he told the UN Press Club, "does not gamble by impatiently accepting bad footholds and poor grips."

Another lesson he learned from mountain climbing was this:

"The safest climber is he who never questions his ability to overcome the next difficulty."

This too might have come from his experience as a climber:

"It is when we all play safe that we create a world of utmost insecurity."

The world Dag Hammarskjöld was expected to keep at peace was full of tensions which made his task, to say the least, unique.

In Asia and Africa the new nations, most of them having been under the thumb of a European power, came into being with strong feelings of resentment, pride and independence at the very moment when the sovereign nation-state was becoming outmoded as a result of nuclear weapons and the need for some form of security which went beyond that of allied national armies and the balance-of-power seesaw. Human existence itself was threatened by the emergence of two superpowers vying with each other for dominance. This heaping up of armaments in two camps and the invention of weapons—not only nuclear but chemical and biological—which could erase man from earth made the old game of power politics unendurable at the very moment when it had reached a peak of fear, force and fury.

In this situation the enemy—Russia or the United States— came to take on more and more the qualities of a demon who could only be expunged since his nature could not be changed. On the one hand he was the brutal suppressor of human liberties embodied in a one-party oligarchy; on the other, the white supremacy imperialist attempting to make the world safe for the wealthy while the poor grew poorer.

While the superpowers girded for a battle they claimed not to want, it became clear that the old game of power politics could no longer keep the peace, if it ever had. The competition broadened out into every field—in aid to developing countries, scholarships, cultural programs, scientific advance. It seems to have spread almost unconsciously into nonmilitary fields as a way of sterilizing the cold war. And this was all to the good. Far better to throw another hundred scholarships into the breach, or to rush in another ballet troupe or a musical comedy, than to deploy troops and weapons.

Yet anyone could see that the continuing weapons buildup would eventually lead to a war no one would want and no one would be able to prevent. The very strength each side relied on to keep it safe would, by its fantastic overgrowth, bring about its own destruction. The growing psychosis of fear was leading the superpowers to erect a monstrous framework of so-called deterrent power which in the end would drive them to self-destructive war. Egg-heads of the atom blithely devised theories of deterrence which depended upon each side's behaving in a perfectly rational manner, when it was apparent that each was far gone down the road to irrationality so far as its image of the other was concerned.

Meanwhile the new nations were interested, not in the power struggle between these two titans, but in their own internal changes—the breakdown of tribal or village life, the movement into cities with its effect on family life and the role of women, the development of industries, the growth of government services, including especially education. These changes often involved a revolt against old systems of landlordism and usury, against the economic dominance of the white outsider, against any sort of external influence or control. Hatred of the old imperialism often led to a friendliness toward communism simply as a gesture of revolt against the old master.

Often the new nations were very small (Togo 1,500,000; Mauritania 1,000,000, for instance), dependent for economic aid upon foreign powers though fiercely determined to be independent, straining toward the "take-off" point when their economy would begin to produce enough goods and jobs for all. Lacking adequate private capital, most of them had to depend upon state financing, which meant that they must follow a welfare pattern shaped to a Scandinavian, British or New Deal pattern or go communist. Remarkably, not one of the nations coming to independence since the war has gone communist. The passion for national independence has perhaps been their chief protection, for they have plenty of evidence (in Latvia, East Germany, Bulgaria) as to what happens to an "independent" small communist country.

That these countries understand the communist goal of world dominance seems clear from their behavior.

In the bipolar power struggle, Russia has been unable to carry out her ultimate design of a wholly communized world. Her strategy has therefore been to alternate between bluster and compromise, threat and accommodation.

"We will bury you," says Khrushchev, but meanwhile we can also get along with you. The vision of a wholly communist world has had to adapt itself to the recognition that, since all-out war is impossible, communization will have to come by nonmilitary means and perhaps by occasional small, manageable wars.

Communism was also beginning to have some internal problems of its own. Although the big split between China and Russia had not yet developed, it was growing clear that nations like Yugoslavia and Poland did not want to be submerged within a smothering superstate, but wanted to enjoy their nationhood.

So it was evident, when Dag Hammarskjöld came to New York, that some substitute must be found for the old balance-of-power system—something that would possess its own dynamic to carry it beyond the bickerings of nation-states.

But nationalism—both the nascent variety in the new states and the entrenched variety in the old—had only been sharpened and refined by the big struggle and was unwilling to let go. At the very moment when the only way to maintain the safety of nations was by relinquishing some local sovereignty to an instrument of world sovereignty, the nations were too scared to budge, like an animal that is too frightened to run to safety, or turns backward and gets crushed.

A few hopeful signs were on the horizon, such as the European Common Market and the Organization of American States. These proved that nations would commit themselves to joint regional actions and interests. Yet it was becoming clear that survival depended upon an allegiance to interests that were not national or regional but universal—peace, development, literacy, health. Only a united world could guarantee these things. They could not be withheld from any without endangering all, and the welfare of each was wrapped up in the welfare of all—a hard lesson to learn.

Dag Hammarskjöld came to the UN at a time when thoughtful men knew that the world's hope lay in world organization, based upon a world-wide conscience, which would be a dynamic force working through world law and with a world police force for universal peace and progress.

But the world was still a long way from admitting this when he came into office. It still is.

Dag Hammarskjöld's first opportunity to show what he could do came in December, 1954, when the General Assembly asked him to see if he could gain the release of eleven American airmen shot down in 1953 while flying for the United Nations in Korea. Under the terms of the armistice, all prisoners of war were to have been repatriated. But China, having sentenced these eleven as spies, announced that it was also holding four other airmen given up as lost.

Public confidence in the UN, at least in the United States, was already at a low ebb. The great powers were bypassing it. Newspapers were predicting its early death. And now the new Secretary General had been saddled with a nearly hopeless task, for the resolution which asked him to act also condemned China.

"You either condemn or negotiate; you can't do both," he remarked. But he went to work.

Knowing that the Chinese would never negotiate on the basis of a resolution which condemned them, he never sent it. Instead, he cabled Chou En-lai that he would like to come to Peking to discuss the matter personally. Chou replied with two cables—the first inviting him to come, the second stating that the trial and conviction of spies was a purely internal matter. Dag went anyway.

He and his party arrived in bitter cold weather but were cordially received. The negotiations with their long speeches and pauses for translation went on for days. Chou, whose family had been members of China's ruling class for a thousand years, was a tough negotiator and a manipulator of phrases quite the equal of the Swede, whose family background and devotion to public service were strikingly like his own.

"If I express myself in circumscribed terms, it is nothing compared to Chou," said Dag in wondering admiration, after a few earnest sessions. Chinese diplomacy, he discovered, was so subtle as to make him feel a barbarian. He had to leave Peking without any solid commitment, which made it necessary for him to be noncommittal when he reached New York on January 13 (1955).

He believed he had Chou En-lai's promise to release the airmen a few at a time, but it was up to China to make the announcement as and when it chose. If either the UN or the United States acted as if they had forced China's hand, Chou might back down.

At his press conference the next day Hammarskjöld made it clear that peacemaking could better be accomplished by quiet diplomacy than by open bluster.

"Open diplomacy, or the false kind of publicity at the wrong stage, prematurely, has often frozen positions in a way which has rendered the situation much more difficult," he said. A difficult idea to put in a headline!

The Chinese, determined to show that no one could boss them around, took their time. President Eisenhower and Secretary

Dulles counseled patience and restraint. The State Department let it be known that we would welcome a United Nations cease-fire in the Formosan Straits, but this was soon rebuffed by Red China.

Finally, at the end of May, four fliers were released.

Dag flew off to Sweden—to attend a meeting of the Swedish Academy, of which he was a member. Or so he said. Actually, he wanted to talk with the Chinese Ambassador, General Piao. Still no commitment.

Then a Chinese official, happening to meet a friend of Hammarskjöld at an embassy party, learned that Dag would be in Sweden again around the time of his birthday, July 29. The Chinese, who seemed unduly interested in the birthday, asked what he would like for a present.

"Release of the airmen," said the friend.

On July 25 both Washington and Peking announced that they would soon meet for negotiations in Geneva. The conference began July 31.

On August 1 Dag received a message that the Chinese would soon release the airmen—not because of the Assembly's action, but to strengthen good relations with the Secretary General on the occasion of his birthday.

"I hope that this measure taken by the Chinese Government will have favorable effects on our present talks," said Wang Ping-nan, the Chinese negotiator.

So Dag Hammarskjöld's first important mission ended in success. More important, it was now clear that the Secretary General could achieve results where the Security Council or the Assembly could not. The office of the Secretary General was in itself a powerful force for peace.

The next test was a big one.

On October 29, 1956, the Israeli army moved into the Sinai Peninsula, over-running the Egyptian army. Two days later France and Great Britain attacked Egypt. Russia and the United

States united to put a resolution through the Security Council expressing grave concern and authorizing the Secretary General to make whatever recommendations he thought helpful. The Council was asking Dag to do what it could not accomplish itself—prevent an imminent and perhaps disastrous war. Fortunately Dag Hammarskjöld had kept in close touch with the UN Truce Supervisory Organization, established in 1949, which policed the Israeli-Egypt armistice, had recently visited the Middle East, and was therefore well acquainted with all the factors in the present emergency. When Great Britain and France blocked the resolution, Jugoslavia, with able assistance from Hammarskjöld behind the scenes, proposed carrying the issue to the General Assembly under the "Uniting for Peace" resolution. After a wrangle, the resolution carried.

John Foster Dulles, ill with an attack which soon sent him to the hospital, rose to call for a cease-fire and withdrawal of all forces behind the previously established armistice lines.

"I doubt that any representative ever spoke from this rostrum with as heavy a heart as I have tonight," he said, "unable to agree with three nations with which we have ties of deep friendship . . . and two of which constitute our oldest and most trusted allies."

It was nearly 2:30 in the morning of November 2 before the Assembly voted, but it voted overwhelmingly for the cease-fire resolution.

In a long night meeting on November 3, Lester Pearson of Canada proposed a United Nations Emergency Force (UNEF) to see that hostilities were brought to an end. This was voted early in the morning of November 4.

Dag Hammarskjöld now went to work setting up the force. "We had to work under heavy pressure," he later recalled, "at great speed and with a considerable risk of making mistakes or running into misunderstandings." Meanwhile the General Assembly voted him the power to work out the nature and composition of the force as he thought best.

By November 5 the four governments involved had notified the Secretary General that they would agree to a cease-fire. This important result had come about in part at least because of Hammarskjöld's effective work behind the scenes. By November 6, he presented his plan for UNEF, approved the following day. He and his staff had worked almost without sleep—twenty hours at a stretch for four days—to produce it.

The General Assembly left a great deal of responsibility in Hammarskjöld's hands, trusting him to issue whatever regulations and instructions might be necessary. One test of his skill is that the French delegate "welcomed" his efforts and even traced the idea of an international army to a French proposal forty years back.

Hammarskjöld accomplished what no single government could have done. He had devised a police force under the authority of the General Assembly although the Charter made no such provision. And the fighting had stopped.

Eight days after the UNEF framework had been erected, the first UN soldiers landed in Egypt. They could have landed five days earlier if Egypt had given her consent. Canada, Colombia, and the four Scandinavian countries supplied the troops; General E. L. M. Burns of Canada was appointed Chief of Command. American planes brought soldiers from as far away as Bogota, Colombia, and Agra in India. Italy gave permission for troops to be landed at Naples so that they could hop to Egypt the moment permission was given. Meanwhile 1,000 helmet liners were sprayed a distinctive blue so that UN troops would be immediately recognizable.

On November 15 the first troops glided in—ninety-five Danes and Norwegians who stepped out of two Swiss planes in full battle dress. The next day Hammarskjöld landed himself, to help decide exactly what the troops would or would not do.

"This is the first time there has ever been an international police force," he told them, congratulating them on their historic mission.

He then went to Cairo to reassure Egyptian leaders that the UN mission would see that foreign troops withdrew completely from Egyptian soil. More than four thousand UN troops took up their stations in Egypt. By March 8, 1957, Hammarskjöld was able to report that the Israelis had left.

Activation of UNEF within a week's time remains a spectacular achievement, proving that the UN can work quickly and effectively. During all these tense months Dag Hammarskjöld played a unique role. He could negotiate like a foreign minister, but with the weight of the General Assembly behind him. He could speak for the united will of all the nations in his peace-keeping role. He proved that the UN was indeed an effective force for peace. And he did all this without causing any government to lose face.

When he followed up this triumph by organizing almost overnight a salvage fleet of thirty-two vessels to clear the Suez, the ability of his office to do miracles in the workaday world as well as in negotiation was clearly established.

But the ground of Hammarskjöld's success was in establishing a firm legal position which kept him from having to surrender to expediencies as they arose. His solutions were practical, but they could be defended by the rules of the game. This was his job— to interpret the rules and see that they were followed.

As a negotiator, he was careful to leave doors open even when agreement appeared impossible. After Suez, he paid a state visit to Great Britain, walked in the Negev with Ben-Gurion, and dined at the Quai d'Orsay in Paris, thus making clear his friendly feelings for the governments he had had to discipline.

It was part of his method to anticipate world crises. He visited troubled areas and came to know the problems, conditions and leaders at first hand.

The revolt against Soviet Russia's economic, military and political control of Hungary in October, 1956, confronted the UN and its Secretary General with a new sort of problem, and in the very midst of the Suez crisis. It was the first sizable counter-revolution against communism and the first instance brought before the UN of a people determined to overthrow their government by violence so as to establish democratic self-rule.

When the Security Council met on October 27, the Russian and American delegates locked horns. The threat of a Russian veto made any decisive action impossible. Meanwhile Soviet tanks were ruthlessly destroying Budapest. Bitter debates in the General Assembly ended in resolutions which condemned the U.S.S.R. for forceful deportation of Hungarian citizens and called for aid to the refugees, and for the Secretary General to send observers to Hungary. But this never became possible. While the debate boiled in the General Assembly, Russia tightened her grip on Hungary and crushed the revolt.

Hammarskjöld kept trying to get into Hungary, but the communists knew well enough that his presence would give fresh heart to the people.

There were plenty of neutral diplomats in Budapest from among whom UN observers could have been appointed to make the report the Assembly wanted. Yet in the end the result would have been the same. Nothing but superior military power could have given Hungarians the kind of government they wanted. And the introduction of such power would no doubt have touched off a war.

About the only thing left for the UN to do was to take care of the 190,000 refugees who managed to escape—two per cent of the Hungarian population. It did a good job, though no job dealing with so many dispossessed human beings can ever begin to be adequate.

Hungary demonstrated the hopeless imprisonment in their own country of a freedom-loving people and dramatized the plight of millions more. As Mr. Nehru told his parliament, the story of Hungary was one of Soviet suppression of a change in government that the majority wanted. The lesson was a sobering one for many newly independent nations. The UN had gone on record by large majorities for each resolution that condemned this ruthless suppression of a people's will.

In the summer of 1958 Lebanon asked the Security Council to do something about the United Arab Republic's interference in its affairs. Cairo radio was openly attacking the Lebanese government and there was fighting in the mountains, allegedly as a result of arms shipped in by the U.A.R. which had recently been formed by the union of Syria and Egypt. The root of Lebanon's trouble was its almost equally divided population of Christians and Muslims—the former pro-Western, the latter naturally strong pro-Arab and Nasserist.

Dr. Charles Malik, the Lebanese representative, told the Security Council his country was suffering from "massive illegal and unprovoked intervention" on the part of the U.A.R. which, he said, was sending in arms, training men for subversive activity, and conducting violent press and radio campaigns which urged the Lebanese to overthrow their government.

Lebanon's only fault, he said, was its independence and its friendship for the West.

"We plead guilty on both of these counts," he said. "Our case then is a test case. It is the case of every small country in the world. If intervention in the affairs of one small country should be allowed to work its way without hindrance, how can any other small country feel secure again?"

After some bitter exchanges between the U.S.A. and the U.S.S.R. and between Iraq and the U.A.R., Sweden offered a resolution which satisfied everybody. An observation group (UNOGIL) was to go to Lebanon immediately, make certain that no arms or agents were entering the country illegally, and keep the Security Council informed through the Secretary General, who was to be responsible for setting the whole thing in motion.

Lebanon would have preferred a fighting force, but Dag insisted that the UN's job was to observe.

It is a reasonable guess that the Swedish delegate had discussed his resolution first with his countryman, the Secretary General, who was eager to placate both Lebanon and Egypt. Dag Hammarskjöld felt that if Nasser was sure Lebanon was not teaming up with the newly formed Arab Federation (Iraq and Jordan) to overthrow him with the West's help, he might end his provocations.

First, Dag established the legal status of the observation group through an exchange of letters with Dr. Malik. Then he chose three executive officers—a Norwegian, an Indian and an Ecuadorian. Within ten days sixty-nine observers from nine countries were on the job. Dag Hammarskjöld flew to Beirut himself in order to brief the observers and talk with Lebanon's President Chamoun. He also visited Jordan, Israel, and then Egypt, where he talked for four hours with President Nasser.

In time the observation group grew to about six hundred observers drawn from twenty-one countries. They set up and staffed forty-nine observation posts, using eighteen planes and nearly three-hundred ground vehicles. They did not find the massive infiltration Lebanon had claimed, but rather an undeclared civil war.

Meanwhile the situation worsened with the murder of King Faisal and the overthrow of his government in neighboring Iraq. On July 14 President Chamoun urged the United States to send troops within forty-eight hours. Otherwise he felt certain that his regime would be overthrown.

Twenty-one hours after the decision had been reached at the White House, Marines came ashore at Ouzai Beach. Diners at the fashionable Pigeon Rock restaurant nearby watched 3,600 of them wade ashore girded for battle, surrounded by hundreds of good-natured Lebanese who not only welcomed them but helped them push two of their sand-mired vehicles onto firm land. The Marines had hardly reached shore when vendors swooped down offering Cokes for sale. Strange sort of crisis!

On the same day the American intervention was explained to

the Security Council by Ambassador Henry Cabot Lodge, grandson and namesake of Wilson's opponent.

"We are the first to admit that the despatch of United States forces to Lebanon is not an ideal way to solve present problems," he said. "They will be withdrawn as soon as the United Nations can take over." The next day he proposed a resolution which would set up a UN security force.

On the following day British paratroopers landed in Jordan at the request of King Hussein, who felt sure that he was about to be invaded by the U.A.R. After a good deal of bickering and maneuvering had occurred at the UN, Dag Hammarskjöld offered a plan to calm the Middle East. The heart of it was an appeal to the Arab states to follow the principles already enunciated by the Arab League—mutual respect for each other's territory and sovereignty and no meddling in each other's affairs. On this basis the UN would assist the Arab states toward economic cooperation and improvement. And the big powers would agree to keep hands off so that the people might shape their own destinies.

At this point the United States announced that 1,700 of its Marines would soon be leaving Lebanon. Addressing the General Assembly on August 13, President Eisenhower proposed a United Nations peace force to prevent outside intervention in the Middle East and an economic development plan to improve living standards in all the Arab nations. He suggested that the Secretary General consult with all the countries concerned to see whether a regional plan could be worked out.

After a good deal of backstage negotiating, ten of the Arab nations came forward with a "Good Neighbor" resolution of their own. This in itself was an accomplishment in view of the disharmony that had existed. The larger problem was to get a resolution which would not only satisfy the Arab nations but would pave the way for the withdrawal of British and American troops, make sure the U.A.R. did not move in, and establish a presence which would guarantee safety and neutrality. The resolution

[328]

made it the business of the Secretary General to see to the practical arrangements. As usual, where the situation looked difficult, the Assembly found it wise to leave details to him.

Without the constant attention of the General Assembly, focusing world interest and opinion on the Middle East and bringing the activities and attitudes of the various governments before public scrutiny, no such settlement would have come about. But without Dag Hammarskjöld's quiet behind-the-scenes negotiating with each of the parties—all suspicious and edgy—the result would have been impossible. Throughout the crisis he had worked for a settlement all parties could accept.

For once he allowed himself to boast a little. "Yesterday was one of those days in the life of this Organization when it showed its invaluable contribution to present politics in the international field and to present diplomacy," he said.

Egyptian newspapers which had bitterly attacked the United States and Great Britain changed overnight to praise the UN action and the solidarity displayed by the Arab states.

The United States would have preferred a resolution approving its intervention; Jordan wanted a denunciation of the U.A.R., which in turn wanted the intervention denounced. Without the UN, accusations, reprisals and continued unrest would have been the fate of the Middle East.

When Dag Hammarskjöld visited the area in the late summer of 1958, King Hussein of Jordan was surrounded by hostile neighbors—Iraq, Syria, Israel, even Saudi Arabia. Probably two-thirds of his own people opposed his government. Dag's mission was to arrange for the withdrawal of British troops, calm down the bitterness between Jordan and the U.A.R., and devise some sort of UN presence that would keep the peace.

His visit ended in setting up the first UN mission not based on a resolution of the General Assembly or the Security Council, but on his own authority. It was typical of Hammarskjöld in its subtlety and restraint. Actually it amounted to no more than a United Nations presence—a representative who acted like an ambassador from the UN to the Middle East. In the event, the main jobs of his staff were to monitor Arab broadcasts, as a way of discouraging hostile and inflammatory talk, and to restore traffic between Jordan and other Arab countries which had been cut off by the prevailing hostility and suspicion. Fortunately he was on hand to deal with the crisis when King Hussein's plane was nearly shot down by Syrian fighter planes, and greatly moderated that explosive incident. The very presence of the UN turned out to supply the necessary calming influence, as Hammarskjöld had hoped.

Another victory for the Hammarskjöld brand of quiet diplomacy, now forgotten, was the Beck-Friis Mission to Cambodia and Thailand in 1959. Differences had arisen over trade and transportation, prevention of epidemics, ideologies, and the ownership of a hallowed temple. Negotiations had broken down, and, after frontier incidents and demonstrations, diplomatic relations had been suspended.

Letters of complaint came to the Secretary General from both sides. Instead of making a public issue of it, Dag quietly discussed the matter with Cambodian and Thai representatives and with members of the Security Council. He proposed to appoint an impartial observer to look into the facts, made Baron Beck-Friis of Sweden his personal representative, and advised the Security Council of the action he had taken.

Beck-Friis left for Bangkok January 15, 1959, and spent a little more than a month in the two countries. With both sides eager to cooperate, difficulties were adjusted and normal relations restored. The case demonstrated the virtues of quiet diplomacy and the value of a respected third party which symbolized the peace-keeping power of a world body whose services were always available.

Said Dag Hammarskjöld: "You can see how much more effective and smooth-working such a technique is than the regular one, which involves all the meetings and debates and so on."

By far the most difficult crisis Dag Hammarskjöld had to deal with, and to which he ultimately gave his life, was the Congo. Anticipating trouble in the areas moving toward independence, he had already visited Africa to study its problems and needs. A UN presence in the form of economic and technical aid would help greatly, he decided. But events moved too fast.

From the moment when the Belgian Congo became the Republic of Congo on June 30, 1960, trouble flared up. The country was completely unprepared for independence. It had but sixteen university graduates—no doctors, lawyers or engineers. On July 11 the mineral-rich province of Katanga declared its independence. Premier Patrice Lumumba urgently requested military support from the UN. Belgian troops meanwhile extended their control around Leopoldville and elsewhere. On July 13 the Secretary General called the Security Council into emergency session, recommending that military aid be sent. Mongi Slim of Tunisia proposed a resolution which covered what Dag had in mind—calling on Belgium to withdraw its troops, authorizing that UN forces be sent in.

Hammarskjöld went to work with his usual concentrated efficiency to build the second United Nations peace force. Ironically, the Russians who would have liked to veto it were obliged to go along because it was the anti-colonial countries which had asked for it.

By July 18 more than four thousand troops had been promised from five African countries and 3,500 were already in the Congo. They did not arrive a moment too soon. Belgian and Congolese troops had already clashed. Belgians were fleeing, shops closing, business at a standstill. On his way to the Congo soon after, Dag Hammarskjöld stopped in Belgium to extract a promise that Belgian troops would leave as soon as the UN could replace them. Then came the difficulty over Katanga, and Tshombe's refusal to allow UN troops to enter.

Hammarskjöld flew back to New York. The Security Council authorized him to return to Africa and enter Katanga with troops but not to intervene in the internal conflict.

On August 12 he flew into Katanga with 220 Swedish troops and was warmly greeted by Premier Moise Tshombe. Within two days 2,000 more UN troops flew in, the airfield was in their hands, and the outlook good. But Hammarskjöld had infuriated Lumumba by announcing that the UN presence was not to be used to influence the outcome of the internal conflict but to preserve order until the Congolese could make their choice of leadership clear. Lumumba now began to make bitter and irresponsible attacks on the Secretary General and to deluge him with impossible demands, such as turning over all airports to the Congolese army and using UN aircraft to carry Congolese forces wherever they might be needed to preserve the peace. It was now clear to Hammarskjöld that Lumumba in his drive for dictatorial power was ready to wreck both the Congo and the UN. Sir Claude Corea and Mongi Slim, spokesmen for the Afro-Asians on the Security Council, publicly rebuked Lumumba.

Differences arose between Ralph Bunche, UN Special Representative, and Major General Henry Alexander, who commanded Ghanaian forces, over the exact role of UN troops. Perhaps their duties and objectives should have been spelled out more clearly, but at the time the urgent need was to introduce a presence which would insure peace and order.

Then came Khrushchev's visit to the United Nations, his disgraceful attacks on Hammarskjöld, his shoe-pounding, and his effort to castrate the UN by making a mere figurehead of its Secretary General.

In his reply, the Secretary General pointed out that the accusations against him had been put forward "without any single substantive fact." Speaking with icy dignity, he showed that the

U.S.S.R. again and again had voted in the Security Council empowering him to proceed as he had.

"A weak or non-existent executive would mean that the UN would no longer be able to serve as an effective instrument for active protection of the interests of those Members who need such protection. . . . It is not the Soviet Union or, indeed, any other big powers who need the UN for their protection; it is all the others."

When he said, "I shall remain in my post," a storm of applause filled the hall.

"I shall remain in my post," he began again, "during the term of my office as a servant of the Organization in the interests of all those other nations, as long as *they* wish me to do so." An ovation followed in which nearly everyone but the Soviet bloc joined.

The fact that the Soviet Union was aiding Lumumba, Belgium Tshombe and the United States Kasavubu, did not make matters any easier for the UN Peace Force. Kasavubu, President of the Congolese Government, was at swords' points with Premier Lumumba. Also, the UN's top three officials in the Congo all happened to be Americans. Despite their disinterested behavior, this was seen as tilting the whole operation toward the West and was no doubt a factor in the Soviet Union's bitter attack against the Secretary General, culminating in the demand for a troika to replace him. After Colonel Mobutu ordered the Soviets out of the Congo, they turned their heavy guns on Dag, determined to destroy him. The United States made matters worse by supporting President Kasavubu's demand that his delegation be seated by the Assembly. He won, but at the cost of splitting the African states and thus destroying Dag's long efforts at conciliation.

Meanwhile the UN agencies were doing their best to prevent the spread of disease and starvation, an aspect of the work that caught very little attention. UNICEF, WHO, and FAO moved in to help the several hundred thousand people who were wandering homeless after their villages had been destroyed.

[333]

When the Belgians withdrew, only one qualified agriculturist remained to take the place of 542 Belgians. Not one Congolese could run or repair a tractor, yet five million acres of cultivation had been mechanized. To fill in the gaps, an international staff of 750 experts was almost miraculously assembled. They took over the hospitals, food distribution, airports, telecommunications. They set up training courses in farm mechanics, public works, land reclamation. They prevented chaos.

Nevertheless, towards the end of 1960 the political situation grew worse, not only in the Congo but at UN headquarters, where both the General Assembly and the Security Council, divided by cold war conflicts, failed to give the Secretary General a vote of confidence or a new directive. In the Congo itself UN troops were being taunted and abused.

Oddly enough, it was American support which both kept the UN operation going yet made it the object of communist abuse. The United States wanted to see order restored to the Congo and was willing to bear a heavy share of the burden. When Adlai Stevenson became Ambassador to the UN, the United States began to plan its policy so as to cooperate with the Afro-Asian states and with Hammarskjöld. The Soviet Union preferred to capitalize the anti-colonial opportunities inherent in the situation. The unfortunate murder of Lumumba early in 1961 dramatized all the conflicts and suspicions.

The Soviets accused Hammarskjöld of being an organizer of the Lumumba murder. They demanded his dismissal, announcing that they would no longer consider him a UN official. The response was an overwhelming vote of confidence in the Secretary General.

A few days after Lumumba's death had been announced, the Conciliation Commission which had been making on-the-spot investigations turned in its report. It urged a summit conference of Congo political leaders to work out some sort of federation which would preserve both unity and representation of the various factions. Congolese forces were to be immobilized and

[334]

UN forces would supervise an end to hostilities among them. No military aid should be sent into the Congo except through the UN.

After considering this report, the Security Council passed a resolution calling for all appropriate measures to prevent civil war, for an end to all military operations, and for the use of UN force if necessary to end the fighting. Sponsored by Afro-Asian countries (Ceylon, Liberia, U.A.R.), the resolution gave the UN more power than it had previously had to establish peace in the Congo. Twenty African states meeting at Monrovia firmly backed the UN effort. Despite errors and conflict, civil war had been forestalled.

Eighteen Congolese leaders meeting in March hammered out a confederation agreement, but Tshombe, President of Katanga, later backed out. The attempt to preserve order without active intervention had failed. In April President Kasavubu signed an agreement accepting the UN Security Council resolution of February 21, which authorized UN troops to use force if necessary to prevent civil war. On September 13 UN troops therefore attacked Elizabethville in order to end Katanga's secession. The fighting spread throughout Katanga. It was on a mission to help resolve this problem that Dag Hammarskjöld lost his life on September 18, 1961.

No one will ever know why his plane crashed; no indication of sabotage was found, only a long gash of broken trees and torn earth scarred the African jungle where it went down, stopping just short of a giant anthill. Of the fifteen dead (one more died later), only Dag was unburned and immediately recognizable.

His death was a true sacrifice to world peace. He made world history by demonstrating that a resourceful, quiet, and sometimes purposefully obscure Secretary General could do a great deal to keep peace in the world by skillful use of the tools the UN Charter makes available. In each crisis he seemed to make the instinctively right response. His trip to Peking succeeded in releasing the UN airmen where formal diplomacy or public denunciation would have failed. His ability to form the UN Emergency Force in forty-eight hours to meet the threat in the Middle East, his construction of the UNOGIL to patrol the Lebanese border, the modestly conceived presence in Jordan, the calm solution of the Cambodia-Thailand dispute, all demonstrated his genius at avoiding dangerous confrontations, working instead quietly behind the scenes.

Because conflict is news, the public is most aware of the UN when it is least successful. But under Dag Hammarskjöld the world organization built up a repertory of effective techniques for the resolution of tensions which is a permanent heritage. And in the Congo, where he gave his life, he demonstrated his courage in facing the larger issues and in working valiantly to solve them too.

Dag Hammarskjöld stepped aboard at a time when impatience with the cold war and its many frustrations had led the great powers to the point where they seemed likely to scuttle the UN if it did not founder in the storm. He left it strengthened by the integrity and subtlety of his own personality, his capacity for endless maneuver, tireless diplomacy, subtle adjustment, political sensitivity, legal knowledge, an incredible memory for detail and a steady vision of a world in which peace had to be maintained bit by bit because there was no other way. Idealist and pragmatist, he knew how to snatch small advantages and build them into firm results.

He so enlarged the status and function of the Secretary General's office that he was able to act when Council and Assembly were caught on dead center. While he always sought instructions from them, he was also ready to act on his own to the full extent that the Charter permitted. This made it possible for him to do on his own authority things that needed doing but which, because of cold war tensions, the Council would not authorize.

He saw his authority as embedded in the whole Charter, and he took it as his duty to act in the spirit of the prologue, "to save succeeding generations from the scourge of war." Authorized by the Charter to "bring to the attention of the Security Council any matter which in his opinion may threaten the maintenance of international peace and security," he also saw it as his duty to be personally familiar with the world's trouble spots and the leaders there.

He had hoped to make the Security Council a body which regularly met to discuss situations before they erupted into crises and to take preventive steps, but the great powers were not ready for this. De Gaulle, for instance, made no secret of his contempt for the UN, while even the United States was of a divided mind, with Adlai Stevenson and Harlan Cleveland ready to accept Dag's vision, but conservative pressures on the White House and in Congress pushing the other way.

Speaking in California, Dag Hammarskjöld tried to make it clear that negotiation is not surrender.

"To negotiate with someone never means to me I had to like him or approve of him, much less that I was willing to sell out my principles.

"Terrible wars have been fought in the past because people thought they could not live in the same world together," he said. But eventually "they found that it was not only possible but necessary to accept the principle of diversity in human society."

If international negotiation could only be centered in the UN, he felt, the Charter with its emphasis on peaceful solutions would provide a positive background—a framework and a presence quite different from the spirit in which two opposed powers habitually negotiate with each other.

He had already demonstrated that where international tensions were high and the great powers opposed in their interests, as in the Middle East, the UN presence was the only way out. Especially in areas where the old colonialism was withdrawing, nothing but a UN presence could prevent new forms of imperialism or outright bloody battle, with clandestine cold war aid coming in from outside—a situation already familiar in the countries which had once comprised Indochina. The UN could then be used as a shield against the cold war.

The UN, said Hammarskjöld in a speech honoring George de Hevesy when he received the Atoms for Peace Award in 1959, is something like Niels Bohr's model of the atom—not final or correct in all its details, but providing an approach leading to a satisfactory solution. "The UN is part of the great pattern of change of our time." It recognizes and gives expression to the interest in peace which unites mankind.

A few months later, in Denmark, he spelled out his vision of the UN as an open channel for continuous consultation. The diplomats at the UN, he said, make possible a diplomatic conference which instead of meeting to deal with a crisis is always in being. Much of the exchange is confidential—in fact its value comes in part from being unpublicized. Here exchanges are possible "even across frontiers which otherwise appear impassable." Used as an unofficial sounding board, the UN often helps to shape national policies or prevent unwise actions. At the usual foreign minister's conference, delegates may simply fail to agree. But at the UN they must at least reply. And the presence of so many member states exerts an influence toward agreement.

Within this framework, the Secretary General takes his stand on the Charter and is able to build an independent influence for the UN as it evolves. Thus, he is able to engage in "preventive diplomacy," sending his personal representative on a good offices mission to any area where a conflict appears likely.

Throughout the Hammarskjöld speeches of the later years there runs a clear conviction that the UN is a live and developing organism, strengthened by every use that is made of it, every challenge to which it must respond. This, indeed, was very much in line with his personal philosophy of creativity. Like Schweitzer's, his philosophy was centered in a deep reverence for life and for the life force which manifests itself both in spirit and in matter, finding expression in the fine arts and in the equally fine art of government to which he had devoted his life. It is not surprising that he loved poetry, music and nature, for he was an artist in government. Not only in the intricacy of his diplomatic footwork, or in the occasional outcroppings of poetry in his speeches, but in his conception of the creative task he was undertaking as the builder of a political vehicle which might carry mankind over the hump to safety instead of down the iced slope into the abyss.

He liked Bergson's philosophy of creative evolution and *élan vital*, and he believed with Pierre de Chardin that man is evolving into newer and better types and toward a higher degree of social organization. A deep philosophical foundation as well as an almost mystical faith supported his actions as Secretary General.

"We all know," he had said at a staff meeting a few days before his death, "that if we feel that what we do is purposeful, not to say essential, for the progress of man and human society . . . we are willing to accept hardships and serve gladly for the value of serving."

It was the evolutionary aspect of the UN that he chose to emphasize in his speech at the Chicago University School of Law in June, 1960.

"Still there is no international society," he said. Man has developed through the family to larger and larger social units, "but we, like our ancestors, can only press against the receding wall which hides the future."

We can, however, see in the UN the beginnings of a constitutional framework for international cooperation. The necessary institutional framework is also being built through the European Common Market and other regional groupings. These institutions, he insisted, must develop without a preconceived idea of their ultimate form.

So with the UN. It too is an "experimental operation on one of the lines in which men push forward in the direction of higher forms of an international society."

"Working at the edge of the development of human society is to work on the brink of the unknown." Such a situation calls for

[339]

"steadfastness of purpose and flexibility of approach." Admitting that the Secretariat had been "a little too much of a one-man operation," he was convinced that through the UN men have "conquered essential new ground for our work for the future." And finally, he expressed his "faith in the ultimate result of the creative evolution in which it is our privilege to cooperate." Here indeed was the ground of his faith. He was sure that in time men would create "an international constitutional system surmounting the nations."

The fullest statement of his concept of what the United Nations ought to be occurs in the Introduction to his Annual Report for 1961.

"I don't see what I can write after this one," he told Andrew Cordier. It was, in any event, to be his last.

In this carefully drawn document he described two concepts of the UN. The first views it simply as a conference machinery for resolving international conflicts with a view to peaceful coexistence, the Secretariat representing within its ranks the same interests and ideologies which create the tensions. This view is anchored in the time-honored concept of sovereign states in perpetual armed competition.

The other view sees the UN as a dynamic instrument of governments "through which they should also try to develop forms of executive action, undertaken on behalf of all members . . . in implementation of the principles and purposes of the Charter." Such a conception will produce "continued growth to increasingly effective forms of international cooperation" served by a Secretariat guided solely by the principles of the Charter and the decisions of its main organs, and the interests of the Organization itself.

Such a concept moves beyond national sovereignty and "opens the road toward more developed and increasingly effective forms of constructive international cooperation."

The Charter, Hammarskjöld pointed out, projects into the international arena principles and purposes already accepted as

[340]

of national validity. It accepts the principle of equal political rights and implies an endorsement of equal economic opportunity. So the UN has worked to raise standards in underdeveloped areas and has contributed to the self-determination of former colonial territories.

Having declared itself against war, the UN has tried to see that nations which resort to it do not achieve their ends. The Security Council is there to substitute negotiation for conflict, the International Court of Justice to see that the rule of law works in the international sphere. Although the General Assembly only recommends, its votes have more and more often come to be binding.

The Secretary General found in Article 25—"The members of the United Nations agree to accept and carry out the decisions of the Security Council in accordance with the provisions of the present Charter"—a bridge from conference to parliamentary status. Some members try to sidestep this provision, but if they would only implement it, the UN would become more effective. It is not the UN that is at fault when recalcitrant members ignore its decisions.

Article 24 gives the Security Council the primary responsibility for maintaining international peace. In practice, the responsibility has been carried out by establishing on-the-spot subcommittees for fact-finding or negotiation, as well as observation missions and police forces. The Secretary General has had to interpret his duties under the rather vague but therefore potentially broad terms of Articles 98 and 99. Criticism of his actions has usually been based on thinking of the UN as a conference rather than an organic body. But Article 100 clearly establishes the international nature of the Secretariat, which neither seeks nor receives instructions from national governments. Each member nation agrees to respect the international character of the Secretariat.

Dag Hammarskjöld managed to make it clear that he stood for a dynamic, living organization which would develop in response

[341]

to the challenges it had to meet, evolving in time as a guarantor of world peace.

The death of this quiet, undemonstrative, withdrawn man, whose words had so often seemed to hide both himself and his meaning, struck the world's people like a personal blow.

"My God, Dag's dead," people told each other.

"You'll never see anyone like that again," said one of his co-workers. "He had fantastic spirit, discipline, energy, and intellect, and you very rarely find all these qualities in one person. He was a diffident, unpretentious, slim figure, but you always felt his grandeur. . . . He's made the UN an indispensable machine, and here it is.

"I never heard him say he was tired. . . . He would think of all the history, all the problems, all the long-term probabilities, all the practical possibilities for action by the UN, and then how to get support to do something about it. . . . He was a force—for justice, common sense, and decency."

Andrew Cordier, who had worked with him through all the difficult years, paid him this eloquent and moving tribute:

> "Dag Hammarskjöld's death marks the close of an era of unparalleled richness—in the charting of new paths of diplomacy, in combining rare gifts of energy, wisdom and intelligence to bring crises under control and to promote progress for human betterment. . . . His accomplishments . . . [were] like snowflakes . . . countless small, almost unnoticed achievements joined with decisively constructive results on great issues."

Dag Hammarskjöld's accomplishments stretch far beyond the record of these few pages, as his influence will stretch far into the future of human history. He set up, for example, the first international Atoms for Peace conferences. He organized an International Administrative Service to see new nations through their early crisis period.

History often seems to make men. Do men also make history?

[342]

Chance lighted upon Dag Hammarskjöld to be Secretary General of the United Nations. It is ironic that many who voted for him thought they had chosen a weak man who would serve them chiefly as housekeeper. Instead, they got a man uniquely fitted to move the UN forward in the direction of what some of its founders, at least, had hoped it might become, and what all men everywhere must really want: an international body able to rise above nationalism and power blocs so as to prevent the scourge of war.

That Dag Hammarskjöld did push history in this direction there is no doubt. Looking back, we can see how all his previous training helped to fit him for the post, and how even his supposed shortcomings became assets—his impersonal style a defense against being identified with any one nation or ideology, his celebrated vagueness a way of insulating against open conflict, his legalism a way of cooling hot disputes and bringing the opposed sides into harmony.

The components that go to make a human being are so many and often so undetectable that character often appears to be a mystery. But in Dag's case many of these formative influences can be detected—the family tradition of selfless service to the state, which he transferred to the world; the autocratic pattern of the public figure who was his father vying with the poetic and emotionally warm nature of his mother to produce in himself a lasting tension between outer stiffness and inner sensitivity, between law and poetry, devotion both to duty and to the arts, which symbolize man's contact with ultimate reality.

One sees how the law, which is one way man orders experience, was balanced in him by a devotion to the arts which also seek to pierce the mystery of existence by searching out the forms which characterize it. The aesthetic sense, which came out in him so many ways—his personal attention to choosing and placing paintings and statuary for the UN buildings, for example—gives us a valuable key to the man. Just as nature clearly demonstrates order as the principle of creation, so man through his sciences and his arts responds to that order by making it more visible, more deeply felt. Dag was an artist in politics, where a good performance requires skills equal to those of the composer, the singer, the poet.

To conceive rightly was to execute expertly. Dag was meticulous about his conception of problems and often inspired in the artistry of his response. A passion for order lay behind his long working hours, his good housekeeping in matters both great and small. He wanted a tidy world. More, he was willing to help make it. All his eight and a half years at the UN were an effort to tidy up the world's messes—to sweep world events clean with the broom of law. In the process, he built a better broom, one which we fail to use at our peril.

Peacemaking is an art. Like all arts, it must either be growing or dying. Dag helped it to grow. Both creator and performer, he had the world for his audience. Did we understand the professional excellence of his work? Perhaps not; yet, like any landmark in art, it stands there for others to measure themselves by and to learn from.

This man, by what we call chance but which may in a higher artistry be design, came happily to fill the job best suited to his very special nature. He devoted himself to it in a spirit of unconscious sacrifice which can only be described as religious. He died too soon, but perhaps not too soon to have saved mankind. Though we still totter on the brink, he gave us a breathing spell, and if we would only follow his example and his method, we might yet build the UN into the kind of international body which can prevent disaster by subjecting nation-states to the rule of law instead of letting them vie with each other to be the strongest, and thus to prepare for war.

Having designed the meditation room at the UN, Dag wrote the inscription carved in black marble at the entrance:

"This is a room devoted to peace and those who are giving their lives for peace. It is a room of quiet where only thoughts should speak."

[344]

In that silent room to which Dag often came when he had a problem to resolve, we still feel his presence. Sitting there, we might remember the line of a Swedish poem he loved:

"The greatest prayer of man does not ask for victory but for peace."

16. Peace Is the Way

 If we should try to reduce to a sentence the essential teaching of each of these great peacemakers, the result might be somthing like this:

Ikhnaton: The world is one; can man then fight himself?

Buddha: Peace comes only by overcoming desire.

Asoka: Man must achieve nonviolence by the practice of it.

Jesus: Love thy neighbor as thyself.

St. Augustine: True peace is found only in the City of God.

St. Francis: But we can discover it in ourselves through loving service.

Penn: Force may subdue, but love gains; assume in others the same good motives you find in yourself.

Thoreau: Protest evil and injustice—even when it is embodied in the law.

Tolstoy: Abandon the privileges that make for strife; resist not evil with evil.

Nobel: Combine to resist aggression; encourage the best minds to work for peace.

Carnegie: Educate; arbitrate; federalize; rationalize.

Angell: Face the fact that no one wins wars any more.

Wilson: Combine to deter the aggressor; cooperate to assure self-determination and world democracy.

Gandhi: Work upon the goodness in your opponent, and work nonviolently.

Hammarskjöld: Stand on firm legal ground, but reach as far as you can to develop a law above that of nations which will build a consensus for peace.

Despite the pessimism with which we tend to view our own age, it has developed several remarkable instruments of peace which man had never successfully developed before.

We have the United Nations and its agencies, cooling disputes before they kindle into war or restoring order where the dispute has gotten out of hand; or providing technical assistance which will raise standards of health, education or agriculture and thus cure sore spots before they become sources of infection.

We have foreign aid, and with it a new moral commitment to help those far distant from us for whom a little while ago we had no sense of responsibility at all.

We have the Peace Corps, a practical yet inspiring answer to the question, "Am I my brother's keeper?" and an example, at last, of that moral equivalent of war for which William James was searching.

We have agencies like the Common Market and the Alliance for Progress which indicate an awareness of the inadequacies of nationalism and the necessity of going beyond it.

We have a much broader concept of cultural and educational exchange than ever before. The number of persons who travel between countries and who live for a significant length of time abroad is still too small, but it is growing. We may hope for the day when working vacations will put the farmer, the factory worker, the teacher in a foreign land long enough to feel at home in it, and to do this not by thousands only but by millions.

And we have weapons of ultimate destruction so frightful that

[347]

we know we must keep working for peace whether we want to or not.

One thing all the great peacemakers agree upon: man can have peace only by changing himself. That the change can be made, they illustrated in their own lives.

But it cannot be made without effort, without discipline, without motivation, or without sacrifice.

The effort has to be made all along the line. In education, we have to broaden our vision so as to think about our own country a little less, about other countries a little more. Somehow, we have to overcome the superstition that the United Nations is some sort of subversive organization and see it as it is: a creation for which we were largely responsible and which is of tremendous benefit to all those who want a just, peaceful and prosperous world.

Through trade, commerce and finance we can build firmer international ties. Hundreds of voluntary organizations exist through which such ties can be strengthened—everything from Boy Scouts and Rotary International to the Interparliamentary Union and the many scientific and professional associations.

How does one become motivated toward this open, friendly, international world, leaving behind the narrow, suspicious, chauvinist framework? We need to know more about this and shape our educational planning accordingly.

Although we have been busy in many fields, we have tended to overlook the power and importance of symbols to move us in the right direction. The flag, the national anthem, the Capitol, the Statue of Liberty are strong aids to patriotism. How can symbols of similar effectiveness unite us in a common brotherhood of mutual concern?

Well, as our peacemakers have seen, you have to have a personal commitment that is essentially religious. Each religion is responsible for evoking this commitment in its members. But would it not also be a great force for good if all the religions meeting together would adopt a statement of basic ethical principles to guide us in this new international world?

Already we have the international work of the YMCA, Church World Service, Catholic Relief Services, World Neighbors, American Friends Service Committee and all the other religion-based agencies whose work grows out of a commitment to the brotherhood of man, and these are backed up by other, secular agencies such as CARE, the International Red Cross, Oxford Famine Relief in England, and hundreds more.

All these remind us that the world we hope for is on our doorstep.

We need a concerted ethical-religious jolt to remind us that, as the great peacemakers were always rediscovering, the final basis of peace is moral, depending upon a renewal from within. Without this personal dedication in millions of individual hearts, treaties and negotiation and diplomacy can come to nothing, for they will lack a firm ground of self-sacrificing popular support to stand on.

To put it simply, we must be willing to exchange the love of power for the power of love. Then, as with Gandhi, we may discover that there is no stronger power.

Our preoccupation with techniques, our virtuosity in details, requires a sturdy underpinning of idealism to keep them from being merely mechanical. We need to be continuously clear on what principles we are advancing through our techniques, and whether the choices we make are the right ones. A fifty-billion-dollar military budget piled on top of a supply of bombs that would wipe out humanity several times over is one illustration of how much we need this self-evaluation.

We are standing on two thresholds at once. One leads to all-out nuclear, biological and chemical warfare and the extinction of civilization. The other leads to a world brotherhood in which men, recognizing the dangers and delusions of nationalism, suddenly discover that they can after all federate on a world scale

[349]

and reap the advantages of federation already proved on a continental scale in the United States.

"There is no way to peace; peace is the way."

Perhaps the whole story is told there. We can have peace only by practicing it—at every level, in every way, despite all provocations, in the midst of utter disappointment, at the cost of personal sacrifice. We can have it, that is, only if we truly want it.

"Let us then try what Love will do: for if men did once see we love them, we should soon find they would not harm us," said Penn.

No one has yet found a sounder foundation than this for peace to rest on.

For Further Reading

Instead of listing all the works consulted, I give here a list of the books a reader might turn to next if he wanted to know more about these men. B. S.

IKHNATON:
Bratton, Fred Gladstone. *The First Heretic.* Boston, 1962.
Breasted, James Henry. *The Dawn of Conscience.* New York, 1933.
Weigall, Arthur. *The Life and Times of Akhnaton.* New York, 1923.
BUDDHA:
Burlingame, Eugene Watson. *Buddhist Parables.* New Haven, 1922
Goddard, Dwight, ed. *A Buddhist Bible.* New York, 1952.
Percheron, Maurice. *Buddha and Buddhism.* New York, 1957 (paperback).
Suzuki, D. T. *Zen Buddhism.* Garden City, 1956 (paperback).
Thomas, Edward J. *The Life of Buddha.* London, 1927.
ASOKA:
MacPhail, James. *Asoka.* Oxford, n. d.
Smith, Vincent A. *Asoka.* Oxford, 1920.
Thapar, Romila. *Asoka and the Decline of the Mauryas.* Oxford, 1961.
JESUS:
McCown, Chester C. *The Search for the Real Jesus.* New York, 1940.
Paul, Leslie. *Son of Man.* New York, 1961.
Schweitzer, Albert. *The Psychiatric Study of Jesus.* Boston, 1948.
Steinmann, Jean. *The Life of Jesus.* Boston, 1963.
SAINT AUGUSTINE:
Augustine. *City of God* and *Confessions.* Many editions.
Deane, H. A. *The Political and Social Ideas of St. Augustine.* New York, 1963.
West, Rebecca. *St. Augustine.* New York, 1933.

SAINT FRANCIS:
  Goudge, Elizabeth. *My God and My All.* New York, 1959.
  The Little Flowers of St. Francis (many editions).
PENN:
  Beatty, Edward. *William Penn as Social Philosopher.* New York, 1939.
  Bronner, Edwin B. *William Penn's "Holy Experiment."* New York, 1962.
  Buranelli, Vincent. *The King and the Quaker.* Philadelphia, 1961.
  Hull, William I. *William Penn: A Topical Biography.* New York, 1937.
  Peare, Catherine Owens. *William Penn.* Philadelphia & New York, 1957.
  Penn, William. Of his many works, "The Frame of the Government of the Province of Pennsilvania" and "Some Account of the Province of Pennsylvania" are of interest in connection with his American experience, "England's Present Interest Discovered" and "The Peoples Ancient and Just Liberties Asserted" for his convictions regarding freedom of conscience, and "An Essay towards the Present and Future Peace of Europe" for his league of nations.
THOREAU:
  Canby, Henry Seidel. *Thoreau.* Boston, 1939.
  Krutch, Joseph Wood. *Henry David Thoreau.* New York, 1948.
  Thoreau, Henry David. The essays "Civil Disobedience," "Slavery in Massachusetts" and "A Plea for Captain John Brown" have been reprinted in various collections.
TOLSTOY:
  Rolland, Romain. *Tolstoy.* New York, 1911.
  Simmons, Ernest J. *Leo Tolstoy.* 2 vols. Boston, 1946.
  Stockham, Alice B. *Tolstoi: A Man of Peace.* Chicago, 1900.
  Tolstoy, Alexandra. *Tolstoy: A Life of My Father.* New York, 1953.
  Tolstoy, Lev. The works referred to in the text are found in many editions. Several of his religious writings are assembled in *Lift Up Your Eyes,* New York, 1960.
NOBEL:
  Bergengren, Erik. *Alfred Nobel.* New York, 1962.
  Halasz, Nicholas. *Nobel.* New York, 1959.
  Schuck, Henrik, *et al. Nobel: The Man and His Prizes.* New York, 1962.

CARNEGIE:

Carnegie, Andrew. *Autobiography*. New York, 1920.

Carnegie Endowment for International Peace. *Fifty Years in the Service of Peace and Justice*. New York, 1961.

———. *Perspectives on Peace*. New York, 1960.

Hendrick, Burton J. *The Life of Andrew Carnegie*. Garden City, 1932.

ANGELL:

Angell, Norman. *After All* (autobiography). New York, 1952.

———. *The Great Illusion*. New York, 1910.

———. *Peace and the Plain Man*. New York, 1935.

WILSON:

Bailey, Thomas A. *Woodrow Wilson and the Great Betrayal*. New York, 1945.

———. *Woodrow Wilson and the Lost Peace*. New York, 1944.

Baker, Ray Stannard. *Woodrow Wilson: Life and Letters*. Garden City, 1927–39.

———. *Woodrow Wilson and the World Settlement*. Garden City, 1922.

Cranston, Alan. *The Killing of the Peace*. New York, 1945, 1960 (paperback).

Greene, Theodore P., ed. *Wilson at Versailles*. Boston, 1957.

Hoover, Herbert Clark. *The Ordeal of Woodrow Wilson*. New York, 1958.

Lansing, Robert. *The Peace Negotiations*. Boston & New York, 1921.

Link, Arthur. *Wilson*. 3 vols. Princeton, 1947–60.

White, William Allen. *Woodrow Wilson*. Boston & New York, 1924.

Wilson, Woodrow. *War and Peace* (Presidential messages, 1917–24). New York, 1927.

GANDHI:

Fischer, Louis. *The Life of Mahatma Gandhi*. New York, 1950, 1962 (paperback).

Gandhi, Mohandas. *An Autobiography, or The Story of My Experiments with Truth*. Ahmedabad, 1927, Boston, 1957 (paperback).

Jack, Homer, ed. *The Gandhi Reader*. Indiana, 1956; New York, 1961 (paperback).

Nanda, B. R. *Mahatma Gandhi: A Biography*. Boston, 1958.

Sheean, Vincent. *Lead, Kindly Light*. New York, 1949.

Shridharani, Krishnalal. *War Without Violence*. New York, 1939.

HAMMARSKJÖLD:

Hammarskjöld, Dag. *Servant of Peace: A Selection of . . . Speeches and Statements.* New York, 1963.

Lash, Joseph P. *Dag Hammerskjold: Custodian of the Brushfire Peace.* Garden City, 1961.

Miller, Richard I. *Dag Hammarskjöld and Crisis Diplomacy.* New York, 1961.

Index

[355]